GOOD FAITH AND OTHER ESSAYS

For Mary Margaret
whose early death deprived
special children of her love and help

GOOD FAITH AND OTHER ESSAYS

Perspectives on a Sartrean Ethics

Joseph S. Catalano

ROWMAN & LITTLEFIELD PUBLISHERS, INC.

ROWMAN & LITTLEFIELD PUBLISHERS, INC.

Published in the United States of America
by Rowman & Littlefield Publishers, Inc.
4720 Boston Way, Lanham, Maryland 20706

3 Henrietta Street
London WC2E 8LU, England

British Cataloging in Publication Information Available

Library of Congress Cataloging-in-Publication Data
Catalano, Joseph S.
Good faith and other essays : perspectives on a Sartrean ethics /
Joseph S. Catalano.
p. cm.
Includes bibliographical references and index.
1. Ethics. 2. Sartre, Jean-Paul, 1905—Ethics. I. Title.
BJ1031.C325 1995 171'.2—dc20 95-37344 CIP

ISBN 0-8476-8082-7 (cloth: alk. paper)
ISBN 0-8476-8088-6 (pbk.: alk. paper)

Printed in the United States of America

∞ TM The paper used in this publication meets the minimum requirements of
American National Standard for Information Sciences—Permanence of
Paper for Printed Library Materials, ANSI Z39.48–1984.

Contents

Preface

The long essay that comprises the first part of this book was written especially for this volume. It is only a sketch of a Sartrean ethics that I hope to be able to develop in the near future. I take some major liberties with Jean-Paul Sartre's thought, and, in this respect, I want to acknowledge the help that I received in clarifying my perspective. William L. McBride, who provided the introduction, gave useful comments, as did James L. Marsh. Both Elizabeth A. Bowman and Thomas R. Flynn provided very detailed criticisms; I have sometimes credited their help in footnotes, but their useful suggestions led to more extensive revisions than these brief acknowledgments indicate.

The second part of the book is a collection of essays on Sartre's ethics that I wrote over a period of fifteen years. Appropriate acknowledgments are given in the footnotes of these essays and I will not repeat them here. There is some repetition and some change in style among these essays, but I have made only minor editorial changes. These earlier essays are closer to Sartre's own text than my new essay.

I also want to thank Jennifer K. Ruark of Rowman & Littlefield for encouraging this project and Anne Pomeroy for proofreading and for making the index.

Introduction

William L. McBride

It is frequently said, by followers of intellectual trends, that the once-hegemonic influence of Jean-Paul Sartre's thought has dwindled to comparative insignificance. It is true that, even before his death and certainly since then, philosophers in his native France have by no means been lavish in citing him or in noting how much of their own world views have Sartrean provenances, even when that is obvious enough to their readers.[1] By contrast, the French scene of the past decade or so has witnessed revivals of interest in the philosophies of Heidegger, of liberal democratic theory, and of traditional religions, to name only three salient tendencies. In the United States, Canada, and the United Kingdom, on the other hand, Sartre's philosophy was NEVER hegemonic; but even here one is sometimes told by would-be scorekeepers that Sartre is faring poorly in the historical influence game.

In partial rebuttal of this contention, it is always possible to cite statistics. The most impressive are those that have been painstakingly gathered by Michel Contat and Michel Rybalka concerning books, articles, and dissertations on Sartre, in all academic fields and in the various languages, about which they have received information. Their bibliography for the years 1980–1992 runs to over 200 pages, with an average of more than 15 items per page;[2] a supplement printed in 1995 adds over 400 items omitted from earlier bibliographies and nearly 300 for the years 1993–1995.[3] The statistics come to life when one begins to read the titles and the occasional brief characterizations of these entries. They cover all facets of Sartre's long and highly diverse intellectual career, which means that they range over the gamut of topics—ethical, political, metaphysical, literary, religious—that have preoccupied thinking human beings during the twentieth century.

It is not really a matter of a "Sartre revival," since there has really never been a time of Sartre oblivion, but a panoply of fascinating developments has made the last ten years or so especially important in ensuring the continued relevance of his ideas for ethics, politics, and culture. The ongoing posthumous publication of important writings of Sartre himself, notably the *Cahiers pour une Morale*[4] and the second volume of the *Critique de la Raison Dialectique*[5], followed by new translations of these and earlier works (including a Bulgarian translation of *L'Etre et le Neant*, when political conditions in that country at last permitted such a thing to be published[6]); the establishment of Sartre societies and clubs in North America, Germany, the U.K., Italy, and the Congo, to name only those with which I have some familiarity; the launching of a new English-language journal, *Sartre Studies International*; and above all the appearance of a number of new authors who look to Sartre not as a "Master"[7] whose ideas are to be made the object of a reverential hermeneutic but as a brilliant and conceptually daring if often highly contestable deceased colleague with whom it remains possible to think through to new insights about the contemporary world—all of these occurrences add up to a significant international cultural phenomenon that is worthy of study in its own right.

The Sartre Society of North America, which has been active and thriving since its inception, held its first meeting in the fall of 1985 at The New School for Social Research in New York City. Those of us who were involved in organizing and planning it thought of The New School as the most desirable site both because of its location and because of its historic links with the European philosophical tradition. I approached the late Rainer Schurmann, a well-known Heidegger scholar and at the time chairperson of The New School's Philosophy Department, with our proposal, and he agreed to it and facilitated it in its beginning stages. All or almost all of the arrangements of detail were negotiated by the one member of the organizing group who lived in New York City, Joseph Catalano. Professor Catalano had already published, some years earlier, his commentary on *Being and Nothingness*,[8] which so many students have found to be such a helpful guide, and his even more ground-breaking commentary on the first volume of the *Critique of Dialectical Reason* was at the time in production, to be published the following year.[9] At the same time, he had begun the series of original critical studies, starting from the question of good and bad faith, that have eventuated in the present volume.

A remarkable number of the leading North American Sartre scholars have focused their work primarily in the areas of ethics and politics. Many of them receive mention in the following pages. Here, I shall single out, for special reasons, only two of them, so as to avoid the embarrassment of overlooking one or another jewel in this embarrassment of riches while trying to be comprehensive. First, then, let me take particular note of the work of Linda Bell, both her earlier *Sartre's Ethics of Authenticity*[10] and especially her recent *Rethinking Ethics in the Midst of Violence: A Feminist Approach to Freedom*, which makes liberal use of Sartre's thought and was published in this series.[11] Second, I call attention to the even more recently published book by my Purdue colleague, Lewis Gordon, *Bad Faith and Anti-Black Racism*, crucial strands of which are indebted to Professor Catalano's earlier analyses.[12] The present work by Catalano belongs to the same distinguished genre, but has the special merit of leading us back to the existential underpinnings of sexism, racism, and other social manifestations of bad faith by exploring what might be called the foundations of ethics.

Joseph Catalano, for all of his moral commitment (to which I shall return), is first and foremost an ontologist, but one who is concerned above all with the ontology of values. He accepts, on the whole, the Sartrean account of values as anthropocentric, that is, rooted in the free choices of individual human beings, but he finds no difficulty in rejecting certain problematic implications drawn from this view by many of Sartre's critics and even some of his would-be defenders, to wit, egocentric individualism combined with a strong relativism. Against the former charge, Catalano argues—quite convincingly, in my opinion—that there is a very significant continuity between the approach to bad and good faith in Sartre's very earliest writings—not merely *Being and Nothingness* from the early 1940s but even *The Transcendence of the Ego* and the novel, *Nausea*, from the 1930s—and Sartre's later political analyses and radical political commitments of the 1960s and early 1970s. Of the latter charge, which seems unworthy of being dignified with much explicit comment in light of Sartre's repeated public involvements in value-laden social issues, Catalano's deft interpretations and utilizations of Sartrean categories, beginning with bad and good faith, to illuminate and explain the ambiguities of our individual and social lives constitute a powerful and sustained refutation.

It is not my role, as I conceive it here, to anticipate either Catalano's careful arguments, always so straightforward, guileless, and in short self-referentially suffused with the spirit of good faith that he has found in a certain sense to be possible despite the deep and abiding structural obstacles to it with which the world in which we live is fraught, or his penetrating descriptions of some of these bad-faith structures—anti-Semitism, colonialism, mistreatment of the homeless: you must read this book for yourselves! But I think it is permissible for me to refer to the one extended personal account that he provides in his first chapter, dealing with the St. John's University faculty strike of 1966–1967 in which he was involved, because it is so illustrative of the spirit of this book and of his thought. What he so lucidly portrays in this account is the interplay of the two senses of bad faith—"strong," or what in one text he calls, in a memorable phrase, "a kind of self-induced sleep," and "weak," or in other words based in the social structures in which we all must live and hence cannot escape—that his analysis has led him to identify; he also points to the possibility, despite everything, of good-faith behavior. There was the university administration, attempting to exert an oppressive dominance over its faculty and not hesitating, despite whatever moral values its controlling religious order was supposed to profess, to negotiate with them in totally bad faith (it gave the appearance of being willing to listen even while it was drawing up dismissal papers for a number of the leaders of the opposition to its oppression, himself included), and there were the numerous faculty "colleagues" who found various reasons for avoiding taking a stand despite all of THEIR supposed commitments to academic freedom and so on. Professor Catalano uncompromisingly shows the complexities of the situation, its ambiguities, the interrelations of the personal and the social, AND the fact that good-faith behavior was nevertheless not an illusion or an impossibility under the circumstances. He concludes, charmingly, with a refusal in retrospect to condemn his bad-faith colleagues, noting his own comparative inactivity during the (more or less contemporaneous) civil rights movement.

This account, with which I imagine many readers can readily identify even if they were not yet born at the time of the civil rights movement or of this event, well illustrates the proximity of the historical dimension of our lives to the immediate and personal, even while the two dimensions remain comparatively distinct—a point that Professor Catalano constantly stresses. It is the awareness of this that enables him to maintain an exceptionally strong social conscience in a society that seems currently to be immersing itself ever more deeply in the Slough of Bad Faith, a society in which racism and so many other forms of oppression have become positively fashionable in large segments of the political and media leadership. He thus situates himself firmly with the Sartrean tradition of radical social critique at a time when "intellectuals," that is, that dwindling group of individuals who are still willing to be so designated, all too frequently either retreat to the comfortable pose of *Explicateurs de Texte* (the genre of so many of the papers that are presented at the annual meetings of the French Sartre group in Paris[13], as elsewhere in Academia) or become spokespersons (or rather ''spokesmen,'' as they would no doubt prefer to be called) of the political Right.[14]

Not only is Professor Catalano not a mere ''professor'' of Sartrean texts, but indeed fidelity to them is by no means his highest priority. Of course, he has found in Sartre, as I have, a highly kindred spirit from whom he has drawn enormous intellectual inspiration. But he does not hesitate to take positions of criticism with respect even to some of Sartre's best-known ideas (for example, the ''postulate,'' as he calls it, in *Being and Nothingness* that the most general description of human beings' fundamental project is to be God, which he regards as ''lazy''), and above all he is perfectly comfortable with developing new categories and new distinctions that depart from the letter of Sartre's texts, even when he is not sure that Sartre would have taken kindly to these departures. When he does this, to be sure, he lets his readers know just what he is doing: he has a mastery over the texts and the long sweep of Sartre's development, and he does not, in bad faith, deceive either himself or us concerning such matters. What Catalano is ultimately most concerned to achieve in his writings is, not self-referential textual exegesis, but rather the clearest possible explanatory account of the domain of ethics, individual and social, and he believes that the numerous Sartrean texts to which he alludes together furnish a superb basis for moving towards this outcome.

Of just what ''the domain of ethics'' consists, just what this MEANS, has always seemed to me an enormously complex, desperately difficult philosophical problem; at the same time, it is, obviously, at the very core of any philosophy that is oriented towards human action. I therefore find myself frequently appalled by texts, which occur in abundance in the ''mainstream'' Anglo-American philosophical literature, that take the existence and general contours of this ''domain'' as more or less given and beyond question, and then either confine themselves to arguing about whether the utilitarian or the deontological approach is more satisfactory for making ethical decisions or else, assuming the former to be ''correct,'' proceed to engage in cost/benefit calculations concerning specific types of actions. But such writing and thinking misses most of the real drama and depth of human moral choice, the choice of values, which is in many respects THE central philosophical question of what it means to be human. Sartre, throughout his career, was obsessed with this question; it was a generally fruitful and positive sort of obsession; and the section entitled ''La Mauvaise Foi'' early in the masterwork that is *Being and Nothingness* can rightly be seen as the key to his approach to answering it. Professor Catalano, placing somewhat greater emphasis than Sartre on the positive possibilities that constitute good faith while being even more aware than was his predecessor, at the time of that early writing, of the virtually hegemony of bad faith in our social institutions and practices, has used this key to undertake careful, creative, ground-breaking explorations of both interpersonal and historical praxis. The result, in the pages that follow, is a model of a ''good-faith effort'' by a philosopher; but it also, paradoxically in light of its title, far transcends that level of achievement!

Notes

1. A good example is Jacques Derrida, who seldom mentions Sartre in his texts and when he does is usually dismissive of him, but who, when asked, readily acknowledges Sartre's importance for his own philosophical formation. See, for example, *Magazine Litteraire* no. 286 (March 1991), interview with Derrida by Francois Ewald, 19 and 22.

2. Michel Contat / Michel Rybalka, *Sartre: Bibliographie* 1980–1992 (Paris: CNRS Editions; (in English) Bowling Green, Ohio: Philosophy Documentation Center, Bowling Green State University, 1993).

3. In *Bulletin d'Information du Groupe d'Etudes Sartriennes* no. 9 (juin 1995).

4. Paris: Editions Gallimard, 1983.

5. Paris: Editions Gallimard, 1985.

6. *Bitie I Nichto*, vol. 1, trans. and with introduction by Yvanka Raynova (Sofia: Nauka i Iskustvo, 1994).

7. As Sartre remarked by way of commenting on President Charles De Gaulle's salutation, ''My dear master,'' in a disapproving letter to him concerning the Vietnam War Crimes Tribunal in which Sartre was involved along with Bertrand Russell, ''I am 'master' only to the cafe waiters who know that I am a writer.'' (My translation.)—''Sartre a de Gaulle,'' in *Situations, VIII* (Paris: Gallimard, 1972), 47.

8. Catalano, J., *A Commentary on Jean-Paul Sartre's* Being and Nothingness (New York: Harper & Row, 1974; Chicago: University of Chicago Press, 1980).

9. Catalano, J., *A Commentary on Jean-Paul Sartre's ''Critique of Dialectical Reason,* vol. 1: Theory of Practical Ensembles'' (Chicago: University of Chicago Press, 1986). I reviewed this in *Canadian Philosophical Reviews* 8 (Nov. 1988): 430–32.

10. Bell, Linda, (Tuscaloosa: The University of Alabama Press, 1989).

11. Bell, Linda, *Rethinking Ethics in the Midst of Violence: A Feminist Approach to Freedom* (Lanham, Md.: Rowman & Littlefield, 1993).

12. Gordon, Lewis, *Bad Faith and Anti-Black Racism* (New Jersey: Humanities Press, 1995). See especially n. 42, 189–90, for an indication of his indebtedness to Catalano.

13. There have been some outstanding exceptions to this generalization, of course, in each of the years in which I have attended, and in any case there exists a vast variety of *Explication de Texte*, some of which can be extremely valuable. But at the June 1995 meeting there was widespread disappointment even with the session celebrating the fiftieth anniversary of the journal that Sartre edited for so many years and used as a forum for literary and ethico-political "Engagement," *Les Tempes Modernes*, because so little of this spirit seemed to be left in the remarks made either by one of the original members of the editorial team, Jean Pouillon, or by the current editor, Claude Lanzmann, who were the two panelists.

14. In his last period of active writing, roughly 1968 to 1974, Sartre frequently made a distinction between the "classical" and the "revolutionary" intellectual, indicating that he had "crossed over" to the latter category, to the extent to which this was still possible at his age and for someone with his background. Today, I am suggesting, it is the future of the generic category itself that is in question.

PART ONE

Mediations: A Sketch of a Sartrean Ethics

Introductory Remarks

What should we expect from a Sartrean ethics? Should we expect an emphasis on freedom? Yes, but one would have to take into account also Sartre's sensitivity to Freud and Marx. Further, since Sartre wrote directly or indirectly about ethics for more than fifty years, it would be surprising if his moral perspective did not develop and mature.

Perhaps the question one should ask is what one should expect at the end of the quest for a Sartrean ethics. Will Sartre offer us norms and values and a priori rules of conduct? He may not offer them specifically, but they are part of his moral picture. As a phenomenologist, Sartre does not deny that phenomena and the everyday claims of morality are part of our lives, but for him moral norms are part of our lives only insofar as we have made them to be so. Even a priori demands of morality have been historically constituted and are sustained by us daily. It is impossible to overemphasize this last point. Those who look for neo-Kantian, neo-Aristotelian or Heideggerian roots for morality should look elsewhere; in Sartre's strong anthropocentrism neither God, Nature, nor Being exists as a guide that can lead us toward a more moral life. On the other hand, this same anthropocentrism reveals that values exist in the world independently of our private conceptions. Values, positive and negative human relationships such as love and hate, violence and fraternity—indeed, all that is good and evil in human lives—are for Sartre the products of human efforts, considered both individually and collectively.

Ethics seeks to establish more than accepted norms of behavior; it aims to inform us not only about how we do act but also about how we should act. This pursuit of values is also on Sartre's moral agenda, because it too is part of our everyday lives. Once again, however, he tries to make us see how we have forged for ourselves not only accepted

3

norms of behavior but ideals. For example, we create a world in which we lie and yet we hold onto the ideal of telling the truth. We want both, not out of sophistry, but out of comfort, and then, because we recognize the bad faith of our comfort, we want to go beyond it. We begin to desire a space and temporality in which our inventiveness is not a choice of lying or telling the truth, but in which communication is of itself disclosure.

Sartre thus wants to unveil the adventure of moral creativity and to grasp how we collectively shape new ideals out of old ones and how we then maneuver beyond them. Indeed, we are inventive even in our attempts to escape being free. A strange creativity is present in bad faith, that is, in the ways we individually and collectively forge the chains that bind ourselves to ourselves.

With all this emphasis on creativity we seem to be admitting that Sartre has an absolute notion of freedom and that he absurdly claims that we can do whatever we want to do. This never has been Sartre's view, if, in fact, it ever has been anyone's philosophical view. Sartre always has claimed that human existence is thoroughly situational. To put the matter somewhat differently, our freedom is not merely embodied, for such a view implies a force that is limited by being here rather than there; rather, freedom is the name we give to our individual and collective inventiveness. In the concrete, this creativity is revealed in the way our bodies interact with each other; it is also shown in the ways our bodies touch matter and alter it into a world.

"Altering matter into a world," "creating norms and values," "binding ourselves to ourselves"—all these may seem to be very strong claims to make about mere mortals, and we may now want to say that freedom is indeed absolute. Let the claim stand, and let it be the Sartrean recognition that human freedom is all the freedom there is and that both history and nature are human adventures.

Many ethical perspectives are concerned with the various ways we use our freedom, and once again the question arises about the distinctiveness of Sartre's ethical views. I see a twofold uniqueness in his moral outlook. First, we have an intimate moral bond with others because the very context within which our own freedom works is fixed by others as they act both individually and collectively on us. Second, what I think is unique to Sartre are the many attempts he makes to align himself alongside the oppressed. I thus see Sartre extending to us an invitation to attain a particular moral sensitivity, namely, one that invites us to view the world from the position of the most disadvantaged members of society. This does not mean that he regards the disadvantaged and oppressed as especially enlightened, but only that he sees the struggle against oppression to be enlightening, because this struggle reveals freedom finding a way out of its chains. I thus see a Sartrean ethics requiring of those reflecting on ethics that they become both aware of their place in the social structure and sensitive to the degree to which their social standing may affect their ethical concerns.

If I had to hint at a Sartrean justification for attaining this perspective—if I had to sketch answers to the question, why should we help the poor and oppressed?—I would return to my initial point about how dependent we are on others, and I would note that the look of the oppressed reveals us to ourselves as oppressors. I would also call attention to the degree to which our own privileged existence is based on the poverty and oppression of others. Concern for the oppressed seems to me to arise from a strict sense of justice, since we benefit from their oppression.

On the other hand, I see our bond with the oppressed to exist first and foremost not in any general moral principle, but in the structure of oppressive and repressive acts as such.[1] These acts mirror our inhumanity. Sartre is not an irrationalist because he advocates that actions are what are primarily intelligible. We can, of course, reflectively formulate moral principles, but this is a secondary enterprise. For the most part, however, I think that Sartre's moral thought is mainly directed toward revealing the intelligibility of our individual and collective actions as these forge, for better or for worse, the ideals of what it means to be human.

Ethics thus involves a subtle dialectic: we have to consider how a particular act is related to a moral principle, but we then have to examine the principle as something we forged. Indeed, any moral principle formulated by an individual works within a social web of moral ideals that have been constituted by past human actions and that are themselves held in existence by our present actions. Social ideals are thus quasi-historical a priori that we can examine and, to use a Sartrean expression, surpass, but that we cannot completely ignore.

Needless to say, all of the above is an interpretation. One elicits a Sartrean ethics only from Sartre's texts, and that itself implies a view on these writings. In what follows I try to be explicit about my perspective. I also make an effort to keep my debates with other Sartre scholars to a minimum, but these debates are there mostly in the emphasis that I put on certain aspects of Sartre's thought. I would not even mention this disagreement over interpretation of texts except that it leads at times to a good deal of explanation about matters that might not be of interest to all. When that happens, one might want to skip paragraphs or sections, as, for example, the next section.

1. Reading the Sartrean Canon

Any attempt to sketch a Sartrean ethics confronts both textual and contextual matters. The textual issues arise from two sources. The first is that Sartre never presented us with a completed ethics; the second is that, nevertheless, his works consistently deal with moral themes. This textual concern is further complicated, because to the extensive writings published during his lifetime we must add posthumously published works, which, as of the time of this essay, continue to appear. As a whole, these writings are so varied in both tone and format—including recorded conversations, addresses to students and colleagues, massive psychological biographies, diaries, and extensive but abortive attempts at constructing a formal ethics, as well as more formalized and finished philosophical studies—that one has to take a stand on their relative importance. I will soon clarify my view of the relative merit of these works.

The textual issue is, I believe, hindered rather than helped by Sartre's own remarks about his efforts. Sartre never rejected, in any sustained and formal way, his attempts at developing an ethics. Rather, he sometimes called his early efforts a "failure" or "idealistic." At other times he simply considered them incomplete. The point is that Sartre did not destroy them; he allowed them to stand, envisioning that when they were published posthumously they would have their own finality as efforts that another thinker might complete. Further, we must keep in mind the casual and circumstantial nature of these comments about his own writings, frequently made in interviews.[2] Unlike Heidegger, Sartre did not always have posterity in mind when he wrote or spoke. He addressed specific persons with a particular context in mind. What Sartre might call "idealistic" when talking to a Maoist, he might not consider so if he were addressing a more formal philosophical audience. Also, in many respects Sartre is his own harshest critic; we see him always attempting to struggle against his former views so that he might accomplish something new. Still, when interviewers attempted to lead him to reject totally the philosophy of *Being and Nothingness*, he always qualified his own view of the evolution of his thought and emphasized the continuity of his philosophy.[3] On the other hand, my qualifications are not meant to minimize the development of his thought. My point is simply that this development should be determined by the texts themselves and not by Sartre's comments about them.

I wrote in the opening sentence to this section that contextual as well as textual issues confront any attempt to sketch a Sartrean ethics. By contextual I mean the inner dialogue within the text itself, the thinkers whom Sartre is using mainly to delineate his own position. This contextual issue is itself complex, because where Sartre is considering Kant, Kierkegaard, Marx, Freud, or Heidegger, it is Sartre's view of these thinkers that is immediately and obviously relevant. One can write an extensive monograph, as indeed Robert Denoon Cumming has done, on the significance of Sartre's appropriation of other thinkers and thus introduce a multileveled contextual dialogue, but I will not attempt that.[4]

Now for my general perspective on Sartre's ethical writings: I choose the major philosophical and uniquely biographical works published during his life over those already posthumously published or those about to be published. This may seem like a preposterous view, since we have no explicit knowledge about the content of certain unpublished works, such as an extensive tract on Nietzsche that has not yet been located. My outlook would indeed be questionable if the books that Sartre published late in life did not themselves address moral concerns, but Sartre was working on his massive study of Flaubert almost until he became blind, and that work has just about everything in it: it is a work of deep moral concern. It would be very strange if Sartre was writing but not publishing moral tracts that ran counter to the works that he was allowing to be published.

These then are the major stepping stones in my attempt to sketch a Sartrean ethics: *Being and Nothingness* (*BN*), *Genet: Saint and Martyr* (*Genet*), the first volume of the *Critique of Dialectical Reason* (*Critique*), and Sartre's massive work on Gustave Flaubert, *The Family Idiot* (*Flaubert*).[5] Of less importance for me are the posthumous works. Of these the most significant are the already published *Notebooks for an Ethics* (*Notebooks*), the partially published—as of this writing—*1964 Rome Lecture* (*Rome lecture*) and *Morality and History* (*Cornell lecture*), and last and for me indeed least the recorded conversations with Benny Lévy (*Lévy conversations*), sometimes romantically cited as the Last Words, a very un-Sartrean expression—there are no last words in a life; there are only words that come last.

I want to make clear, however, that I do not regard the posthumously published works as unimportant; rather, I am addressing a certain recent tendency among some Sartreans to look for a magic key to Sartre's thought. So far, where I have seen this to have occurred, it has always been accomplished by minimizing the insights of the major works published during his life, particularly *Being and Nothingness* and the first volume of the *Critique*.[6] Indeed, what disturbs me is that those who advocate a sharp break in Sartre's thought seem to do so by diluting the content of *Being and Nothingness*. The result is that the thought of the later Sartre never reaches what is for me the sophisticated thought of the early Sartre. Starting with a simplistic view of *BN* as portraying a lonely, disembodied freedom inventing the world for itself in the face of other people who are mere objects in the world, Sartre supposedly matures. He learns that he has a body and that other people are more than objects. Finally, we are told, Sartre discovers the importance both of family relations and of history. This so-called advance is frequently presented as a movement toward a neo-Aristotelian and neo-Kantian perspective that is ultimately so vacuous that one wonders why anyone would want to bother about it.

The division that I see between the early and late Sartre is not that of a sharp break in his thought, and I will return to this point both here and in the essays in the second part of this book. Nevertheless, I should note that although the division does not, for me, represent a rupture in his thought, it is more than a simple chronology. The division between the early and late Sartre points to a maturing that occurs on at least three levels. The first and most general level represents the completion of Sartre's break from Husserl's eidetic reduction, that is, Husserl's attempt to get to the essence of a thing by eliminating the way our individual psychological perceptions color phenomena. Of course, Sartre never accepted the details of the phenomenological reduction; what is still present in *BN* is a partial belief that one can ascribe a single essence to such complex phenomena as interpersonal relations. Thus, Sartre attempts to deduce the underlying structure of these relations from the look.[7] Sartre's mature thought completely breaks from the eidetic reduction, and what takes its place is a distinctive dialectical nominalism that appears fully developed first in the *Critique* and then in *Flaubert*. On the second level, Sartre becomes increasingly aware of the degree to which one's own consciousness is structured by others who attempt to mold it after their own likenesses or in accord with their own needs. Thus, from *BN* to *Genet* and then finally to *Flaubert* Sartre gradually begins to detail the ways in which our parents, our friends, and our social and historical milieu alter our childhood lives and, to a great extent, fix the context within which our freedom operates. On the third level, as Sartre moves from *BN* to the *Critique*, I see him to be forging a technical distinction between the social and the historical realms and a corresponding distinction between simple action and praxis. Briefly, I take praxis to be the action of an individual working through a group to relieve our historical condition of sustained scarcity.

I have elsewhere defended the notion of a basic unity in Sartre's thought, and I think that what I do in this essay is in line with such a view.[8] If I here take some interpretative liberties with Sartre's thought, that is another matter.

I am attempting to encompass a large and extensive corpus that spans the major part of Sartre's writing career, and I need a more carefully defined focus if my sketch is to have any unity. Sartre scholars will recognize that my use of the term *mediation* in the title implies that I take the *Critique* as my focal point, and this is indeed true. I will soon explain in some detail my use of Sartre's notion of mediation, but here it is sufficient to say that I understand it to imply that there are different levels on which our moral concerns arise. The three levels that I consider are the immediate or local level, the historical, and the psychoanalytic. The immediate or local is for me also the social, that is, I am making a technical distinction between the social and the historical, and I think that this distinction is consistent with Sartre's own thinking. I will also, however, be extending Sartre's initial notion of mediation so as to use it both as a means of outlining an overall ethical perspective and as a way of unifying his own works.

My claim is that it is fruitful to view many of the moral insights of *BN* as well as the *Notebooks* as directed toward our experiences in their local and social environment, and from this perspective the early ethics can be said to be idealistic. Such idealism refers only to the fact that we have agreed to limit our moral questions to our immediate concerns, such as our relations with our family or friends. Thus, when properly placed, this idealism is harmless; it merely points to the fact that we cannot conceptually handle everything at the same time. On the other hand, I see the *Critique*, the *Rome* and *Cornell* lectures, and the *Lévy conversations* to be broadly directed toward the historical dimension of our actions. The level of the psychoanalytic is introduced in *BN* and developed in *Genet*. I view Sartre's work on Flaubert to be an ambiguous attempt to unite all aspects, the local, the historical, and the psychoanalytic—ambiguous because, as Sartre notes, Flaubert's age was especially neurotic, and, as a successful writer, Gustave Flaubert was in this age in a special way. But this claim about *The Family Idiot* and my general use of mediations are substantive judgments about Sartre's ethics for which this essay can only lay the groundwork and, hopefully, serve as an invitation for future study.

2. Mediations: An Introduction

The most technical use of mediation in Sartre's philosophy occurs in the *Critique*, and it concerns the formation of the group-in-fusion: each individual within a group becomes what Sartre calls a "third," and through the mediation of these thirds the group is capable of a distinctive action, or, more technically, "praxis." I will discuss Sartre's third and my extension of it in the next section. Here, with a minimum of explanation, I use the third simply to clarify the three levels of action, the social, the historical, and the psychoanalytic.

In the abstract this distinction between the social and the historical could appear to be arbitrary: large-scale social relations can indeed be historical; but following what I see to be Sartre's usage in the *Critique*, I find the distinctive feature of the historical to be an awareness of a large-scale condition of a humanly constituted scarcity. That is, in what I call a historical relation, we become explicitly aware of a deep-rooted fracturing within our humanity that is caused by the way we individually and collectively sustain a more or less worldwide condition of scarcity. In contrast, immediate or social relations are those that pass through this scarcity. Thus, although scarcity is always present, altering our interpersonal relations, the condition of scarcity is not, for me, always the defining feature of a situation. I give below examples to illustrate this distinction between the social and the historical.

I begin by examining the relative independence of social interpersonal relations from either the psychoanalytic or the historical ones. Because these three levels interact, I also must consider the relation between the social and the psychoanalytic on the one hand and the social and the historical on the other. This implies that I show how repression or well-being are, in each case, relatively distinct and yet how they interact. My emphasis, however, is on indicating to what extent the three realms are distinct. The interrelations can be complex, and I will only hint at them. I view Sartre to have accomplished just such a task in *Flaubert*.

The textual basis in Sartre's works for my claim that the social realm has a relative autonomy from the historical is in the *Critique*. Sartre opens the chapter, entitled in English "Human Relations as a Mediation between Different Sectors of Materiality," with the words: "Immediate experience reveals being at its *most concrete*, but it takes it at its most superficial level and remains in the realm of abstractions."[9]

Consider a family dinner. Let us grant that it is a particularly happy occasion and that all are enjoying themselves. This experience is certainly concrete, and we can say that immediate bonds of reciprocity exist among the members of the family. The happy times, however, occur through a practical abstraction from the historical situation: there are the numerous homeless people who are not able to enjoy a family meal; there are the countless starving children throughout the world; there are acts of oppression, repression, and persecution. The locked doors of a home or an apartment that keep one secure also keep the rest of the world at a safe distance. Nevertheless, on their own level the interpersonal relations can be genuine and the pleasures they give can be real. My point is that Sartre is not a reductionist: the historical is always present, but it is not always what is characteristic of a situation.

I think that one can make a case that a happy family dinner becomes a weak group-in-fusion. This group, which is explained in detail in Sartre's *Critique*, arises within a relatively tight environment, and it brings about closer bonds of reciprocity than those that normally occur in social relations. In my extended use of the third, which, to repeat, I will comment on in the next section, each member enjoying the family dinner becomes a third bringing about a weak group-in-fusion. This fusion cannot affect the historical situation, but it does allow a measure of respite from the pressures of the world, and the respite is genuine. This point was brought out in an article by Alessandra Stanley on the front page of the "Week in Review" section of *The New York Times* for Sunday, 1 January 1995. The article, entitled "A Toast! To the Good Things about Bad Times," began:

> Moscow
> In Soviet times, the real living room was in the kitchen, a cramped, dingy space where friends laughed, drank, smoked, sang, quarreled and talked intensely into the night, night after night. Back in the days when nothing was permitted, only relationships could flourish. Russians cultivated those friendships with fierce attention, focusing their ample free time and creative energy on the never-ending conversation in the kitchen.
> Now the conversation has ended.

The conversation ended because, while the competition to succeed brought some Russians new modern kitchens, it also required of them long hours of work. Obviously, people can become politically impotent either by being alienated from the superstructure of the state or by being kept so busy earning a living within the infrastructure that they have no time or energy left for genuine political concerns.

Sartre offers a somewhat more general example in the *Critique*. In the quote I give below, Sartre refers to seriality, and I will later examine this notion; however, the specific context of the quote occurs within his discussion of "other-directed" behavior. Sartre's example is of buying and listening to one of the "top ten" records—each person buys a record and listens to it because each believes that everyone else is doing just that, and thus each buys and listens as if he or she were the other buying and listening. He writes:

> But although this initial behavior towards the object which is prized or acclaimed is totally alienated, it does not determine the actions of small groups or of practical individuals, in so far as these elementary units lie *below the level* of seriality. There is a kind of pleasure or displeasure in the listener which, apart from his alienated evaluations, expresses either his personal valuations . . . or perhaps that of his family group. (*Critique*, 646; Sartre's italics)

Advertising, the subtle pressures to belong, the entire large-scale social effort to make money on the record—in short, the weight of a good part of American history—bear down on you to act as others do and buy one of the top ten records. You give in, and from this historical perspective your action is alienated. But you enjoy the record anyway.

I am concerned with saving an ethical space for our interpersonal relations. My claim is that good and bad faith, authenticity and inauthenticity—some of the structures of consciousness dealt with in the essays in this volume—are applicable first and foremost when limited to the local context of our actions, such as family, friends, and neighborhood. I would say the same about Sartre's interpretation of play.[10] Of course, all these notions can be extended to our historical existence, and I do this myself in some of the essays in the part 2.[11]

Now that I have pointed to the relative autonomy of the social from the historical, I want to consider how interpersonal relations within the social realm can be affected by a distinctive family or social repression that is not reducible to historical oppression and how, unless the repression is extreme, the individual can still rework it for his or her own ends. This is not to justify the repression or to say that the individual does not suffer because of it. In such situations there is tragedy, but, as with Genet, one can still live authentically. Whether Sartre would regard Gustave Flaubert as authentic, I am not, at present, prepared to say. Nevertheless, despite being unloved, Flaubert wrote, and he did not wallow in passivity. Further, it is clear that, despite his constituted passive nature, he enjoyed his writing. Toward the end of book 2 of *The Family Idiot*, in a section called "On Gratuitousness as Categorical Imperative," Sartre writes: "To be sure, he did not write in obedience to a transcendent demand but from exuberance . . . even when he hasn't a subject in his head."[12]

This exuberance was an aspect of Flaubert's project; it was the way he surpassed the influences of his early childhood, specifically his constituted passivity. This exhilaration matured until, under the influence of what Sartre calls a half-hearted but nevertheless decisive friendship with Alfred, Flaubert forged it into an a priori demand on his own freedom.

> Until now he has written without difficulty. . . . Yet his painful liaison with Alfred and the fear that Alfred's suicidal immobilism inspire in him throw him back on the ethic of effort and merit. Gustave is a *worker*, work is isolated and affirmed for itself: "Nothing is continually satisfying but the habit of persistent work." . . . Gratuitousness imposes itself, then, as a categorical imperative. (*Flaubert*, 2, 418–19)

Sartre goes on to explain this self-imposed demand. Flaubert works under an a priori command that imitates the Kantian categorical imperative. He realizes that the true work of art cannot come from lived experience but only from the command to produce art, and thus, "what Flaubert himself begins to understand is that the sole motive of the artist must be an a priori determination of pathos . . ." (*Flaubert*, 2, 418–19).

The point is that while Flaubert's early childhood was almost engulfed with role-playing in a way that went beyond that engaged in by most children and while this role-playing was a distinctive passive response to the role-playing of his parents that in turn embodied certain demands of the age, Gustave was himself and not his brother. The "original project" of freedom spoken about in *BN* is indeed present in *Flaubert*, but it is now in the form of what Sartre calls a spiral existence that includes mediations: Flaubert lives his constituted passivity on different levels of his life, surpassing it here only to find that it encompasses him again on a different level, but always reworking it as he moves from actor to author and poet, and then finally to artist. Flaubert's passivity becomes more deeply sadomasochistic until it finally centers on writing as pure style, that is, a style that negates its content even as it puts this content forward as the author's work.

How is Gustave given a quasi-passive nature? It is not genetic, but constituted. Toward the end of *BN* Sartre had earlier introduced a study of a passive constitution in the example of a person hiking who decides to rest while his companions of similar physical constitution move on. In answer to the question, "Could the hiker have continued to keep up with his friends?" Sartre answers, "Agreed. But *at what price?*" Such a decision would have required a new orientation of the hiker's body with the world—an orientation that could itself be made only by considerable effort and that could have become comprehensible only by the application of an existential analytic.

> Therefore if I apply this same method to interpret the way in which I suffer my fatigue, I shall first apprehend in myself a distrust of my body. . . . Hence my fatigue instead of being suffered "flexibly" will be grasped "sternly" as an importunate phenomenon that I want to get rid of. . . . We are not attempting to disguise how much this method of analysis leaves to be desired. This is because everything remains still to be done in this field. (*BN*, 457)

Sartre's massive study on Flaubert can be understood partly as an attempt to develop his existential methodology and to reveal how we "exist" our bodies in relation to the world and before others. This development implies certain qualifications on Sartre's initial view of the project. These qualifications begin in his study of Genet and are examined in some of the essays included in this volume. Briefly, the alteration of the project, in both *Genet* and *Flaubert*, is mainly along the lines of showing how interpersonal relations can affect our very selfhood. Thus, in *BN* the implication is that the hiker chose to have a passive constitution. The study of Flaubert reveals that Gustave was constituted passively mainly through his mother's unloving behavior toward him; his own freedom was the way he reworked his passivity to serve his own ends. Sartre indicates the kind of love that Gustave lacked when he writes:

> If the mother loves him, in other words, he gradually discovers his self-object as his love object. A subjective object for himself through an increasingly manifest other, he becomes a *value* in his own eyes as the absolute end of habitual processes. . . . Let a child once in his life—at three months, at six—taste this victory of pride, he is a man. . . . He will preserve even in misfortune a kind of religious optimism based on the abstract and calm certainty of his own value. . . . We shall say, in any case, that an adventure begun in this fashion has nothing in common with Flaubert's.[13]

Flaubert's distinctive passivity, the concrete form of his alienation, was thus not caused by his historical period, as neurotic as this was. Gustave's passivity came instead from his parents, particularly his mother. Gustave could have been subject to the same historical alienation of his bourgeois class without suffering from the distinctive kind of unloving acts that he received from his parents. Indeed, if Sartre did not believe this to be the case, if he thought that some simplistic dialectic could explain it all, the study of Flaubert would not have to be as massive as it is.

Gustave's freedom was the way he reworked his passivity to serve his own ends, surpassing it now only to meet it again in a different form and to surpass it once more as he lived within what Sartre calls a "spiral existence."

> The *person*, in effect, is neither completely suffered nor completely constructed; furthermore, the person *does not exist* or, if you will, is always the *surpassed* result of the whole mass of totalizing operations by which we continually try to assimilate the nonassimilable—primarily our childhood. . . . From our present point of view, we might well conceive this circular movement in a three-dimensional space as a multicentered spiral that continually swerves away from these centers or rises above them by making an indefinite number of revolutions around its starting point. (*Flaubert* vol. 2: 6–7)

The above discussion of Sartre's *Flaubert* is directed to showing how family relations are relatively independent of the historical situation. The historical situation, however, is always present, and it gives the general form of our alienating practices. But this alienation does not explain the substance of the relations as these concretely appear in this family as distinct from another. To repeat, Gustave suffered from lack of love. This lack of love had the general form of the historical situation. But this lack of love that Sartre also calls "dutiful love" could have been, and should have been, direct loving acts. True, these loving acts would still have shared in the alienation of the times. Nevertheless, to repeat the important point once again, Gustave's passivity arose not from historical alienation, but from the contingent fact that he was not loved as he should have been.

The previous remarks have been directed toward showing that our everyday acts enjoy a relative independence from our historical situation. The *Critique* and the *Rome* and *Cornell* lectures, however, give examples of how our everyday lives are sometimes thrown into the historical realm. The frequently quoted example in the *Critique* of storming the Bastille is a good example of the way history can intrude itself into the fabric of ordinary lives, but I prefer to cite and elaborate on an example given by Elizabeth Bowman and Robert Stone in their overviews of Sartre's *Rome lecture*. The case concerns a group of mothers in Liège, Belgium. While pregnant, the mothers had taken thalidomide, and their children were born deformed. Although of generally traditional moral backgrounds, they committed infanticide. Bowman and Stone write:

> Despite failing by the Kantian criterion, Sartre insists the infanticides *were* normative. Kant erred in taking the normative to be restricted to the repeatable. The acts of the Liège mothers lacked the "tranquility" of justification available when one behaves in the light of or in the creation of a value. These acts were instead "anguished" because historical; that is, dated and unique. For Sartre, their nonuniversalizable-yet-normative maxim is "I kill my child today so that tomorrow no mother will be tempted to kill hers."[14]

Bowman and Stone here interpret Sartre's claim that the action is anguished, because it is historical in the sense of being dated and unique. I think that their interpretation is acceptable, but the infanticides were historical for another reason. By taking thalidomide the mothers were thrown out of their family environment and forced to participate in the historical dimension of their lives. The world of insufficiently tested products becomes for them no longer a passive background that they dimly experience, but an active force molding their lives.

We should note Sartre's approach to the infanticides—the way he aligns himself with the women, attempting to understand the morality of their actions. He seeks to reveal the intelligibility in their praxes. Sartre sees a fundamental difference between what he calls violence and antiviolence. Violence is what the oppressor does to the oppressed; antiviolence may be the oppressed's response. While Sartre always condemns violence, he is more open to the morality of antiviolence. It is also important to note the qualification implicit in the remark that a "tranquility" could be available when creating values in more normal circumstances. I see this tranquility to imply not an affirmation of the Kantian categorical, but an acknowledgment of the viability of the way freedom functions within a local context.

My distinction among the three levels—the social, the historical, and the psychoanalytic—can be viewed as involving a twofold extension of Sartre's notion of spiral existence as developed in *Flaubert*. Sartre's notion has to do with the way we reappropriate our past, surpassing it toward new projects only to find that our past is there again in a new form that we must once again surpass. My first extension of this notion is simply to note that from another perspective we also find ourselves now dealing with our family and friends in everyday happenings, now facing the historical dimension of our lives, and now the psychoanalytic. At different times each is determinative of the morality of our actions. When we attempt to unite these aspects so as to give us a view of the whole person, we must do so without reducing one aspect to another. We can thus extend the notion of authenticity to be the way we handle the demands of the social, psychoanalytic, and historical levels of our life within a dialectical unity.

My emphasis on the three levels of existence also implies that circumstances may justify a person living a life basically on one level. Admittedly, my examples have not really illustrated this. I simply point to the situations of the poor, of those having to take care of handicapped children, and of those with severe psychoanalytic problems, and I suggest that it is unrealistic to expect them to have any moral concerns other than the alleviation of their personal inhuman situation. I do not, however, have in mind the middle-class person who thinks that he or she must have every modern convenience before turning attention to our historical situation. Where do we draw the line? I do not think that an ethics can answer that specific question, and Sartre was aware of the tension that, as he said in *Genet*, makes morality both necessary and impossible. More explicitly, in *What is Literature*, he states:

> Such is the present paradox of ethics: If I am absorbed in treating a few chosen persons as absolute ends, for example, my wife, my son, my friends, the needy person I happen to come across, if I am bent upon fulfilling all my duties towards them, I shall spend my life doing so; I shall be led *to pass over in silence* the injustices of the age, the class struggle, colonialism, Anti-Semitism, etc., and, finally to *take advantage of oppression in order to do good.*[15]

I think that Sartre's remarks are to the point, and I see authenticity, in the extended sense, to be our good-faith efforts to handle this tension between the needs of those close to us and the needs of those oppressed throughout the world. I see myself to be merely offering a different emphasis. The tension that Sartre refers to is, for the most part, the kind of moral conflict that is experienced by a person of good conscience who is not suffering severe oppression or extreme psychoanalytic difficulty. In one sense I am merely situating Sartre's comments by calling attention to the historical and local situation of the person experiencing the moral conflict. It is my view that, for the most part, ethics concerns those of us who have a relatively decent standard of living and who are in basically good health. I want to abstract here from political oppression, because that is a complex issue that I am not prepared to deal with.

But, for the homeless, for the countless starving people throughout the world, I think that they are justified in helping themselves and their friends. The most disadvantaged people of the world are the main recipients of oppression and, if they can pass over it to obtain some small relief, they are justified. That the poor can, at times, unite to help themselves is an achievement of such exceptional sacrifice that it should not be expected; rather, it is our obligation to help the oppressed because we benefit from their inhuman condition.

Of course, I am also making a few other points. I think that one who chooses to live a life within the tensions of authentic existence can and should experience the genuine good times that temporarily pass through historical oppression. Even more important, I want to call attention to the fact that nothing justifies making interpersonal relations repressive, not even a commitment to relieving the world's oppression. Nothing, not even historical alienation, justifies a parent's unloving acts toward his or her child.

Finally, with the corpus of Sartre's work in mind my claim is that, to a great extent, the emphasis on freedom given in *BN* is still present in the later works, but it is shared among the members of one's family and friends. The specific context within which Gustave Flaubert must work out his free acts is set not by history, but by the free acts of his family and friends. Of course, the historical dimension is also present, fixing the broader context of his life; but, as the *Critique* makes clear, we are collectively responsible for even this dimension. Freedom is always present in Sartre's works; it is simply more complex. Indeed, as I indicate in the last section, human nature itself is an adventure of freedom.

3. The Look

In this section I want to examine the metaethical dimension of our everyday reciprocities. The key works are primarily *BN* and secondarily the *Notebooks*. In *BN* the important section is part 3, "The Existence of Others," particularly chapter 1 "The Look."

The general movement of the chapter on the look is to show that each human existence is a contingent event, an event that once given affects the very subjectivity of another's existence. Our very selfhood depends upon how we respond to the silent presence of others within our consciousness. I also see the import of this chapter as laying the framework for what I take to be a basic Sartrean view that the moral aspect of an action is completely constituted by the action itself with no aid, guidance, or help from a transcendent reality. I thus understand a Sartrean ethics to imply that the drama of human life is real in the sense that our life—not only with its specific hopes and ideals, but in the creation of the possibility of these ideals—exists to a great extent as an inner dialogue with others. It is of irreducible value whether our parents and friends are in good faith or in bad faith, whether they nurture our freedom or attempt to suppress it. The significance of this claim will become clearer as I proceed.

Sartre's rejection of Husserl's and Hegel's being-for and Heidegger's being-with should be seen as drawing our attention to the importance of the specificity of the other's existence for our lives. It is all very well to say with Husserl that intentionality spontaneously reveals a world of artifacts and thus an interpersonal world or to claim with Hegel that the development of self-consciousness requires that we are each essentially a being-for-another, but in both cases we lose sight of the concrete other, the other who can use an artifact just as easily to kill us as to feed us.

My point about considering the specificity of the other can perhaps be made clearer by considering Sartre's critique of Heidegger. For Sartre, Heidegger's being-with brings us closer to the concrete other than either Husserl's or Hegel's being-for. Sartre's discussion is interesting, because on the surface it seems that he should approve of Heidegger's views.

> For Heidegger, to be is to be one's own possibilities; that is, to make oneself be. . . . Authenticity and individuality have to be earned: I shall be my own authenticity only if under the influence of the call of conscience . . . I launch out toward death with a resolute-decision . . . as toward my own most peculiar possibility. At this moment I reveal myself to myself in authenticity, and I raise others along with myself toward the authentic. (*BN*, 246)

Clearly, even according to Sartre, Heidegger has read Kierkegaard, and one might wonder what more Sartre could want as a basis for the reality of interpersonal relations. What Sartre wants is still the drama of each life and cooperation only as part of that drama. Thus, Sartre adds that for Heidegger: "The original relation of the Other and my consciousness is not the *you* and *me*; it is the *we*" (*BN*, 246).

The issue of what is at stake in Sartre's critique of Heidegger can be put in the following question: Can I help you to become authentic through the mere fact of making myself authentic? If Heidegger is right, the answer is "Yes." I tune myself authentically towards my death; I face my freedom and *by this very act* I reach out and help raise you to authenticity. I do not have to dirty my hands by actually doing anything concrete for you. If you are poor, I do not have to feed you; if you are oppressed, I do not have to relieve your oppression. If the *we* is an original a priori bond implying a positive moral content of cooperation, then all forms of mysticism and tutored passivity as a remedy for the world's problems are justified. The mystic praying in his cell and the Heideggerian poet in her room reach out to God or Being, and, because of the silent dedication and perfection of the mystic or poet, God or Being graces others.[16]

I also do not think that one saves the Heideggerian day by claiming that being-with is ontological and that its empirical implementation is up to us. This is obvious. What is at stake, however, is whether we ourselves create the very conditions for the possibility of our actions or whether we merely fulfill those that await us. A Sartrean perspective requires that we see that ideals and the possibility of cooperation are themselves established by human action. The groundwork for this view of human action creating its own untranscendable values is given in *BN* and examined in the essay in this volume, "On Action and Value." Of course, in the *Critique* and in the *Rome* and *Cornell* lectures Sartre continually extends and deepens his view of how we collectively forge the ideals that outline our very humanity.

I think a rejection of an a priori ontological "we" is central to Sartre's philosophy. From *BN* to *Flaubert* I see Sartre claiming that we have a very intimate bond with others; indeed, I would say that the bond is tighter than that which is described by either Heidegger, Jaspers, or Buber. For Sartre each person needs the other in order to be human. As I repeatedly claim throughout the essays in the second part, Sartre denies that we have a privileged access to our own consciousness.[17] True, we know ourselves more intimately than others know us, but not more objectively. We need other persons for discovering how we appear in the world; indeed, we need the other for becoming a person, for acquiring our very selfhood. Why not then simply call this intimate bond *ontological* and admit that there is an ontological *we*.

The reason is partially one of terminology. As the term is used by Heidegger and, indeed, by Buber, it signifies not merely an intimate bond with the other, but a nurturing bond that is a priori and that has its roots in some transcendent reality. The implication is that we are born into a fraternity in which God, Being, the Thou, the Encompassing, or some other superhuman reality unites us as brothers and sisters and that our evil actions merely cover over this natural state of cooperation. Sartre's rejection of the ontological we is thus a rejection that Nature or Being can ever cause any moral union among people. I see Sartre holding to this view right up until the conversations with Benny Lévy, because even when Sartre implicitly refers to a "human nature," he means the human reality as molded by our collective praxes. For Sartre, Nature itself is a human adventure.

Nevertheless, the movement from *BN* to the *Notebooks*, then to the *Critique* and *Flaubert*, and finally to the *Lectures* and the *Lévy conversations* indicates a deepening of the we-relation: with the mediation of the third Sartre sees that human relations can be a union of subjects so that the *we* becomes more than the sum of individual selves, more than a union that is the object of the look; but this more intimate union is still produced by our actions and by circumstances. The same is true of all modifications of the Sartrean *we*.

I consider the above description of the we-relation to be part of Sartre's anthropocentrism. As used in an ethical context, the term implies that we have no morally positive ties with any transcendent reality. In this section in *BN* I see Sartre pressing this point home by his insistence that the image behind Heidegger's intuition is that of a crew. A crew would not be a bad Sartrean image for cooperation if the emphasis were on the long history of workmanship that went into making a boat in which people could work together as a crew. The boat and oars, the slots for the oars, the seats properly arranged for teamwork, all these preexist for Heidegger, and one merely has to decide to be cooperative or not. For Sartre, however, we make the rowboat itself, that is, we forge the very possibilities of cooperation. As an image of an original relation among people, a crew, or an ontological being-with, renders the sacrifices and efforts of people who have worked to make cooperation possible into a shadow dance.

I thus see a strong anthropocentrism in Sartre's philosophy, and I see it as modifying even the kind of subdued transcendence referred to in a quote of John Wild given by William McBride in his excellent article, "Sartre's Debts to Kierkegaard: A Partial Reckoning."[18] I want to give McBride's cautionary introductory sentence before giving my own comments. McBride writes:

> Finally, he [Wild] turns to a third way of understanding transcendence, strange and unfamiliar and therefore not to be named, with the following Wildian formulation of which neither Kierkegaard nor Sartre would, I believe, have altogether concurred but which captures important elements of

the intellectual connections that I have been attempting to bring out in this section.

McBride then quotes Wild:

> According to this way of understanding, there is something radically tran-
> scending us and separated from us, which is nevertheless both present in
> and absent from our history. When present, however, it never merges with
> man but rather maintains a certain distance. From this distance, it may
> excite men and lure them on to acts of self-transcendence without interfer-
> ing with their freedom and responsibility, nay, rather eliciting and
> strengthening these, if man will listen to the call. But whether he listens
> or not, it is up to him, for he is responsible.[19]

My Sartrean gloss on this quote is that such transcendence does indeed exist: it is the legacy of all those who have struggled against oppression and whose efforts exist as part of the totality of worked-matter
that is our history. This "call to conscience," which is reminiscent of
Heidegger's poetic tie to Being, Jasper's Encompassing, and Buber's
Thou, is, in my Sartrean view, the totality of individual acts of inventiveness and struggle against oppression as these are fortuitously embodied in books, laws, and customs—in short, in the totality of both the
infrastructure and superstructure of our lives.

I thus think that we should modify Sartre's view of our social structure to include the residue of efforts of those who have fought historically constituted scarcity. Our present laws against discrimination are
not as effective as they should be and indeed they should not be necessary, but given the general oppressive nature of our society, it is better
to have them then not have them. If there is to be hope for greater
change, let us not minimize what little we have done. Unfortunately, it
is still true that the overall efforts of our society continue to be directed
toward sustaining and deepening the very inhumanity that the few fight
against.

Our attempts to rework matter so that it reflects our more humane
ideals are fragile. Large-scale efforts at censorship and long periods of
oppression and pauperization may eliminate them: "Tomorrow, after
my death," Sartre writes, "some men may decide to establish Fascism,
and the others may be so cowardly or so slack as to let them do so. If
so Fascism will then be the truth of man, and so much the worse for
us."[20] This remark from Sartre's "Existentialism is a Humanism" has
scandalized some readers, because it seems to leave the "truth" of
human reality dependent on the concrete actions of others. Although

the essay is admittedly loose and informal, it is on this point indicative of the strong anthropocentrism of Sartre's thought.

The look is both ontic and ontological. The look of the homeless and superrich are not the same: each reveals us to ourselves differently. The look draws our attention to the specificity of our neighbor and the way his or her existence contributes to the forging of our very selfhood. In particular, the look reveals our own body to us as beautiful, homely, or just ordinary, and it requires of us to learn about these unrealizable aspects of our life. "The Other is, to be sure, the condition of my being-unrevealed. But he is the concrete, particular condition of it" (*BN*, 269).

As I walk home to my Manhattan apartment and pass the homeless, I think that Sartre is right. The homeless concretely reveal to me what it means to have a home. Normally, I walk simply as one walking; but now I am for myself this strange being, a person with a home. When I try to realize this new existence, however, the looks of the homeless alienate me from my home. Their looks are different from those of the blind and the sick because the homeless are such partly through me. Some time ago I happened to meet a neighbor as we were entering our apartment building. We had passed two homeless men camping by our door. When we were securely in the lobby, he turned to me and said, "We should not have to look at *that*." I do not think that it was merely the ugliness of the homeless that bothered him but rather the way their existence makes strange the everyday act of entering our home. Indeed, I find it difficult both to see myself responsible for the homeless and to hold authentically onto my quality of having a home. When I am within my apartment, I let go of the images of the homeless and I forget about the distinctiveness of having a safe home. Secure behind closed doors, I put the dangerous "other" out of sight. Nevertheless, before going to bed, one checks the locks.

The presence of the homeless, of those in need, of those willing to risk life to rob me of my security, haunt my existence, and reveal to me the fragility of my body. Extending this perspective momentarily to our historically constituted structures, we are thereby brought in contact with the contemporary Manichaeism elaborated on in several of the essays in this volume. This Manichaen aspect of our society makes it easier for me to hate than to love. It alters the environment so that I am inclined to believe that good happens by itself if only evil and laziness can be kept in check. The need for more prisons, the belief that the poor and the homeless are so because of their own fault, racism and hatred of women, the fracturing of humanity through scarcity—all these are not merely psychological phenomena; they are some of the ways we mold and sustain our social structures. The present rise of much of the right-wing conservatism is based on our need to hate. In the article "Why America Hates New York," in the 23 January 1995 issue of *New York Magazine*, Tad Friend, referring to the growing popularity of Newt Gingrich's supporters in his home territory of Cobb County in Georgia, writes: "It may be that in New York City, hell is other people, but in Cobb, hell is often other *kinds* of people" (35, author's italics).

It is perhaps by now obvious that I do not follow those Sartreans who view the look as degrading or as unnecessarily emphasizing objectification. I should also say that I do not follow Sartre himself when, in *BN* and in the *Notebooks*, he tends to identify the look with objectification and alienation. This claim requires a good deal of justification on my part, but I first want to sketch my general argumentation and then I will develop it in the following section.

I think that there is a tension in *BN* between a true Sartrean phenomenology that respects contingency, the irreducibility of individual phenomena, and one that uses language contextually. The Sartre of *BN* had not yet developed the dialectical nominalism of the *Critique* nor the distinctive use of language of *Flaubert*; nevertheless, it is clear that basic terms such as the "for-itself" and the "in-itself" have no univocal meaning but are relational depending on context. On the other hand, in *BN* Sartre is still partially under the influence of Husserl's eidetic reduction. In the chapter "Concrete Relations with Others" I see Sartre somewhat forsaking his own phenomenology as he attempts to get at one essential structure underlying all human relations. He also allows himself to become too influenced by Heidegger, albeit negatively; in place of the Heideggerian being-with that implies an unjustified moral togetherness, Sartre substitutes a notion with a negative moral connotation, namely, conflict.

For me, though, the most significant confusion occurs because Sartre has not yet laid the framework for the distinction between the local, the psychoanalytic, and the historical that I see to be implicit in the *Critique* and that I am developing in this essay. These levels are confused in *BN*. Specifically, the historical conflict that Sartre sees in the world he puts in individual relations. Because we have constituted many of the moral historical a priori to be alienating, because essential aspects of institutions, such as the institution of marriage, are oppressive, and because our humanity is fractured by a sustained scarcity that leads to the oppression of the poor and the repression of women, Sartre concludes that the specificity of interpersonal relations must be identical to the historical archetypes. This reductionism is actually against the spirit of his own phenomenology. I thus see Sartre vainly trying to get out of his initial confusing of the social with the historical in the *Notebooks*, and perhaps that is one of the reasons why he never completed the work nor allowed it to be published in his lifetime.

Sartre's confusion between the social and the historical realms is the partial motivation for my reconstruction of the social aspects of *BN*, but before continuing along these lines I want to give some introductory and qualifying remarks. First, I wish to make clear that I am definitely not condemning the entire content of *BN*. I think the book as a whole develops a viable ontological anthropocentrism. Indeed, Sartre's own later and critical judgements of *BN* are always qualified; it is the social aspect of *BN* that he judges to have failed, and not the entire ontology.[21] Indeed, even when dealing with our interpersonal relations, Sartre's remarks are frequently to the point both in *BN* and the *Notebooks*. From my perspective these remarks have to be carefully situated within either the social, historical, or psychoanalytic realm or the dialectical tension that occurs between them. With all their problems and weaknesses I am grateful for the chapter on interpersonal relations in *BN*.

Why bother trying to reconstruct what Sartre himself has regarded as a failed attempt? Why not simply admit that the early Sartre was wrong about interpersonal relations and move on, the way he apparently did in the *Critique* and *Flaubert*? I have two reasons. First, there is an ambiguity in Sartre's own thoughts that I think can be resolved by reinterpreting the section on the ''we'' and the chapter ''Concrete Relations with Others.'' Second, I think that the *Critique* and *Flaubert* are written on different ontological levels than *BN* and thus there is a need to bring the ontology of *BN* in line with these later works. I think that if Sartre were rewriting *BN* from the perspective of his later thought, he might do it somewhat as I am suggesting.

I have two more qualifying remarks to make before continuing with my reconstruction: I should note that the usual Sartrean gloss on the *Notebooks* in general is that Sartre is trying to give us the ''ethics of deliverance and salvation'' that he referred to in the footnote to the concluding words of the section ''Concrete Relations with Others'' (412, n. 14). In this view, supported by some of Sartre's own comments, *BN* is written from the general perspective of the bad-faith context of our lives, and thus Sartre needs an ethics of conversion. While I do not think that it makes much sense to say that *BN* as a whole is written from the perspective of bad faith—much of the book lays the foundation of a unique anthropocentrism that is independent of good or bad faith—the view can be both interesting and fruitful as a perspective on chapter 3, part 3, ''Concrete Relations with Others.'' Betty Cannon has done an excellent job in showing how these Sartrean descriptions frequently can be seen as giving many of the characteristics of neurotic relations. I also think that Cannon is right when she sees that the basis for help and cure of these neuroses is also to be found in *BN*, specifically in the notion of a free project with its possibility of conversion, and some of my remarks in this collection are in a similar vein.[22]

Finally, I want to qualify the judgment that the descriptions of our concrete relations with others in *BN* are solely about relations in bad faith. Many of the descriptions seem to be very much to the point of what actually happens in our relations with others and to be so in a way that does not seem to be limited to bad faith. In the article on Sartre and Kierkegaard already cited McBride notes that the remarks in *BN* about making ourselves into fascinating objects in order to be lovable to another does not of itself seem to be in bad faith.

4. Reconstructing the Look

I want to reconstruct the social aspects of *BN* so that the deep ontology of that part of the work is more in line with the ontology of the *Critique* and *Flaubert*. There are two key related elements of this reconstruction. The first is to introduce into *BN* the insight of the *Critique* that ideals are historical a priori constituted and sustained by us. The second is to stress again the distinction between the three realms, the social, the historical, and the psychoanalytic.

From *BN* to *Flaubert* Sartre is concerned with the dialectic between the ideal of an action and the action itself. I suggest that the overemphasis on the negative aspects of the social realm in *BN* arises because, while the ideal of an action is historically constituted, it was postulated as the structure of an individual consciousness. Relations such as the masochism and sadism that are described in both *BN* and the *Notebooks* as necessary qualities of individual projects are, in fact, historical a priori. These a priori can be seen has having their own dialectic and as leading into the kind of failure that Sartre describes as typical of individual relations.

Indeed, looked on as historically constituted ideals, the chapter ''Concrete Relations with Others'' now takes on a new and perhaps more interesting appearance. Many of our institutions and customs are laden with a false love and with the sadomasochistic structures of interpersonal relations that Sartre describes. It is easy to become drawn into this disastrous social dialectic that moves from love to language to masochism or from indifference to desire to hate to sadism. We should not, however, confuse the historical realm with either the social or psychoanalytic realms. I suggest that once we eliminate the confusion between the historical on the one hand, and the social and psychoanalytic on the other hand, we see that each and every interpersonal relation does not have to be characterized by the historical dialectic.

I present the above analysis as an explanation for the confused tensions revealed in those passages in the *Notebooks* that deal with a conversion to authenticity. The question that one has to answer is, if the alienation is historical, how can an individual conversion be possible? I think my perspective helps solve the dilemma. Historically constituted alienations do not necessarily give the substance of interpersonal relations. Family relations can suffer from repressions that are distinct from the historical scarcity that fractures our humanity or they can be blessed by loving relations that are quasi-independent from this same alienation.

Of course, the general form of the repression can be traced to a historical a priori that creates the condition for its possibility. The ideal of love can be confused with the act of love only because an alienating ideal of love exists in the structure of our society. Thus, if Gustave's parents had chosen to love him, this love would have reflected historical alienation. Still, it would have been love and not dutiful unlove. The substance of repression or social well-being is therefore neither deducible from nor reducible to historical conditions. Thus one can experience a conversion from a social, that is, locally constituted, repression while still confronting historical alienation. I anticipated this view in my essay "Good and Bad Faith: Weak and Strong Notions," included in the second half of this volume.

I now begin my more detailed analysis of interpersonal relations by noting Sartre's own ambiguous comments about them. Despite the fact that he claims that the ideal of love fails, he distinguishes this failure from the love of failure as it exists in masochism. He notes: "Masochism therefore is on principle a failure. This should not surprise us if we realize that masochism is a 'vice' and that vice is, on principle, the love of failure" (*BN*, 379).

In general, I do not recommend relying very heavily on any one statement of Sartre's, since he writes contextually; but here I think the distinction between a simple failure and the love of failure, as well as the related distinction between an action and the false ideal of the action, reappears frequently throughout *BN*. In the essay included in part 2 of this volume, "On the Possibility of Good Faith," I found in the chapter on bad faith in *BN* a distinction between the ideal of good faith and good faith itself. The ideal of good faith, in this context, is a bad-faith ideal.[23] Consequently, one can fail to perceive oneself to be in bad faith, because bad faith is a way of conceiving good faith. However, I do not want to duplicate my remarks about good faith here.

My point is that if I am right about the distinction between the ideal of good faith (bad faith) and good faith itself, as I believe that I am, then even in *BN* Sartre has opened the door to a description of good-faith acts, even if he has not chosen to discuss them. I think that the reason he did not describe them is that he saw that, as members of a culture, we seem to act more in bad faith than in good faith. Again, my point is that from the perspective of the *Critique*, we can see that in *BN* Sartre confuses the social and psychoanalytic with the historical.

The distinction between the ideal of belief and belief itself comes across clearly in *Flaubert*. To refer again to the example in book 2, Sartre distinguishes between filial love and filial piety. ''Filial love can be sincere, that is, *felt*. Filial piety, by contrast, is ''show'' (*Flaubert,* 23). Filial piety is a show because the ideal of what this love should be is more real than the concrete acts of love. It is not ideals that Sartre is opposed to—every act implies an ideal. What Sartre condemns is making an action to be a mere instance of an ideal. This makes change impossible and sets repetition as the goal of life. Gustave suffers because his father wants him to be like his brother; the brother was a repetition of the father and this was to be Gustave's fate, a fate that, unfortunately, his mother also wanted for him.

In the limited context considered above, I agree with Sartre's own remarks that his discussion of social relations in *BN* suffers from ''a bad realism.''[24] I understand this bad realism to consist in postulating historical alienation as characteristic of the substance of every interpersonal relation. Similarly, a priori structures of consciousness, such as that the for-itself seeks the impossible ideal to be God, are also, for me, first and foremost a historical structure that becomes in *BN* the characteristic of the individual. I want to expand on this view of consciousness as a failure to be God.

Over the years my own gloss on Sartre's view that the self aims at the impossible ideal of a for-itself that is also an in-itself has been to distinguish between failure as thematized and as simply lived. That is to say, ontologically, I saw this failure to be simply freedom and in turn I saw this freedom to be the lack of identity of a self with its own selfhood. Thus, even within the context of *BN* one can claim that, insofar as this failure is simply lived, it is passed through without explicitly mediating our actions. I said that this was my usual commentary. Now I am more inclined to simply drop the notion of consciousness as a failure to be God and to substitute in its place our own creation within the practico-inert of bad-faith ideals. Specifically, under the influence of our Platonic-Christian heritage we have forged ideals within the social structure—ideals that are reflected in our laws and customs—that incline us to see an ideal to be more real than an action in such a way that the action tends to be a merely repetitive instance of the ideal, with no element of inventiveness.

I thus think that it is fruitful to interpret the chapter "Concrete Relations with Others" within the context of the distinction between simple action and the ideal of the action. It is also important to revise one's view of ideals and perceive them as historical a priori constituted and sustained by collective praxes. The following passage, while admittedly not representative of the chapter, points in this direction.

> This unrealizable ideal which haunts my project of myself in the presence of the Other is not to be identified with love in so far as love is an enterprize; i.e., an organic ensemble of projects toward my own possibilities. But it is the ideal of love, its motivation and its end, its unique value. (*BN*, 366)

Love as an ensemble of projects is just the complex of loving acts. There is no value here apart from the acts of love. But love as an ideal has a value over and above the acts of love, namely, that the lover wants the beloved to grant, by one grand act of loving, the security of being confirmed once and for all as a justified existence. Still, given the distinction between loving acts and the ideal of love, why does Sartre not describe it more fully, and why does he give us the impression that love as an ideal is itself ontological. Aside from the usual explanation hinted at by Sartre himself and accepted by many Sartreans, that in *BN* Sartre was intent on describing relations in bad faith, I can only repeat my own nuance to this accepted explanation: We are inclined to seek false ideals because they are part of the public realm and thus an essential part of our historical situation. From this perspective Sartre had not yet worked out the notion of the practico-inert elaborated in the *Critique*— that is the distinctive alienating features of our social structure—but something like this notion was already functioning within *BN*.

Regardless of the reasons for Sartre's emphasis on bad faith in *BN*, the important point here is that when Sartre focuses simply on the distinction between loving acts and the ideal of love, two forms of love emerge as equally possible, although, perhaps, not equally probable. We are capable of loving acts even though the historical situation inclines us to repetitive acts that merely mimic an ideal. Thus, despite the historical pressures, Gustave's parents were responsible for giving him a passive nature. Specifically, in Flaubert's case the look or touch of his mother was not a confirming one. I add touch, because in the quote that follows Sartre refers to the mother's "handling" of the infant. I see no great import in this change from a look to a touch, because the look directs us primarily to the other as a happening and not as an object.

> Indeed, the Other is there, diffused, from the first day in that discovery I make of myself through my passive experience of otherness. That is, through the repeated handling of my body by forces which are alien, purposive, serving my needs. Even on this level, however basic, love is required. Or rather, the attentions the baby receives *are* love. (*Flaubert*, vol. 1: 129–30, n. 2)

I think that Sartrean conflict can benefit from the same reconstruction as that of the look. I will again introduce my interpretation by noting some ambivalence in Sartre's own use of conflict. In the long section in the *Notebooks* that deals with children Sartre writes: "There is violence in the relation of parents to children,"[25] but then he qualifies his remarks.

> I do understand that there are two kinds of parents. 1st, those who conceive of the Good as already existing. . . . Here education is negative, destructive, and one places one's confidence in an already existing order (as in the case of an auto-da-fe or anti-Semitism). 2nd, those more liberal who want the child to be able to choose his own good when he grows up. (*Notebooks*, 191)[26]

Even liberal parents have to give a child direction; an adult's reason is, in fact, more developed than the child's. Conflict is, in a sense, unavoidable. How then does one deal with children ethically? In his answer Sartre indirectly initiates his critique of Kant, which he is to continue in both the *Rome* and *Cornell* lectures.

> We have to renounce seeing the future man in the child as an absolute end that justifies every means, instead considering that this end can be attained only if, in each case, the situation of the child is the means of his concrete and real emancipation. The future has to be seen through the perspectives of the present, we have to comprehend that it is *the future of this present*,

giving each present along with the future it foreshadows an absolute value. (*Notebooks*, 194)[27]

A child is a child and not an immature adult. Thus, a parent should not sacrifice the child of today to the adult of tomorrow any more than a revolutionary group should sacrifice the humanity of today to the humanity of tomorrow. But discipline and sacrifices can be asked. The child has to be stopped from harming himself, but this intervention is not to be taken as an excuse for considering him ignorant of all his actions.

One has to admit, however, that the general movement in the *Notebooks* is away from the notion of conflict as essential to human relations and toward showing, in such phenomena as the gift, that we can overcome the conflict and sadomasochism initiated by the look.[28] Again I return to my reconstruction: I think a basic confusion between the historical and social realms has occurred. In *BN* Sartre has substituted historically morally oppressive conflict with ontological conflict. In this respect my analysis would be similar to the one given above on the confusion between the ideal of an act and the act itself, but the situation with conflict is more subtle, and the point I wish to make can be brought out by reflecting on the following passage in *BN*:[29] "Now at last we can make precise the meaning of this upsurge of the Other in and through the look. The Other is in no way given to us as an object. The objectification of the Other would be the collapse of his being-as-a-look" (*BN*, 268).

There are two important points I want to make about this passage. First, on the basic ontological level of the look the other is not given as an object. The look is primarily an ontological bond that arises because one owes one's very exteriority to the other, an exteriority that is an essential aspect of one's very selfhood. It is important to note that this awareness of our exteriority is not the same as objectification. Our exteriority is the lived body as it exists before others. But it is the lived body that faces the other and not a mere object. I do not experience shame because you have objectified me as shameful but because you reveal me as possibly shameful to myself. Thus Sartre says in the above quote, "The objectification of the other would be the collapse of his being-as-look." That is, if I can degrade you into an object, then your look becomes a mere object that I can now deal with as such. My shame becomes just your private opinion of me and not, perhaps, my very exteriority. Once I make you into an object, I can claim that I do not truly appear as shameful to other people.

We can also somewhat reverse the reasoning given above in the following way: objectification is the collapse of the look, and it is also a necessary consequence of the look. The ontological level of the look is not stable; it leads to a dialectic of objectifications. It is here that Sartre sees conflict arise. For example, I try to escape your look and your revelation of me as shameful by making you into an object. For the Sartre of *BN* conflict is now necessary because my attempt to regain myself will always involve a bad-faith attempt to degrade your revelation of me into a mere object.

The dialectic of objectification following the look, however, does not necessarily lead to conflict or sadomasochistic relations. Of itself, the movement between subject and object, between facticity and transcendence, between interiority and exteriority that follows the look means merely that I have to make a continual effort to get to know how my acts appear to the other. This effort can be painful because frequently I am tempted to hold on to a bad-faith view of my own actions; nevertheless, it does not necessarily lead to the kind of conflict described by Sartre in *BN*.

In summary, I think that my reconstructed version of the chapters "The Look" and "Concrete Relations with Others" allows us to retain the essential aspect of the look: the other is there as distinct from me, and cooperation, the unity of ends, is something established by the mutual efforts of those involved. In the language of the *Notebooks*, you freely make an appeal making my end your end, and I accept your help. Such cooperation is both ontic and ontological; it establishes the conditions of its possibility as well as its actuality. "Indeed, human reality being ontic-ontological, one of the structures of surpassing that it brings from its situation is the passage to the universal" (*Notebooks*, 422).

I see the look, that is, my reconstructed version of it, to be present in the *Critique*, because the genuine we of the group is again the product of effort. Finally, in *Flaubert* the look reappears as the difference between unloving looks that harmfully mold the child's body into a passive object and loving looks that forge it into an active center eager to enter into the world with hope and confidence.

Why then do I want to keep the look as an essential aspect of interpersonal relations? Only the look cuts through the Heideggerian *mitsein* and all forms of mystic unions among selves that tend to justify passivism as a way of helping others. Further, once we recognize that in *BN* and in the *Notebooks* the social realm has been confused with the historical and the psychoanalytic, the look becomes not only viable but consistent with Sartre's later philosophy. The basic notion of the look is to reveal the other to me as irreducibly unique and as yet tied to me in an adventure that has the well-being of our very selfhoods at stake. For me, what Sartre calls "recognition," "praxis," and "spiral existence" all depend on the deeper ontology of the look.

I also like the notion of conflict, but I would want to distinguish between a healthy conflict and bad-faith one. A useful conflict exists between our unmediated experience of our body and the way this experience is seen by others. This conflict exists even if someone praises us, because we still have to discover the meaning of that praise. I must continue to exert effort if I am not to become totally alienated from my exterior. Further, this process of getting to know about myself from others can be painful. No matter how much others help me by making my project their project, true growth implies some pain. This point is brought out in a brief biography of the composer Walter Piston given in Manhattan's Museum of Modern Art calendar "Summergarden 1995": "A kind and gentle teacher, his criticisms could be pointed yet were never harsh." Strong, caring relations must, at times, be "pointed." If I call this feature of interpersonal relations a type of conflict, it is a conflict that is not a violence.

In the final analysis, however, I am willing to sacrifice names for notions and realities. By whatever names and by way of a final repetition, the main issues I am concerned with are as follows. First, it is through the look that the other appears to me as a contingent and unique event in my life. Although contingent in origin, the other is nevertheless bound to me in an adventure that is of our own making, an adventure in which we can expect no help or guidance from any transcendent reality, whether God, Being, or Nature. Second, we live within the milieu of historical a priori constituted and sustained by us. These a priori give us the ideals that we must transcend, and, unfortunately, they reflect for the most part a humanly made scarcity that fractures our humanity into the favored and the unfavored. Third, the social, historical, and psychoanalytic realms are distinct although related. There is thus a substantive difference between repressions that arise because of interpersonal family relations and those that are caused by historical alienation. For example, parents who decide that raising their children is more important than the pursuit of wealth make a morally correct decision. They escape, to a great extent, the alienating attempt to keep up with and even surpass the social standing of their neighbors. Likewise genuine conversions are possible even though the converted state will exhibit the genuine features of the historical alienation characteristic of the age. Of course, a true and full authenticity will always involve a dialectic among the three realms. I discuss this dialectic briefly in my concluding remarks and deal with it in the essay "Authenticity" contained in part 2. When I wrote that essay, however, I had not worked out clearly the distinctions among the three realms.

5. The "Third" and the Dimension of History

In Sartre's view a society consists of groups and the collective. Groups are in varying stages of activity, and, as a social structure, the collective is passive. Groups arise from the collective and fall back into it, and there is a dialectical tension between the two. The collective is, in a sense, the remnants of degenerate groups, and, as such, it consists of buildings, newspapers, and the entire physical structure of a society, as well as the people within it. We are members of a collective precisely as we share in this complex, for example, by buying a newspaper or by taking a bus to work.[30]

There exists in the *Critique* a rather sharp dichotomy between actions that take place in groups and those that occur within the collective. In both the fused and pledged groups, our actions are able to overcome to some extent the alienations that exist in many of our social structures. As members of the collective, however, our actions share in these same alienations; for example, we suffer from a distinctive political impotence arising from a false sense of privacy. If we read a politically oriented story in a newspaper, we have no easy way to join with others and register our opinion. If each neighborhood had its own assembly hall in which it was customary to meet, we could more easily participate in group action, or, if citizen groups were common, we could more effectively fight the organizations that take advantage of the poor. The rich can afford to organize support for their benefit, leaving the individual citizen relatively impotent.

Thus, for Sartre, our democratic society mystifies its citizens to privilege the very privacy that the wealthy use to their advantage. As members of the collective, we participate in the degenerate forms of groups and suffer from the effects of oppressive groups. We act serially, that is, separate from each other, and in this impotent condition we await our turn to get relief from our condition of scarcity.

When we act as members of groups fighting oppression, however, we can partially affect the alienating features of the social order, or what Sartre calls the practico-inert. Indeed, only in strongly organized groups, the group-in-fusion and the pledged group, do our actions unite in a genuine we-relation. Each member of the group is a third mediating every other action; that is, each action is approved and supported by every other member of the group. Each individual thus has a power that he or she does not have as members of the collective; indeed, each is a sovereign third mediating the action of every other in order to produce a result greater than the same individuals could perform as members of the collective.

My motivation in extending Sartre's views is to qualify this sharp distinction between actions that take place in the collective and those that take place in active groups. This dichotomy does not seem to reflect much of our behavior. Specifically, I think that we sometimes act within the collective in a way that is not purely alienating and that approximates being members of a group. I am not here returning to my distinction between the local and the historical and claiming again that our actions among our family and friends are relatively independent from the historical realm. Rather, I am making a distinction within the historical realm itself.

My point is that although we may not be members of a group-in-fusion or a pledged group, we nevertheless sometimes act as members of weakly united historical groups that fight oppression. We are not totally isolated nor are we actually united. In order to explain this weak union, this ambiguous we-relation that is more than a mere object and yet not a true union of selves, I need to view the third to be not merely a person in a group but any situation that can mediate the members of the collective into a weak union. Before I examine Sartre's own notion of the third and my extension of it, however, I want to describe briefly the general context in which the need for a third arises. This discussion requires that I once again examine my distinction between the social and the historical realms.

The broad context of my distinction between the social and historical realms is related to the debate about whether society is monistic or pluralistic. From my perspective there is an important sense in which the pluralists are right. A pluralist tends to reduce the unity of history to a psychological phenomenon; actions of individuals are the only reality. A nation or a broader unity such as Western history has, for a pluralist, no distinct unity over and above the collection of individuals and artifacts that constitutes it.

The most obvious context in which to understand pluralism's rejection of historical unity is Hegel's "spirit." What is significant about this historical spirit is that the end of history is in some sense already present, just as the fully grown tree is in some sense in the acorn. This oversimplifies Hegel but it nevertheless helps in understanding pluralism. In a similar way one can understand dialectical materialism as putting Hegel's spirit in the class struggle. Again, in some sense the end of the struggle is already present.

I see Sartre to be partially on the side of the pluralist. He consistently rejects Hegel's spirit and dialectical materialism.[31] For Sartre the only history we have is the history we make and the end is never guaranteed. Still, Sartre is not a pluralist. History has a real unity, even if it is only a partial unity. Of course, partial or complete, history's unity is of our own making.

I want to devote a few paragraphs to examining Sartre's thought on the unity of history, and I hope that the reason for this digression is clear: my claim that our actions can enter into a historical dimension would be meaningless if history did not, in some sense, exist.

It has become somewhat fashionable to claim that finally, late in life, Sartre saw the importance of history and he thus wrote his *Critique*. Supposedly, his colleagues, such as Raymond Aron and Merleau-Ponty, always understood this simple fact, even if they wondered about the nature of historical unity, but Sartre was not stupid. In *BN*, he refers to oppression as a historical force and as a circumstance of our actions. In book 4, he gives a long discussion of "My Fellowman" that begins:

> To live in a world haunted by my fellowman is not only to be able to encounter the Other at every turn of the road; it is also to find myself engaged in a world in which instrumental-complexes can have a meaning which my free project has not first given to them. (*BN*, 509)

The issue then was never the importance of history. In retrospect, we can see that the great hurdle for Sartre was to discover a way of going from collections of individuals to large-scale social structures that were not a simple extension of the dyadic relations following from the look. The look can indeed be extended to the unity of a nation; but not without postulating a superhuman Look such as God. The looks of individuals could never lead to the unity of the modern state. True, I can encompass numerous people within my look and thus unite them within my project. Each person can do the same with me and with every other person, but in this way the state becomes a mere subjective thought.

Nevertheless, I still claim that my reconstructed version of the look is applicable within the historical realm. The look functions on a different ontological level than that of the third of the *Critique*. The look gives us the basic contingency and uniqueness of the other. Indeed, in my view the third presupposes the look, because the third implies that only by distinct efforts and special circumstances can a bond be forged uniting unique individuals in a genuine we-relation—but I anticipate myself.

The third, in fact, appears in *BN*, but there it is used as an extension of the look: I see my relation with you in the look of a third person, and through this look of the third I interiorize my relation to you. For example, someone tells me that I acted unkindly to you, and I examine my actions to find this unkindness. I may or may not discover it. In either case this psychological unity does not seem able to account for true social unity, such as belonging to a country, speaking its language, adopting its customs, and living under its laws. More importantly, it cannot account for the distinctive feature of our history, namely, the condition of a sustained scarcity that goes beyond that of a natural lack of abundance.

Thus, the look of a third can never account for a union that is more than subjective. For example, consider three people, a young man, a young woman, and an elderly man, living on a deserted island. Through the look each become a third in regard to the other two. The elderly man can see the other two as a couple, but this is a subjective view. What does he mean by calling them a "couple?" Perhaps they do not regard themselves as such. There is no objective "couple" in the social structure and thus there is no facticity to be transcended. For me, the three exist on the social realm and not within the historical. My example already extends Sartre's own views, perhaps, and I should now turn to the *Critique* itself.

One of the most important points about the *Critique* is that in place of an organismic or totally pluralistic view of society, it introduces the third as a way of creating historical unities through group praxis. These unities, such as the modern state, are ontologically reducible to the individuals that compose them; nevertheless, they stand out as distinct from the individuals as these are considered to be mere collections. Sartre begins his study with the frequently quoted example:

> From my window, I can see a road-mender on the road and a gardener working in a garden . . . they have no knowledge of each other's presence. . . . Meanwhile, I can see them without being seen, and my position and this passive view of them at work situates me in relation to them: I am "taking a holiday," in a hotel; and in my inertia as a witness I realize myself as a petty bourgeois intellectual. . . . (*Critique*, 100)

As a third person aware of both the road worker and the gardener, I can unite them in my perception, even though they are unaware of each other. The first reaction one might have to this view of the third is that it seems to be a mere extension of the look; but, as Sartre develops the issue, the opposite turns out to be the case. "It is important not to reduce this mediation to a subjective impression" (*Critique*, 103). Even if I am not looking out of my window, the road mender and gardener are united in a practical field in which they work ignorant of each other's existence. The road mender and gardener are such because there exist groups of road menders and gardeners. They have occupations and these occupations have a social standing. As I see them working I become aware of myself as belonging to a certain part of society. Before, I was just writing or reading my books; now I see myself, Sartre says, as a petty bourgeois. I too belong to a group or groups. Of course, by merely looking out of the window I am not actively part of a group. I may simply survey the world outside my room, and what I see is not my participation in a group, but the collectives waiting to engulf me.

I need only glance out the window: I will be able to see cars which are men and drivers who are cars. . . . These beings—neither thing nor man, but practical unities made up of man and inert thing—these appeals, and these exigencies do not yet concern me directly. Later, I will go down into the street and become *their* thing, I will buy that collective which is a newspaper, and suddenly the practico-inert ensemble which besieges me and designates me will reveal itself *on the basis* of the total field. . . . (*Critique*, 323–24)

This passage illustrates the distinction between the social and the historical realms. In my room I can be relatively isolated from the world. True, my relative and temporary isolation is itself part of the social structure. Aspects of this privacy can be alienating, but other aspects seem appropriate for human life. Sartre's main point, however, is that what awaits me when I leave my room is the alienation of the collective precisely as this forms the ensemble of the practico-inert. As I mentioned, our social structure, according to Sartre, is a complex mixture of groups in various stages of activity and union. Although there is no single totalizer, these groups are hierarchically related so that a certain historical unity is achieved. Historical unity is thus, to a great extent, caused by the way oppressive groups sustain and deepen conditions of scarcity. What then is the situation of the average person not actively involved within a group? When we are not actively part of a group, we are not thereby isolated individuals. Sartre correctly notes that isolation as such is a special historical situation that may or may not exist for a particular person.

My qualification on Sartre's view of the collective is that at times our behavior within the collective can have a grouplike quality. Praxes, or actions as they take us into the historical realm, can be either passive or active. As our praxes take place within the collective, they share the alienation and impotence of the collective, and from this perspective they have a passive element. As our praxes are within either a group-in-fusion or the pledged group, they are active.

It is this active aspect of praxis that I want to subdivide. When we enter into the historical realm, for the most part, we do so passively. We act as members of a collective, each person isolated from the other, as happens for example, if we buy a newspaper or take a bus to work. I think, though, that there are times in which we act neither as members of an active group nor as purely serial members of the collective. I want to suggest that there are many times when we are partially active even though we are in the collective. My qualification is meant to draw attention to our actions when they occur within a very weak group. These weak groups are different from something like a family dinner or gathering of friends that I said could be looked on as a weak group-in-fusion. The point that I made in the introductory section on mediation and in my reconstruction of the look was that a kind of happiness can be achieved among friends and family, a happiness that is genuine even if it does not alter historical oppressive conditions.

I claim, therefore, that a quasi-active praxis takes place within the collective. For example, when I write, aware of the hidden male orientation and domination of many of our terms, when I consciously try to avoid using *he* or *man* when I mean a person, I am a member of all those who are making some effort to relieve the oppression of women. I write alone and yet I am not merely serially related to every other writer. My language thus becomes a mediation through which I enter the historical realm; or, if I decide not to buy a product or enter a store because the employees are on strike, I act individually and yet I support the group action of the strikers.

The sharp dichotomy in the *Critique* between group praxis and serial behavior is occasioned by Sartre's desire to focus on the unity of the practico-inert. This unity can be revealed as an antipraxis that returns to fight against our own good intentions. Sartre gives the example of the deforestation that occurred when Chinese peasants cut trees to cultivate land. The subsequent flooding destroyed the cultivated land. Anti-praxis is a true feature of our social structure, even though the message of the *Critique* is that we can be dialectically aware of it. Also, Sartre was very much aware of the common failure of intellectuals to become closet critics. He saw the need for action and indeed there is no substitute for direct group action. Nevertheless, there is a sphere of praxis that is above collective action and not quite the praxis of the active group.

There is thus a sphere of action within the collective in which we do not act as the other, but in which, even though we are here and now alone, we act as a member of a group. We have not made a pledge to belong to a group—indeed, we may never have met the other members—but we know that other like-minded individuals exist and that our action does unite with their actions. If this was not the case, why would we urge people to alter their individual behavior?

This extension of active praxis implies a corresponding extension of the third and the mediation that the third accomplishes. Thus, not only a person but also a situation can be a third mediating a very weak but nevertheless real union. At times, Sartre uses the third as a situation, but it seems to be a negative and passive use, leading to mystification. He implies that a contract between an employer and employee can be the mediation that creates the illusion of justice but that makes the worker into a product.

I think that a more positive extension is called for, not only to make room for the kind of active praxis I have been referring to, but also to account for the unity of history. It seems to me that this unity can be accounted for only by seeing institutions, language, and the entire structure of our society not merely as practico-inert, but also as potential mediating thirds that we use to enter the historical realm. We are thus surrounded by other people's intentions, not psychologically, but insofar as these intentions are embodied in matter and thus give us the a priori conditions of our language and customs.[32]

Indeed, more generally, I view the third as the means by which we enter into the historical realm. Any aspect of the collective can become a third in the sense that it makes us explicitly aware of our fractured humanity. What we do with this awareness is a moral issue. I agree with Sartre that we should, as much as possible, align ourselves with the oppressed of the world.

It is now possible for me to apply my extended use of the third to the distinction between love as an act and love as an ideal. Given the notion of the collective and the practico-inert, we see that ideals are not properly subjective notions. Ideals exists in institutions such as marriage, and these institutions mediate every act of love. In my extended use of the term, a third is silently present within every relation of duality and reciprocity. Loving acts indeed have a directness that, as I said, is genuine when examined within the local context in which they arise, but from a historical perspective they too are mediated. The ideal of love exists not as a psychological barrier that can be disregarded, but as the very milieu of the social structure. Because of this mediation, we should expect to find not only that marriage rites vary in different cultures, but also that direct acts of reciprocity, such as loving acts, are also different. Today, for better or worse, we seem to be witnessing a westernizing of cultures, and we may be heading to that unified history of which Sartre hints in the *Critique.*

The practico-inert mediates all our actions, whether we are aware of these mediations or not. To repeat once again, my point about the genuineness of local interpersonal relations is that while the practico-inert is always present, it is not always of great significance. Direct acts of love tend to pass through the practico-inert, but in passing through they are altered the way sunglasses alter sunlight. If I am looking at a friend through sunglasses, is my look mediated? Yes, but here the mediation does not give the distinctive quality of the act. There is a difference between having an argument and a friendly conversation, a difference between shaking hands and hitting someone violently, a difference between a smile and a smirk, and these differences are neither deducible from nor reducible to any mediation, whether of sunglasses or of the practico-inert. True, every act exhibits aspects of our historical situation; but these aspects do not give the substance of our interpersonal relations.

Thus, what the *Critique* clarifies over *BN* is that the distinction between acts and the ideal of the act is not a personal matter: ideals and the conditions for the possibility of acts exist in the practico-inert. In this sense bad faith is in the environment not by magic, but because we put it there. I am not claiming, however, that all our instituted ideals are in bad faith, but many, if not most, ideals tend to make the ideal itself to be more important than the act in such a way that the act becomes a mere instance of the ideal.

The practico-inert thus gives the general context of our free actions. Although the substance of interpersonal relations is independent from the historical realm, it is nevertheless true that the practico-inert gives the general conditions for the possibility of our actions. More accurately, the practico-inert establishes the basic facticities that I can transcend. These facticities or historical a priori can be changed, but only by a long process of group praxes.

The historically constituted character of our ideals is brought out in Sartre's analysis of the anarchosyndicalism in the *Critique*. This distinctive humanism brought together skilled and unskilled workers, but the humanism relied on the difference between them. The skilled workers naturally regarded themselves as superior to the unskilled, and the unskilled saw themselves as in some way inferior. No doubt the unskilled also considered themselves as equally good persons as the skilled, but they regarded it as fitting that the skilled workers received higher wages and lived more comfortable lives. They found their common humanity in their opposition to the owners of the factories, and their diversity was seen to be part of this unity. The diversity, of course, arose from the machines, from the lathe in particular. The machines required skill, and this demand was interiorized as a natural human quality that some had and others lacked. What was overlooked was that the machines were themselves made by other humans, and thus this demand was thoroughly constituted. Sartre asks whether the workers could have overcome their own division. His answer is that even if they entertained the thought, they would have rationalized it. Practically speaking, they had achieved the only unity possible.[33]

Another example from the *Critique* illustrates how a historically constituted impossibility creates the very possibility of life. A miner in a nineteenth-century coal mining town may have accepted that he could never live as the owners did. This impossibility defined his possibility. This was his situation and perhaps his children would be better off. If the miner begins to grasp, however, that his situation is not merely the way things happen to be but the way the owners want it to be, if he recognizes that his hardships are greater than they have to be because of their greed, and becomes aware that the owners intend him and his family to remain as they are, this impossibility of becoming other than he is is no longer de facto but de jure. He now knows and experiences his hardships precisely as the result of scarcity, a scarcity created by the owners and sustained by them. The miner now has a practical awareness of his place in history.

In the following section I give an example of what I consider to be the praxis of a group-in-fusion. However, I now wish to examine some of Sartre's own examples that illustrate, admittedly somewhat indirectly, how individual actions become praxes, that is, how acts enter into the historical realm.[34]

In the *Rome* and *Cornell* lectures Sartre gives two examples that illustrate the relation between inventiveness and preestablished norms as these affect our interpersonal relations. Both examples concern lying.[35] In the first, 90 percent of a group of high school women admit in a questionnaire that they lie, but 95 percent of the same group also think that lying should be condemned. In the second, a Puritan husband, committed by his religion to telling the truth, lies to his wife about her cancer condition, which will lead to her death within a year. In both cases Sartre rejects the view that the women and the husband are engaged in casuistry, for they hold firmly to the norm of saying the truth. How then do they excuse their actions? They don't. They want the norm, and they want the freedom to break it. Indeed, the norm of telling the truth creates, for them, the freedom to tell a lie.

If casuistry is not involved, mystification and bad faith are nevertheless present. The husband's lie is an invention that sustains a norm while breaking it. In sustaining the norm the husband confronts the unconditional aspect of the moral life. Nevertheless, his lying now forces him to face explicitly the human source of the norm of telling the truth as well as its social-political context. He and his middle-class wife have been protected from the despair that many know as a condition of life. The poor and oppressed live daily with the despair that arises from an early death. Because the husband does not want to drop his middle-class security and because he does not want his wife to suffer the despair that others cannot avoid, he lies. More important, he robs his wife of her freedom. He imagines that she is as weak as he and that she cannot live with the knowledge of her coming death. By failing to reinvent his place in society he robs his wife of her possibility of reinventing the meaning of her life. In a similar way the lies of the high school students involve mystification: they want both to lie and to keep the security of the adult world.

These two cases do not participate in the historical realm as clearly as the infanticides referred to earlier. The actions remain within the local milieu and are successful in this context, that is, successful as lies. Nevertheless, as lies, the acts do confront the socially constituted ideal of telling the truth.

The examples of the infanticides and lying illustrate how we challenge and manipulate socially established norms, but even in the case of the Liège women's infanticides, no attempt was made to alter or change established norms. The infanticides were an anguished protest against an impossible situation, a protest that was seen as not repeatable. The question arises, however, whether our actions can effectively challenge socially established values. That is, can alienation be eliminated on the historical level? As I have already said, Sartre's answer is a qualified yes. In apocalyptic moments that occur in a group-in-fusion, the alienation is overcome by the way each person uniquely unites to another as a third. To repeat, the third is each person in the group precisely as each mediates the action of every other person in the group. The awareness of this mediation is not merely psychological; it is the very union of the group-in-fusion. Group action, or, more technically, praxis, becomes more than a collective action. A true unity comes into existence and this unity can overcome, temporarily at least, historically constituted alienation. Sartre's own example is storming the Bastille, but I want to give a more personal one.

6. The Group-in-Fusion and the Apocalyptic Moment

One way of looking at the *Critique* is to see it as delineating the large-scale social conditions that permeate our everyday lives. Where these conditions are alienating, as they frequently are, the praxis of what Sartre calls a group-in-fusion may challenge to some extent this historical situation itself. When this happens, it should not be surprising if the challenge gradually becomes integrated within the larger historical structure. A total revolution might accomplish more, but these are rare. Even when the praxis of the group-in-fusion with its characteristic apocalyptic moment subsides, however, usually something has happened to the social order—hopefully, it has become a little more humane. Without these group praxes the society in which we live would be far more alienating than it is.

I would like to begin with a sketch of some of the alienating structures given in the *Critique* and then move on to a more personal example of a group-in-fusion. Some of my remarks will be repetitive, but I want to bring them together.

The right of privacy hides a distinctive, historically constituted form of behavior that Sartre calls "seriality."[36] Sartre appropriates the term *seriality* from the mathematical distinction between cardinal and ordinal numbers. Cardinal numbers are a simple ordering: one, two, three, and so on. The primary insight here is that each number represents a set of elements and that all sets that can be put into a one-to-one correspondence with these elements have the same number. On the other hand, the serial use of numbers implies a distinctive sequential ordering among numbers: the first, the second, the third, and so on. Sartre's point is that the social structure tends to order us serially. A group of ten people is not simply a collection of ten individuals; rather, the ten will be related among each other as first, second, third, . . . through tenth.

Serial ordering cannot be deduced from the look. That is to say, it cannot be deduced from either reciprocity or alienation as these occur within the context of our immediate, abstract relations with others. Rather, seriality arises from the particular way we have molded our environment historically, and it is thus not a question of a private or psychological understanding of human relations. We discover seriality in things and in the way we use them; it exists in the arrangement of the workplace and the school and in the entire milieu of our democratic societies.

Seriality is the reverse side of the very privacy we love. Sartre uses the example of queuing for a seat on a bus. In a queue it is important who is first on line, because the tenth person may not get a seat. This ordering is in the queue itself, regardless of how an individual may choose to respond to it. Someone in the front of the line may yield her place to an elderly person, but this is a private response to a public situation that, of itself, calls for a serial ordering. There is no a priori reason for such ordering: our Western history could have developed in this respect more like a traditional Chinese culture, in which the elderly are always given social priority.

Aside from seriality, the practico-inert induces within our large-scale social relations a distinctive form of alienation that Sartre calls ''otherness.'' Again, this otherness is not deducible from the look; it does not arise from the personal way we may objectify another or see another in bad faith. Like seriality, this historically constituted otherness is part of the milieu of our Western democratic societies. For example, a certain job needs to be done—a machine needs to be run or a face-lift given—and, if one person does not do it, the practico-inert creates the condition that another will. What this amounts to concretely is that frequently one performs a task as if one were the other doing it; one performs it as being easily replaceable. Consider, for example, the research on artificial intelligence. To a great extent this work is supported by the military, and the fruits of the research are de facto aimed at developing robotlike planes that will make crucial military decisions. While most of the scientists working in the field claim that they are interested in only the theoretical aspects of artificial intelligence, the fact is that the practico-inert dissolves their personal intentions. Are they responsible for the large-scale goal of their work? I think that they are, even though it is true that each can say that if he or she does not do the work, another will.

Seriality and otherness contribute to a false privacy that renders human action collectively impotent. This impotence can be handled effectively only through a distinctive collective action that Sartre calls group praxis. True group praxis can never be achieved by serially related individuals each deciding in private that they should act as a group. On the contrary, the proper conditions for the fusion of these individuals must exist within the practico-inert itself, and those present must respond to these conditions. This initial response, which Sartre calls the apocalyptic moment, is such that individuals act in their own place as if they were in every other place in the group. Although separated somewhat in time and space, each person approves in advance of the actions to be taken by every other person. This approval is not merely speculative, because what the fusion accomplishes is the practical presence of the support of others for one's own actions. By nature, the apocalypse cannot last very long; it is born of extreme need and lasts only during the time of that need. This is as it should be. Only exceptional circumstances can justify such unanimity among people. Afterwards the group can still retain unity through a pledge.

Before I had any knowledge of Sartre's philosophy, I was fortunate to participate in a group praxis that in retrospect I recognize to have contained two apocalyptic moments. I had been teaching philosophy at Saint John's University in New York from 1958 until 1966, and I was tenured. For some strange reason the religious order that was running the university decided in the early 1960s to attempt to make Saint John's into one of the most prestigious Catholic colleges in the United States, and to reach this goal they began extensive hiring. The philosophy department consisted of over forty full-time members, in both graduate and undergraduate teaching. Ironically, with this very expansion the administration began to require adherence to obsolete and ludicrous regulations that had always been "on the books" but had never been enforced. One crucial regulation was the approval of textbooks by the department chairperson.

Because of the attempt to enforce these regulations, a tension spread throughout the liberal arts college and graduate school, and a series of meetings was held for almost a year with the purpose of clarifying the kind of university that the administration envisioned. Toward the end of the summer it became evident to a number of us that the university had the contradictory goals of wanting to be a first-rate Catholic university and still retain its extremely conservative outlook on education. Nevertheless, we thought that it was still possible that the university would recognize the absurdity of its position.

To make evident to it the degree of our discontent, a group of about thirty faculty scheduled a walkout that was to take place during the presidential address that inaugurated each new academic year. The plan was that one of us would stand up immediately after the president had been introduced and adjourn the meeting before the president could speak. We knew that unrest was widespread among the faculty, but we were not sure how many would participate in the walkout. We sat in the front rows and, as scheduled, directly after the president was introduced, one of us stood up and adjourned the meeting. Then, together with the persons to the right and left of me, I got up, put my seat back and started to walk toward the exist with our small group. The seats were similar to those at movie-houses in which you push back the cushions, except that these made a very clear snap as they were put back. At first, there was a moment of silence, and then gradually I heard other seats go up, a few here and there, and then suddenly there was a wave of motion and sound. By the time I reached the exit almost three hundred faculty members had followed.

In response to the walkout the university called in an outside observer and, with apparent overtures of good faith, resumed meetings with the faculty. After months of meetings it again became evident that the administration had no intention of changing its stand on the most basic issues of academic freedom. We then began to consider forming a chapter of the American Association of University Professors (AAUP). The administration panicked. In its mind the AAUP was infiltrated with communists. In response to this new absurdity, someone decided that, if the university was to become upset, it might as well have a good reason and that it would be fun to form a chapter of the AFL-CIO. To the best of my knowledge, no union chapter had been formed yet at the university or college level. Thus, sometime during the early fall of 1966, tentative moves were made to the American Federation of Teachers (AFT) to form a union on the college level, later to be called the American Federation of College Teachers (AFCT).

The original momentum, however, had been lost, and interest lagged. By December 1966 most of the inner group had acknowledged defeat in changing the university, and we began to look elsewhere for employment. Hopes for the expansion of the union on the college level were abandoned.

In December of 1966, during the Christmas recess, a magnificent stupidity unfolded: working in complete oblivion of their success, the administration sent out notices firing twenty-eight faculty members, many who had tenure. We were to be paid for the entire year, but we were forbidden to enter the campus. Our grades and examination material were to be mailed to the dean of the liberal arts college. No reasons were given for the dismissals, and, in order to avoid making it seem too obvious that the dismissals were aimed only at the union organizers, two or three faculty members who were quite unsympathetic to the union were included in the dismissals.

When I got my notice, I was elated, because I already had another job in mind, and I could now take the rest of the year off with pay. I called a few of the inner group; they too had been fired, and we all thought it was great fun. Somehow, even though the notices had been sent during the Christmas recess, the word spread. Within a few days I was called by one of the senior faculty members of the graduate school, who had not been fired but who assured me that the faculty were behind those of us who had been dismissed. I did not have the heart to say that, as far as I was concerned, Saint John's was a lost cause. I attended the meeting that was called, however, and when I saw the major part of the liberal arts college present, I knew that I was the one now being fused.

The AFT now saw that it had a real chance to make the union viable on the college level, and it gave us its complete support. At our first meeting we decided to pool salaries and divide monies as needed. Other AFL-CIO unions supplied additional funds, and some faculty members with large families actually made more on strike than while working. We formed an off-campus university and also maintained picket lines around the clock until the end of the academic year.

At the first full-scale meeting we decided that we needed some organization, a formal president, vice president, and so on. Up until that time, first one of us would take the lead, then another, but aside from the general recognition that there was a small leading cadre, no single individual was acknowledged to be in charge. I distinctly recall the moment when we chose our president. Nominations were called for by the AFL-CIO representative, and there was a moment of silence. It was clear that those assembled were expecting the initiating group to choose from among themselves. We looked at each other, and then instinctively our eyes turned toward Father O'Rielly, a Plotinus scholar, a very mild-mannered but firm man who, although he had never taken the lead in the formation of the new union, had always been ready to do whatever had been asked of him and who never pushed his own cause. Perhaps we thought that it would be fun to have a priest in charge of the first strike against a Catholic college. O'Rielly was a perfect Sartrean leader, in charge when we required someone to be in charge and otherwise a good listener and mediator.

We lost the strike, but the union was formed. The AFT still exists, and although I have seen it go through many of the stages of the kind of degenerate institutionalization that Sartre speaks about in the *Critique*, I think that the academic world is better with it than without it.

All of us paid a price for our group praxis, some much more than others. Many never got another teaching job. Regardless of the fact that Saint John's was severely censured and regardless of encouraging interviews, many discovered that, when it came to actually receiving a contract, most administrations did not want to hire potential union organizers.

During the time of the strike individuals had to make ethical choices. Teachers with families to support had to decide whether the immediate needs of their families outweighed the need to support those who had been unjustly fired. There seemed to be no general rule by which to characterize those who quit in protest over the firings. Some had large families and, after the strike money ran out, faced real crises; others, with apparently little to lose, continued teaching through the strike. The firings were handled so stupidly that most of the liberal arts faculty who stayed had to find some way to appease their consciences. Some took out an ad in *The New York Times* urging the university to reconsider the dismissals. Others claimed that they were doing their best to work within the college to get us back. Needless to say, such actions did not seem enough for those on strike, and many personal ties that were sustainable during the walkout were broken during the strike.

It is appropriate in an essay on morality to write a few words about those who did not support the strike. Here, however, I want to make a distinction between the moral obligation inherent in a situation and personal responsibility. I believe that ethics can judge both the general moral responsibility inherent in a situation and the personal responsibilities of the people involved, but there are areas of ambiguity. The strike against Saint John's University of New York was both part of the general unrest of the 1960s and apart from it. The civil rights movement and the general emphasis on freedom of expression that were characteristic of the 1960s made a college strike feasible. Still, there was no direct connection between the general movement of the sixties toward freedom of expression and the unrest at Saint John's. Our concerns were with the minimal standards of academic freedom—the right to choose your own textbooks—and not with the civil liberties of the oppressed and repressed.

Nevertheless, some of us were also involved in a small way in civil rights marches, and I want to treat both the Saint John's affair and the civil rights activity together. In both cases I believe that we must distinguish between those who are actively oppressing and those who go along. Those who actively oppress must be judged to be culpable. As for those who go along with oppression, I suppose that one should examine how closely they are connected with the oppressors, but I do not want to pursue that line of thought. My perception is that to escape blame in an oppressive situation, one must do something to fight it. In retrospect, I did little for the civil rights movement except to go on a few marches, and thus I find it hard to condemn those who stayed at Saint John's while making some protest over the firings. Of course, what is morally useful is not whether one experiences feelings of guilt but whether one fights oppression. I recall Buber writing somewhere that guilt and responsibility are useful only if they lead to a real change in one's life so that the acts that brought about the guilt will not be repeated.

Given my distinction between the local and historical realms, a happy family dinner or a joyous meeting with a friend can be a weak group-in-fusion. Such a mild group, however, is very different from a strike against an oppressive institution. On the one hand, the locked doors that create the temporal space in which the dinner takes place bracket but do not dissolve the concerns of the world. Similarly, a meeting with a friend can suspend but not heal psychoanalytic pressures. On the other hand, a strike or therapy can eliminate oppression and alter moral structures themselves.

Therapy, however, concerns only one individual, whereas a strike involves a group of people. Keeping to Sartre's technical distinction between action and praxis—namely that praxis is action in a historical context—we can say that therapy is action because it aims at a relatively immediate end, the healing of *this* wound and the alleviation of *this* pain. What is distinctive in praxis insofar as it works through a group-in-fusion is that it generates power that is greater than the sum total of the individuals within the group, and it is this power that can alter the practico-inert.

Group praxis is real; nevertheless, ontologically, only individuals exist. The group is not an entity over and above the individuals within it. As I said, one of the major contributions of Sartre's *Critique* is its explanation of how individuals can become united so that each shares the power and freedom of every other without thereby dissolving individuality into some type of organismic unity. Indeed, it is only through group praxis that true individual autonomy can occur, because the individual within a group-in-fusion can challenge institutionalized structures in a way that an isolated individual cannot. An individual acting on his or her own initiative can leave an oppressive institution in protest, but the institution remains intact.

The paradigm cases of group-in-fusion are revolutions of entire peoples. Needless to say, such revolutions are not guaranteed success. Further, it becomes difficult if not impossible to keep the revolutionary group from imitating the practices of the oppressive structure that it is fighting. Sartre gives some general guidelines for the degree to which a revolutionary group can morally indulge in violent practices. Simone de Beauvoir originally gave somewhat similar guidelines in a book that has not been given the full attention that it deserves, namely, *The Ethics of Ambiguity*,[37] and these and Sartre's own cautionary remarks in the *Rome* and *Cornell* lectures have been amply commented on by Sartreans such as Bell, Bowman, and Stone.[38] Sartre indicates, perhaps, the gist of the moral insight in his comments in the *Notebooks* on treating children. These passages were quoted in the section above called "Reconstructing the Look"; the point was that it is never justified to sacrifice the child of today for the adult of tomorrow. A child is a child and not merely a potential adult. In a similar way a revolutionary group can never sacrifice people for a future humanity. This does not mean that sacrifices cannot be demanded of people and that one cannot hope for and aim toward a future. Rather, the point is that this future cannot become more real than the present. The issue is, I think, similar to that of making ideals to be more real than actions. When the ideal of love becomes more real than loving acts, love itself becomes a sham, and when a future humanity becomes more real than the needs of present people, the revolution has not merely imitated institutional praxes, it has become a reflection of the degenerate institutions it opposes.

I understand Sartre to be claiming that the most important issue in the struggle against oppression consists in the praxis itself as an invention, that is, as a way out of oppression. A drowning or choking person cannot wait for a convenient time for rescue, and oppressed individuals cannot and indeed should not wait for the world to change and become enlightened before fighting against their subhumanity. To continue the analogy, just as it is foolish to require a drowning woman to demonstrate to us what her life will be like if she is rescued, so too is it foolish to require oppressed people to prove to us that they know how to use their freedom before helping their revolutionary efforts. I think that this is the direction of William L. McBride's own view in his *Sartre's Political Theory*.

Sartre's fundamental political commitment to "socialism and freedom" entails striving to "liquidate the practico-inert" wherever this can be identified and dealt with in the present, without regard to the eventual form(s) that society could optimally take in a distant and in principle unknowable future. (McBride, *Sartre's Political Theory*, 146)

Of course, even in a socialist society there would be structures and thus something analogous to our practico-inert. But what de facto characterizes our practico-inert is the humanly produced scarcity that fractures our humanity into the favored and unfavored. Sartre's general moral efforts are directed to revealing this "cultured" scarcity; however, Sartre's morality goes farther than simply asking us to be sympathetic to the struggles against oppression. Sartre sees in these struggles the inventiveness that is characteristic of our general efforts to create a better ideal of human existence, one that he calls "integral humanity." The emphasis here is on creation—our creation—of our own humanity. Here, I think, we can have two views on this creation of a new humanity. One is the grand hope of revolutionary new humanity, and this view would seem to follow Sartre's desire in the *Critique* to reveal an intelligibility in history as a whole. The other is what I call a deflationary perspective. This perspective, which underlined my commentary on the *Critique*, does not deny the grand view but it seizes on the more mundane aspects as perhaps just as important. The *Critique* works quite well if we forget about history in general and limit its insights to Western democracies. By "working quite well" I mean simply that it helps us to understand ourselves. In a similar way I emphasize below a deflationary view both of Sartre's remarks in the *Rome* and *Cornell* lectures about our integral humanity and of his comments on fraternity in his conversations with Benny Lévy. I attempt to show that we perhaps thereby gain more than we lose.

7. Integral Humanity and Fraternity: Inventing Needs and Values

The human organism is the original Midas: everything that it touches alters into a human relation, and it is itself the root of every relation. This anthropocentrism does not imply that we do not have ties with matter. Indeed, there exists a virtual infinity of such ties, and what we call nature results from our singling out specific bonds with matter.

Even our need for food is humanly constituted. Sartre writes: "Everything is to be explained through *need*; need is the first totalizing relation between the material being, *man*, and the material ensemble of which he is a part'' (*Critique*, 20, Sartre's italics). Need is a totalizing relation; that is, need arises from a free project, both individually and collectively considered. Our need for food is totally on the human level: it is the demand for food that has been cultivated; it is the need for money to buy such food; in short, it is the need for food in a social-political milieu and not in a state of nature.

Indeed, the so-called state of nature does not exist; it is a pure abstraction, or, to put it differently, there are as many states of nature as there are relations to organisms. In relation to the human organism, the apple in the tree is food only if one decides to reach for it and make it such. Unlike other animals, the choice of staying in one place and cultivating food is the choice of forming a distinctive kind of humanity, an agricultural rather than a nomadic one.

I see the analysis of need in the *Rome* lectures to follow closely on the *Critique*. "The root of morality," Sartre says, "is in need, that is, in the animality of man. Need posits man as his own end" (*Rome lecture*, 100).[39] Sartre is not here qualifying his philosophy of freedom by acknowledging our biological needs. He did not, as Thomas Anderson claims in his *Sartre's Two Ethics*, discover late in life that we need food as well as freedom.[40] On the contrary, Sartre is focusing on the way biological needs become part of the human adventure.

Of course we must eat to live, but the "must" of this claim is ambiguous. Let us examine the conditions that "must" be present in order for us to live. There are a virtual infinity of such "musts," and they each become realized only if free human praxes single them out: our lives require the proper functioning of gravity only because our science can make gravity a felt need.

Surely food, however, is a felt need regardless of science? Regardless of science, perhaps, but not regardless of our free praxes. Let me explain. An infant needs food; but suppose that, for the most part, its need for food is anticipated. Further, suppose that it matures in an environment in which food is always present. Then food as a need does not exist. We do not have to wait for a utopian society to see such a situation realized; most middle-class people live in such a world. Are they never hungry? Not really. For the middle-classes and the wealthy hunger is a good appetite. For the poor, however, hunger is a raw need. The hunger of the poor is like the pain of the tortured: The body is fixed in its animality, but this animal condition has nothing to do with the hunger and pain of dogs and cats that live normal animal lives. The animality of the poor, the extremely oppressed, and the tortured is humanly constituted. People should not need food any more than they should need air, gravity, or sunlight. The existence of such need points to the oppressive way we have forged our humanity, and the satisfaction of this need is, effectively, the eradication of a cultivated scarcity and the movement to an integral humanity.

Integral humanity is what we lack, and what we have in relation to it is subhumanity. The evidence of our subhumanity is the hierarchical division between the favored and unfavored. We have so constituted this division that the most unfavored have raw needs. All of us participate in this extreme subhumanity: the unfavored because they must endure it, the favored because their position requires this extreme oppression.

Indeed, we create a system of oppression, and then we view the system as natural. Within this so-called nature, we repeat our acts, because we are, in Marx's terms, the product of our product. Is Sartre here referring to an elitist notion of freedom? Must we reject the familiarity of repetition, the comfort of routine, and the stability of accustomed relations? I think not. But everything depends on where one is placed. Gustave Flaubert's self-chosen imperative made creation and inventiveness one with discipline. Further, throughout *Flaubert*, Sartre's distinction between loving acts and the ideal of love reveals that the distinction between repetitiveness and inventiveness is not mainly a question of breaking norms, although, as with the Liège women, this is sometimes required. The distinction between repetitiveness and inventiveness is one with the distinction between acts that merely imitate an ideal and acts that reinvent the ideal to fit new circumstances. This claim involves no Godlike activity: to love a child as a child is simply to reinvent filial love continually.

More generally, our good-faith acts are inventive insofar as they are a form of play, and, in turn, play may give us a glimpse of the kind of integral humanity that we are capable of producing. In play, rules are part of our creativity. A game, a sport, a hobby are human inventions. The other is there, but the other's presence is not mystified. For example, there is a proper way to hold the tennis racket, and there exists an entire lore about how best to move one's body on the tennis court. One performs these rites more or less successfully; but these rules and this lore are clearly made by us, and in play the weight of history is not mystified, even if it is not always in the forefront of our consciousness. In true play, as opposed to a sport already alienated by false competition, we bend and even suspend rules. We recognize their human origins and see ourselves not merely as instances of a universal form of the sport, but as recreating it anew in the present. In tennis one is free to say, ''Let us not play a whole set,'' or in chess one might say, ''Let us limit the time for a move to ten seconds.'' While play is weighted with history, it is our history, and we insert ourselves within it freely, interiorizing the rules as the very context of our autonomous action. Further, the inventiveness and the autonomy in play, particularly a team sport, exist as part of and through the rules. In the abstract, I could catch the tennis ball and, deciding to play baseball, throw the ball over the net. But this is chaos and not autonomy. Autonomy exists in play when, keeping within the rules, I place the ball where my opponent cannot hit it.

Finally, in play one competes as a human among humans. True, the starving and homeless do not play tennis, and we must never lose sight of this obvious fact. Still, play is one of the things that shows that our middle-class lives are not totally lost in alienation. With the minor exception that someone with more money may be able to buy better equipment, all are equal because the need of all is equal. My need to hit the ball over the net is one with every tennis player's need. Thus, play provides an insight into the kind of inventiveness required to bring about our integral humanity. Bowman and Stone write: ''Humanity cannot be conferred upon us by any system, Sartre insists. If we become human it shall be because we will ourselves have made us so, in effect inventing ourselves.''[41]

Linda Bell, who more than most Sartre scholars has focused on Sartre's notion of play as an insight into authenticity, correctly warns us not to rely too much on play as a revolutionary act that can alter alienating structures. She notes that play, before it can be revolutionary, ''must not serve as a safety valve within the structure of the status quo.''[42] There is no doubt that play usually functions in just this way, and as such it not only does not challenge the status quo, but reinforces it. My own approach, which is, I think, for the most part in harmony with Bell's, is to limit play and authenticity to our immediate social situations. Like Bell, however, I am not concerned with play as such, but with the structure of the playful act. Play may not be revolutionary, but the playful act reveals something of the inventiveness required to restructure our humanity. The playful act reveals that we can carry the weight of history as our own product, a product that we can remold for present purposes.

Unfortunately, inventiveness alone cannot be the key to understanding Sartre's claim that we can remake our own humanity. Sartre insists both that our new humanity will require new needs and that we do not really know what these new needs will be. If we do not know what the future should be like, how can we aim for it? In order to answer this question, let us take a closer look at needs. The proper satisfaction of present needs gives us a clue to what our future ones might be. Quoting Sartre in part, Bowman and Stone write: "[need is] 'the very root of ethics, its gushing forth at the deepest level of materiality.' Need, he contends, 'is never an alienation' " ("Making the Human," 115).

Ordinarily, needs and their satisfaction would seem to be alienating if the situation is alienating. "I *need* a new television set." If you have become accustomed to watching television, the absence of one can be a felt lack, one of Sartre's requirements for need. Bowman and Stone make a distinction between true need and effective demand—"need that happens to be joined to money" ("Making the Human," 115). This is an acceptable distinction, but they also indicate another direction to follow in distinguishing true needs from false ones, a direction that is closer to the *Critique*.

The first step in understanding Sartre's view of need is to again recall from the *Critique* that not only is need a totalizing relation, but that it is the *first* totalizing relation. That is to say, need is our first relation to matter. The temptation is to identify this "first" with our biological needs as these are seen to be quasi-neutral givens, that is, we need food in the same way animals need it; but such a perspective pushes Sartre's thought into an Aristotelianism that is completely foreign to it. I thus want to return to consider biological need as completely humanized.

Need is a *totalizing* relation; that is, need is the primary way the human organism freely relates to matter. Scarcity thus arises as one aspect of this totalizing relation. In the section of the *Critique* dealing most explicitly with this issue, Sartre says that scarcity is "a fundamental relation of *our* history and a contingent determination of our univocal relation to materiality" (*Critique*, 125).

The key to understanding Sartre's ontology is to realize how important it is that something can be both contingent and fundamental to the human condition. Briefly, Sartre's point is that certain collectively constituted structures can become so basic to our historical existence that they effectively define what it means for us to be human. These structures that form what Sartre calls the "practico-inert" are contingent because, when we trace their formations, we see that they did not have to occur. Conversely, the practico-inert appears as necessary, because, once given its existence, it sets the historical context in which our freedom must operate: just as our individual bodies establish the concrete past of our present actions, so too the practico-inert establishes the historical past of our collective actions and group praxes. Recall Sartre's example of the way the lathe and other complex machines required the distinction between skilled and unskilled workers: workers were able to surpass the division imposed by management, but not that of the machines. These a priori historical structures resemble Foucault's historical a priori, with the important qualification that Sartre emphasizes their freely constructed nature and the way that they are sustained in existence as the past of our present. In brief, they are similar to Foucault's historical a priori with due attention to the subject, although this puts the cart before the horse, because Sartre's *Critique* predates *The Order of Things*.[43]

It is true, however, that Sartre frequently speaks as if scarcity refers merely to some abstract, necessary condition of our existence, such as the fact that the resources of the earth are limited. Nevertheless, I think that these various uses are caused by Sartre's distinctive nominalism, which I have attempted to sketch elsewhere.[44] Briefly, this nominalism—that Sartre sometimes refers to as dialectical—is not opposed to universal terms, but rather limits universality to a particular context, and it further roots universality in praxes. With this in mind, I find that the primary use of scarcity in the *Critique* is that of a sustained condition that delineates our basic relation to the world. The sign of this sustained scarcity is that our humanity is fundamentally fractured into the favored and the unfavored, even as far as our biological constitution is concerned. As a totalizing relation, need appears within the milieu of scarcity. This point, I think, is brought out in the 1965 *Cornell lecture*. Again, I quote Bowman and Stone's summary.

> Life in the biological sense can be either an imperative, a value, or a good, depending on the social class of the agent. For the unfavored, life is a fundamental exigency, an imperative. For the middle class, it is a value to be produced and reproduced. For the privileged, it is a good that is automatically preserved by the labor of others and, as such, is a means for realizing other supposedly more worthy norms.[45]

This is the basic notion of scarcity that I had arrived at on my reading of the *Critique* and that I elaborated on in my commentary on this work.[46] The point is that an ontological view of need reveals it to be both contingent and necessary. What this means is that the hierarchical division within our humanity thoroughly alters our present need; that is to say, need is in the form of humanly made scarcity. This cultured need affects the very constitution of our bodies and their relation to the world. I have always understood this to be the import of the footnote in the *Critique* in which Sartre distinguishes his view from that of Marx:

"It must be well understood here that the rediscovery of scarcity in the investigation makes absolutely no claim either to be opposed to Marxist theory or to complete it. It is of another order" (*Critique*, 130).

I understand this different order to be that scarcity is ontological in the sense of being both contingent and necessary. Scarcity is contingent because the precise scarcity from which we suffer has been historically forged. It is scarcity in the form of a vow: the poor *will* always be with us. But this scarcity is also necessary; that is, once forged, it becomes a historical a priori that sets the limits of our humanity. Of course, it can be changed, but only by changing the basis on which our history is founded. Need as scarcity is thus the precise form in which need exists as a totalizing relation.

The fulfillment of our biological needs is thus not homogeneous. Given our technological progress, our basic needs should be much more equally realized than they are. We have created a condition in which life for the poor has become an exigency, a condition that is inhuman, even for a baby. The proper human condition is to have the basic necessities of life easily available. Thus, the primary need of the unfavored is life. On this level the satisfaction of need is its own justification.[47] Because biological life for the most unfavored is a need, life itself becomes mystified as a value that the middle classes have earned and that the wealthy have surpassed.[48] The middle classes and the wealthy view that parents should be able to anticipate the basic biological needs of their children, and they blame the poor for not being able to do this. They regard the poor to be lacking in self-reliance. The poor frequently interiorize this vision of themselves, and they are led to see themselves as responsible for their raw needs.

The notion of scarcity thus goes beyond the mere lack, for example, of the financial means for owning a house or the fact that not everyone can own a home by the seashore. The Protestant ethic affects us to the extent that, even though we can eliminate the scarcity of many goods, we refuse to move in that direction. Our technology has advanced to the stage that we could mechanize the production of food and housing so that we could at least be *aiming* to provide these free to everyone. It is possible to buy a working wristwatch for five dollars. What this means is that somewhere machines are hammering out wristwatches at almost zero cost. If we can do it with wristwatches, we can do it with bread, milk, and even houses. We are not even attempting to do so, because we view the human nature of the poor to be wild and untamed; it is best for *them* to work for the necessities of life.

The great irony of our civilization is that, while Homo sapiens have for millions of years struggled to improve the network of tools so that the necessities of life could be more easily provided for, we now aim our science and technology, for the most part, either toward creating benefits and profits for the few or toward useless repetition. No doubt both of these facets of our tool-making heritage have always been with us; nevertheless, the industrial revolution gave us the means of eliminating most traditional work in a way that was previously inconceivable. We are still unwilling to grasp the full implications that work, in the ordinary sense of labor, is to a great extent no longer necessary. We sustain a condition of scarcity in order to keep ourselves busy trying to remedy it.

Thus, although need is a totalizing relation and the first totalizing relation, need is distinctively human. Our most fundamental and basic relations to matter are established by free collective praxes.[49] Even our animality is constituted. As with scarcity, Sartre is interpreting Marx within his own philosophy of freedom. This need is not ''imposed'' or ''given.'' Who or what would impose it? Nature? Being? Nature and Being are human adventures. Always, Sartre's strong anthropocentrism must be kept in mind. I thus must also take exception to Thomas Anderson's claim that need is unique because it is *''unsurpassable.''*[50] Goals for Sartre have always been referred to as unsurpassable, but the untransendable character of goals is created by our collective praxes.

I thus see the entire movement of the *Critique* and the basic thrust of the *Rome* and *Cornell* lectures as pressing home the point that our fundamental hierarchy is itself a totalizing relation; it is the result of the way we have forged our history. At the risk of undue repetition and boredom for the reader, I would like to attempt once again to elaborate this important point. A semifictitious example may help to clarify how contingent features of our existence can become necessary for our practical life.

There are countless conditions of our existence that we pass through and do not regard as significant. The extension of one's earlobes is important to certain tribes, but in most societies the necessary condition of having earlobes of this or that size is practically ignored. There is, however, no a priori reason why the size of one's earlobes could not be an important criteria for prestige, power, influence, and social standing and the basis for building an interior life of self-esteem. We could, if we wished, trace the ability to extend one's earlobes to genes and thus justify extending natural superiority to those whose behavior allows them to support more and heavier objects with their ears.

One might object that surely such a society would remain primitive, because science and the capability of controlling the environment require the kind of culture that Western culture has, but are we sure of this? Science may require a specific kind of intelligence, but I doubt whether this is true for technology. Even if we granted the point, so what? For the Romans technological skills, political power, and laws defined what it meant to be human, and one could have, as they saw the Greeks to have, all the culture in the world and still be the stuff of slavery. The ability to earn money is our criteron for being fully human, and we attempt to trace this imbecile ability to genes. That being able to make money requires no great intelligence is clear from the simple fact that one can make a fortune selling illegal drugs. A capitalist might object that selling illegal drugs is against the rules, but the proper moral response to this objection is, whose rules?

I think that it is now possible to see in what sense we might be able to bring about integral humanity and how this invention is related to need. The perspective that I offer requires us to see that our actions, institutions, and customs bear the weight of a specific history, namely, the way we made need to exist within the milieu of scarcity. What this means is that, despite great technological advances, a fundamental hierarchical division remains within humanity. In order not to be overly pessimistic, we should note that our ability to recognize this division as oppressive is itself a more beneficial product of our same history. The introductory sections of the *Critique* are devoted largely to showing that our present ability to bring our history within the scope of human understanding is itself the product of history. I take this to mean partly that our efforts at creating a more human condition for all have not failed totally, otherwise the possibility of writing the *Critique* would not have existed.

We thus stand at a point in history in which we can both see how we have constituted our own alienation from our freedom and glimpse how to go about removing this constituted alienation. We have forged a humanity in which, for a large part of the population, needs exist as raw. Hunger freezes freedom to the human body, creating for it an inhuman animal need for the basic necessities of life. No human life is free from contingencies, but hunger and homelessness in the face of luxuries is the result of free praxes. Fortunately, our historical condition does not totally overwhelm our playful and loving acts—those immediate but abstract interpersonal relations that are the substance of so much of our lives. Further, revolutionary acts, with their apocalyptic moments such as strikes, and local group reactions against established norms such as the Liège women's infanticides involve an inventiveness that can lead the way to a new humanity.[51]

I want now to elaborate on what I see to be two senses in which we can refer to integral humanity, namely, a restricted and a grand sense. Revolutionary acts and the structure of play reveal the moral goal of our present humanity: the immediate historical and moral goal of humanity's free praxes should be to eliminate the same scarcity and oppression established by humanity's previous group praxes. To use a Heideggerian expression, we have "at hand" the means to accomplish this goal. All we need is the dedication.

I think that we have to make a further distinction in the goal of our revolutionary acts. Strictly speaking, revolt aims only indirectly at establishing an integral humanity; it is primarily directed toward breaking down oppression. Of course, there is the hope for more—it is the mothers' hope that the infanticides will prevent untested drugs from going on the market; it is the hope of the Algerians that their revolution will lead them to fuller, more human lives—but there is no guarantee of success. Nevertheless, every fight against oppression is genuinely moral, because it is freedom breaking its chains.[52]

Sartre, however, seems also to be referring to an integral humanity that is far more in the future and less distinctively envisioned than what I have already discussed. He claims that we do not know the future needs of this integral humanity. In this grand view of integral humanity the absence of a hierarchical society and the attainment of a direct democracy can be only stepping stones.

Let me try to state the problem as I see it. Need is our first totalizing relation with matter. Thus, integral humanity will require a new need as a primary totalizing relation, one that does not arise from a humanly made scarcity. Let us suppose that all oppression and unjust division among people were removed and that, for the most part, we used our technology more judiciously. To be more specific, imagine a world in which our technology has made our basic needs easily satisfiable and has also provided luxuries for all. Because of robots and computers, we all have food, shelter, information, and friends. In this world, what would our needs be? What would our work consist of? It does not seem likely that everyone will want to be writers or artists. We do not know the character of these new needs, yet we should aim for the condition that will give rise to them, because this condition will signify the end of oppression as we know it.

The final point that I want to consider is the relation of need, scarcity, and integral humanity, as elaborated in the *Critique* and *Rome* and *Cornell* lectures, to Sartre's taped conversations with Benny Lévy. It seems that more, although not all, of these conversations will be published, but at present I am relying on the incomplete transcripts, summaries, and discussions. William L. McBride introduces his own study of these talks with the remarks:

> Earlier in the dialogue, Sartre has conceded that he would once have laughed at the emphasis that he and Lévy are now placing on the need for ethics; his notion of being-for-another in *Being and Nothingness* was a good start, he says there, but it needed development, since it still left consciousness too autonomous. (*Sartre's Political Theory*, 207)

Note that even toward the end of his life, *BN* is still, for Sartre, a good start. It does not bother me that Sartre acknowledges that in his early view consciousness is too autonomous. I see this to refer to the qualifications that come from his study of Genet and Flaubert and from the *Critique*. The good start is the look and all that it implies, namely that the other is a contingent adventure that affects our very selfhood for better or worse.

Having said this, the potentially embarrassing parts of the interviews that seem significant are Sartre's apparent agreement with Lévy about the importance of fraternity. Fraternity rather than conflict now appears to be at the heart of human relations. It seems clear that Sartre is referring to the relations that we should have, as opposed to those that for the most part we do have. I would add my own qualification, that I see Sartre here referring primarily to historical praxis. One of the points of my division between the local, the psychoanalytic, and the historical is that, even in our present alienating age, our immediate actions can be fraternal.

Sartre's comments about fraternity are centered on our need to create a myth that we came from a single origin and that this myth may help us to see our brotherhood. I want to deflate these remarks and align them with the general anthropocentric movement of Sartre's thought that I see developing but not altering throughout his life.

I want to be very clear about this "deflation," however. I have absolutely no objection to the view that Sartre may have begun to take fraternity more seriously in later life; but this is a psychological issue with no particular theoretical content. For me, the issue of fraternity has philosophic interest only if it postulates an a priori moral bond that supposedly unites us as brothers. We are born into a fraternal class from which we may fall but that always awaits us. We can always return home as the prodigal son or daughter. This view is totally at odds with the consistent anthropocentrism that runs throughout Sartre's entire philosophy. I also find it totally unwarranted and an invitation to passivism. Fortunately, I see no reason to claim that Sartre ever held such a position.

The content of the interviews makes it clear that Sartre is working with Lévy within the context of what I call the "grand" view of integral humanity: We have a vision of an integral humanity, a future invention of humanity that we cannot clearly envision but that nevertheless we can aim for by aligning ourselves with the oppressed. The future is open to our inventive acts, and we should work toward that time when the conditions for the development of that humanity can be concretely possible. Temporality, however, is not a moment; its structure is like a vector: it comes from a past and goes to a future and thus reveals the present. If we are going to invent the future, we must also reinvent the past. In our present history, with its milieu of scarcity, the past appears as conflict. This appearance is not an illusion. It is the way we sustain the past of our present. The invention of an integral humanity would thus require a corresponding reinvention of our past: undoing the bonds of scarcity that have forged our humanity, we now see conflict to have been an error that we have surpassed. Fraternity is the root of our interpersonal relations. Was it always there? No, because then history would be an epiphenomenon. Fraternity will be present when, in creating an integral humanity, we simultaneously constitute it as the past of our new present.

In *BN*, Sartre had already said that free action can remake our past. Our past is a mass of countless happenings and choices, and we sustain in existence only those aspects that are relevant to our present goals. When, in my forties, I decided to take up tennis, my ability to keep my eye on the ball and the strength of my forearm shot surprised not only myself but my friends, but I was unable to develop a good backhand. It was then that I remembered the youthful years I spent playing baseball. That memory did not establish the practical way I was able to play tennis; rather, my new project of playing tennis reestablished a certain orientation of my body to the world that, no doubt, was always there in the way I walked and gestured. In a similar way, group praxis can reinvent the past in light of new goals. This invention will not come out of nothing, because fraternity is already characteristic of many of our immediate relations with others.

My view of fraternity as the new past of our yet-to-be-invented future is similar to Kierkegaard's appropriation of original sin. In *Concluding Unscientific Postscript* he reinterprets the biblical tale of Adam and Eve's fall from grace as a myth representing the sin of recollection: life should be a task, and the pursuit of individuality should be the main goal of existence.[53] This quest requires that we do not see our lives to be merely the repeated embodiment of preestablished norms and values. The Socratic quest for truth should be our ideal, not the Platonic gaze at preexisting archetypes of moral values.

Having offered this interpretation of fraternity, I admit that it is forced. Kierkegaard was pressed to make sense of his Christian heritage, and Sartre, perhaps, is here moved to incorporate for himself some of Lévy's Judaism. My own opinion about these conversations is that we should not make too much of them. Not everything Sartre said or wrote was momentous. Lévy was there, and Sartre was bedridden. I think that Sartre was putting into practice some of his own beliefs about generosity and confirming the other in the freedom that he spoke about in the *Notebooks*. I suspect Lévy wanted to use his Judaism to enlighten Sartre about the errors of his ways, and Sartre was not unwilling to attempt such appropriation within the limits of his own anthropocentrism.

As for Sartre's passing remarks about doing a third ethics, well, I suspect that they were just that. Of course, one could always say that Sartre was rediscovering for himself the distinction that I have made between the immediate local context of an action and the historical. The ethics of fraternity would then be a family ethics that can remain locally viable in the midst of historical alienation, but this seem to be basically the ethics of the *Notebooks* with a slightly different emphasis. The context of the conversations, however, seems to be historical, and thus we must insist that de facto conflict, not fraternity, is the past of our present.

A quasi-mystic view, one that has more in common with Plato than Socrates, can claim that our present bonds are truly fraternal despite appearances to the contrary. The price of this claim, however, is the belief in a world beyond our material world, a world that defines our true bonds to each other and to reality in general despite the historical ones we have forged for ourselves. A belief in such a mystical past would involve a mind-boggling conversion for Sartre, and I see no evidence of such in these conversations. Indeed, the commitment to freedom is still present as McBride indicates in his *Sartres's Political Theory*. Referring to the dialogues with Lévy, McBride writes:

> Here, in a remarkable passage, Sartre says: Socialism really only has meaning as the dreamed-of but in fact poorly conceived stage in which man will be free, and what people who want socialism are looking for,

whether or not they say so, is that state of freedom. (*Sartre's Political Theory*, 189)

Conclusion: Forging a Moral Perspective

Textually, I have situated myself within the *Critique*, and from this perspective I have taken a backwards glance at *BN* and the *Notebooks* and a forward look at the *Rome* and *Cornell* lectures, *Flaubert*, and the *Lévy conversations*. Substantively, I have distinguished between the local, psychoanalytic, and historical contexts of an action, and I have implied that one can unite these aspects of action into a single perspective. I have made some passing remarks about this unified moral outlook, and I want to conclude this essay by bringing these comments together and attempting to be more explicit about how I view a Sartrean moral perspective. Nevertheless, this essay is but a sketch.

Underlying all of Sartre's concrete moral phenomenological descriptions is the attempt to demystify norms and values to their human origins and to show further how, individually and collectively, we create and sustain our own bad faith and hierarchical ordering of our human condition. This deconstruction is one with a consistent anthropocentrism that unmasks the positivistic natural hierarchy—minerals, plants, animals, and humans—as a human ordering. It is in relation to our needs and values that humans are on top of the scale. If the criteria were longevity and not consciousness, minerals and not animals would be the goal of our earthly evolution.

The result of both the moral and natural deconstruction is to show that our basic biological needs are themselves the result of a project, that is, a specific totalization of matter. This totalization cannot be reduced to a grand totalizer; it is in fact the way we have forged our history through group praxes. These praxes alter matter the way we alter it in making a craft. We make a craft by embedding intentions in matter, and these intentions can reflect an entire age. A Chinese vase, for example, tells a properly trained eye about an entire epoch. In a similar way we can educate ourselves to see that we have cultivated scarcity. We have created a historical condition in which, for example, food as the satisfaction of hunger exists for the oppressed majority as a necessity, for the mystified middle class as an earned privilege, and for the blessed wealthy as a condition surpassed and unrecognized. Whether one calls this moral hierarchy a division of classes or a distinction between the favored and unfavored seems to me of little moment.

What is important is to recognize that the division is not psychological, but a fracturing of humanity that reaches into and alters the very core of each person's being.

It is not necessary to imagine evil people plotting to keep others oppressed and poor. No doubt such people exist, but the harm they could do would be limited and passing if it did not become part of an institutional structure. This institutionalization was caused by and is now sustained by our individual and collective efforts. Unfortunately, we can make choices about priorities and yet not see in such choices a refusal to help humanity as a whole.

Oppression is thus an irreducible evil. There is no deep-structured *mitsein* to redeem it. It is totally unjustified. There is no excuse for racism, sexism, homelessness, and extreme poverty. For the most part, the affluent middle class and the rich stand in relation to the oppressed as the Germans of World War II stood in relation to the Jews in the concentration camps. The oppression is more mystified and somewhat softer, but it is of longer standing.

Thus, in relation to those who are extremely oppressed, we have no strict rights. A moral perspective requires that we align ourselves with the oppressed, not out of charity but because we owe our very lives to their charity, their weakness, their confusion. It matters little what they do with their freedom, because it is we who are choking them, and their freedom is, at this level, nothing but the cessation of our enslavements and our murders. I think it is bad faith to see the downfall and leveling of civilization in this moral call to aid the disadvantaged members of the human race. What is at stake is not culture but how much of the world's resources a small segment of humanity should be able to use for its own advantages. At the very least, we do not even know what is at stake, because we have not tried hard enough to eradicate oppression. That some individuals and nations have tried more than others is no doubt true, but this may be the distinction only between an Albert Speer and an Adolf Hitler.

Who are the oppressed? To answer this question, I would again turn to mediations, but now with a slight variation. I take it as obvious that women at all levels of the social structure are more oppressed than men. From the widest historical perspective women justifiably can take a united stand against men; but this perspective is not necessarily the most substantively true in every case. A wealthy, white, American woman is not on the same plane as a poor African-American woman; the gender that unites them is torn asunder by a historically constituted and sustained racism. The African-American woman, her husband, and her children are, from this historical perspective, the unfavored and the oppressed, whereas the wealthy white woman is the oppressor. Is not the rich or middle-class woman oppressed? Indeed she is. Her oppression, her constituted subhumanity, is, however, on a different level, and while it demands to be relieved, it nevertheless leaves her morally indebted to the poor African-American family, including the man.

A moral perspective requires that we align ourselves against oppression wherever it appears, but I would say that we have a special obligation in regard to the most oppressed. From a worldwide perspective the most oppressed are the starving peoples of the world, the tortured, and the unjustly imprisoned—most imprisonments are unjust. For these people, life has been reduced to exigency. True, sickness and old age make life an exigency for all, but poverty, torture, and imprisonment are, to a great extent, conditions that are sustained by our own practices.

The concrete determination of who the most oppressed are must be made separately in each case. In the United States of America the most obvious examples are the Native Americans, the Inuit, and the African-Americans. We enslaved the latter, broke every treaty with the former, and did all we could to make the Inuit into caricatures of themselves. We should add to these the homeless, the imprisoned, and those in extreme poverty. Within each oppressed group, women and children will be the worst off. Indeed, even given my qualification that there exists a substantive division between favored and unfavored women, the overall oppression of women points indirectly to the existence of the unified history that Sartre refers to in the *Critique*. This unity is due neither to Hegel's Spirit nor Engel's dialectical materialism. It is, rather, a de facto unity. We simply made it to be the case that, for the most part, in Western and Eastern cultures women are oppressed. Perhaps our Judeo-Christian and Islamic cultures are partly to blame.

I wrote at the beginning of this essay that I conceived a Sartrean ethics to be an education in a moral perspective. I have tried to show how this Sartrean moral perspective reveals freedom at work—inventing behavior, joining with other freedoms to forge values and norms, unmasking the cover-up of its own tracks, and exhibiting the world and history as a human adventure. This freedom is not Godlike. It does not create out of nothing, but it does rework new values, new norms, and a new humanity from the debris of the old, and the old is always already humanized. This anthropocentrism is not a form of idealism, but merely the recognition that our actions go to the heart of being, altering it into a world. Thus, with the maturing of Sartre's moral outlook I find him still true to a claim he made toward the end of *BN*—

one that I refer to frequently in these essays, because it seems to me to go to the heart of his philosophic and ethical outlook: "My ultimate and initial project—for these are but one—is, as we shall see, always the outline of a solution of the problem of being" (*BN*, 463).

Notes

1. The notions of consistency and necessity are within our Aristotelian framework. This does not mean that we can disregard these notions, but we must realize that we have constituted them by more than two thousand years of praxes of the Western tradition. The difficult task is to show how we sustain both our actions and our logical values. Sartre begins this task in some of the footnotes in the *Critique*, but he does not develop it.

2. William L. McBride, in his *Sartre's Political Theory* (Bloomington and Indianapolis: Indiana University Press, 1991), adopts a similar stance on Sartre's works,

> As I have indicated in the introduction to this book, it would be a mistake to situate the occasional essays that were (for the most part) published in *Les Temps Modernes* and later in *Situations* on the same level of philosophical seriousness as the more systematic works, notably the two volumes of the *Critique*. . . ." (88)

McBride's book contains an excellent chronological overview of Sartre's ethics—the best available, I think.

3. In the interview with Michel Rybalka, in reply to R. D. Cumming's question about Sartre's tendency to exaggerate the change in his thought, Sartre replies: "But it was not like that! I was thinking in opposition to myself in that very moment of writing. . . . On the contrary, I think that I underwent a continuous evolution beginning with *La Nausée* all the way up to the *Critique de la raison dialectique*." *The Philosophy of Jean-Paul Sartre*, edited by Paul Arthur Schlipp (LaSalle, Ill.: Open Court, 1981), 12–13, hereafter referred to as *Schlipp*. Surely, of all of Sartre's interviews, this one has special significance.

4. Robert Denoon Cumming, *Phenomenology and Deconstruction* vol. 1: *The Dream is Over*; vol. 2: *Method and Imagination* (Chicago: Chicago University Press, 1991; 1992). At the time I wrote this essay the third volume of this trilogy had not yet appeared. Cumming's study is more than an examination of the contextual dialogue in Sartre's writings. It is an original philosophical reflection about the goal and nature of philosophical writings.

5. I am indebted to Hazel Barnes's excellent study, *Sartre and Flaubert* (Chicago: University of Chicago Press, 1981), for providing an early introduction to this massive work. I have read only the first three volumes and parts of the remaining two; however, my reflections here stay within the safe parameters justified by a casual acquaintance with the work. My essay thus suffers from a

lack of firsthand knowledge of the crucial last volume of this work. I plan to remedy this defect soon and to write an expanded version of this essay.

6. *BN* has a far greater unity than is usually suspected. Sartre moves from the abstract to the concrete in a very distinctive way. The full concrete bodily and social situation of human existence is present from the very beginning, but it is initially passed over until the proper methodological moment for its description arises. ''But what is important above all else, in ontology as elsewhere, is to observe strict order in discussion'' (*BN*, 218).

7. In a conversation about this section Thomas R. Flynn called my attention to the limited use of the eidetic reduction in *BN*, but I do not take Flynn's remark to imply that the beginnings of the distinct nominalism of the *Critique* are not also present in *BN*. Sartre's remarks are always directed only to the point in question. Thus, Sartre never attempts to prove more than is needed to clarify the issue at hand. This has misled many a careless reader.

8. See the introduction to my *Commentary on Jean-Paul Sartre's "Critique of Dialectical Reason*, vol. 1, *Theory of Practical Ensembles''* (Chicago: University of Chicago Press, 1986), hereafter referred to as commentary on *Critique*.

9. Jean-Paul Sartre, *Critique of Dialectical Reason*, vol. 1, *Theory of Practical Ensembles*, trans. Alan Sheridan-Smith (London: New Left Books, 1976), 95; author's italics. See my commentary on *Critique*, 103–6. I think that Juliette Simont approaches my distinction between the local and the historical in her concise and lucid survey of Sartre's ethics, ''Sartrean Ethics,'' contained in *The Cambridge Companion to Sartre*, ed. Christina Howells (Cambridge: Cambridge University Press, 1992). In discussing the *Notebooks*, she says:

If, on the historical level, Sartre's ethical attitude can be characterized as relatively pessimistic, on the contrary, in the individual and interindividual area . . . the value of 'generosity' becomes the conceptual instrument of a new and fresh optimism. (191)

Admittedly, we differ somewhat about the degree of pessimism present in *BN*.

10. See Jean-Paul Sartre, *Being and Nothingness*, trans. Hazel E. Barnes (New York: Philosophical Library, 1956), 580–585. See also my *A Commentary on Jean-Paul Sartre's "Being and Nothingness''* (Chicago: University of Chicago Press, 1980), 218–220, hereafter cited as commentary on *BN*.

11. Indeed, the essay included in part 2 of this work, ''Good and Bad Faith: Weak and Strong Notions,'' outlines just such an extension of the notions.

12. Jean-Paul Sartre, *The Family Idiot: Gustave Flaubert: 1821–1857*, vol. 2 (Chicago: University of Chicago Press, 1987), 417.

13. Jean-Paul Sartre, *The Family Idiot: Gustave Flaubert: 1821–1857*, vol. 1 (Chicago: University of Chicago Press, 1981), 129–30, n. 2.

14. Elizabeth A. Bowman and Robert V. Stone, '' 'Making the Human' in Sartre's Unpublished Dialectical Ethics,'' in *Writing the Politics of Difference*, ed. Hugh J. Silverman (New York: State University of New York Press, 1991), 113, hereafter cited as ''Making the Human.''

15. Jean-Paul Sartre, *What is Literature?* trans. Bernard Frechtman in *What is Literature? and Other Essays*, (Cambridge: Harvard University Press, 1988), 221–22. I wish to thank Elizabeth A. Bowman and Robert V. Stone for reminding me about this reference.

16. In *An Existentialist Ethics* (New York: Alfred A. Knopf, 1967), Hazel E. Barnes develops this theme of a moral passivity in the chapter, "The Temptation of Eastern Philosophy." Her perspective is much broader than the question of an a priori we-relation; she is, in fact, examining the general question of the self's tie to Being; but our concerns meet: "For Eastern thought a buried separated fragment has emerged from the Self like a butterfly from a chrysalis" (247). Barnes's work is thematically organized, and, while it was written before the posthumously published *Notebooks* and before we knew about the details of the *Rome* and *Cornell* lectures, it is a perceptive introduction not only to Sartre's ethics, but to his general thought.

17. See below pages, 135–38, 143, 152, 155, 157.

18. I sketched some aspects of this anthropocentrism in my commentary on *Critique* (50, 120–21, 136, 151, and passim). I have also written an unpublished book-length study.

19. William L. McBride, "Sartre's Debt to Kierkegaard: A Partial Reckoning," contained in *Kierkegaard in Post/Modernity*, eds. Martin J. Matusitík and Merold Westphal (Indiana: Indiana University Press, forthcoming). McBride's reference is to Earle, Edie, and Wild, eds., *Christianity and Existentialism*, 179–80.

20. Jean-Paul Sartre, "Existentialism is a Humanism," in *Existentialism from Dostoyevsky to Sartre*, ed. Walter Kaufmann (New York: New American Library, 1975), 358.

21. See *Schlipp*, 13.

22. See Betty Cannon's *Sartre & Psychoanalysis: An Existentialist Challenge to Clinical Metatheory* (Lawrence: University of Kansas Press, 1991), particularly her example of "Martha," 325–51.

23. Ronald E. Santoni has provided a detailed critique of this distinction in his *Bad Faith, Good Faith, and Authenticity in Sartre's Early Philosophy* (Philadelphia: Temple University Press, 1995), 78–85. Santoni is correct in noting some ambiguity in my use of the term *ideal*. Because an ideal is inherent in praxes, it can indeed be a good-faith ideal. I thought, however, that the context of my study made it clear that this was not the kind of ideal that Sartre was referring to in the section on bad faith in *BN*. Santoni's study, however, deserves a more careful response, but because I have just received his book, I am not able to provide one at this time.

24. *Schlipp*, 13.

25. Jean-Paul Sartre, *Notebooks for an Ethics*, trans. David Pellauer (Chicago: University of Chicago Press, 1992), 89.

26. Speaking about the first relation, Sartre adds:

The father, a Hegelian without knowing it, represents the cunning of reason in his own eyes. That is, he incarnates the universal order that step by step carries the child to the vision of the True, although by roundabout ways. From this point of view, education resembles the politics of the C.P. [Communist Party of France]. In the case of the C.P., one sacrifices the as yet unemancipated working class to a fixed Good which is the classless society. In the case of the child, one sacrifices him every day to the man he will be. (*Notebooks*, 192)

27. In the reference to the child as *him*, a mild sexism is present, and indeed a stronger one in *BN*. I agree with Hazel Barnes, William McBride, Linda Bell, and others who see this sexism as incidental to the moral thrust of Sartre's writings.

28. For example, *Notebooks*, 280–81.

29. I gave this quote in an earlier version of this essay, but again, I want to thank Thomas R. Flynn for a suggestion that led to my thinking differently about the passage. I still do not know whether Flynn would agree with my interpretation.

30. See my commentary on the *Critique*, 142–62.

31. In *Flaubert* Sartre gives his own version of the spirit of an age. For a carefully drawn summary of the differences between the Hegelian and Sartrean use, see Thomas A. Flynn, ''The Poetics of History,'' in *The Cambridge Companion to Sartre* (Cambridge: Cambridge University Press, 1992), 227–30.

32. It now becoming clear that immediate relations of reciprocity occur through mediations. It is interesting that Sartre refers to giving gifts, an example that he had elaborated on in some detail in the *Notebooks*. What makes a gift different from the mere act of handing an object to someone is that the gift participates in an institutionalized notion of a gift. The gift thus shares in a distinctive kind of temporality. The relation of giving something to someone, no matter how pure the motivation, is recognized as a gift only insofar as it reflects the social norms of giving. This means that it takes place within an established context in which goods are exchanged, and ''the gift *is and is not* an exchange'' (*Critique*, 107). The use of money to buy goods, for example, involves a specific temporality: the money that is in the bank already reaches into the future as a possible purchase of goods. Nevertheless, I still would repeat my earlier comments that mediations do not necessarily determine the specificity of interpersonal relations. To give a gift is to give a gift, and, as such, it differs radically from other interpersonal relations, such as stealing something from someone.

33. See the *Critique*, 242–47.

34. See commentary on the *Critique*, 95, 154–55, and 262–63.

35. Part of the *Rome lecture* is published as ''Determinism and Freedom,'' in *Selected Prose: The Writings of Jean-Paul Sartre*, vol. 2, ed. Michel Contat and Michel Rybalka, trans. Richard McCleary (Evanston, Ill.: Northwestern University Press, 1974), 241–52. The fullest account is in Bowman and Stone, ''Making the Human,'' 61–70. I indulge in some interpretation of their account.

Sartre also gives an interesting example of West Virginia's vote for John F. Kennedy.

36. See the *Critique*, 256–57.

37. Simone de Beauvoir, *The Ethics of Ambiguity*, trans. Bernard Frechtman (New York: Philosophical Library, 1948), particularly 90–128.

38. For example, see Linda A. Bell, *Rethinking Ethics in the Midst of Violence: A Feminist Approach to Freedom*, foreword by Claudia Card (Lanham, Md.: Rowman & Littlefield, 1993), 159–93.

39. The quote is from Thomas Anderson's *Sartre's Two Ethics*, (Chicago and LaSalle: Open Court, 1993), 121. Readers familiar with Anderson's work will note my disagreements with his overall neo-Kantian and neo-Aristotelian view of Sartre's thought.

40. Anderson writes that "it is necessary to find at the most profound depth of human reality, that is, in its very animality, in its biological character, the roots of its ethico-historical condition" (*RL* 73, Anderson's reference and translation for *Rome lecture*), *Two Ethics*, 118; but, in the next sentence Anderson gives the following qualifying remark: "If we just stopped here, he [Sartre] adds, what we have presented so far would be an overly idealistic account of the human condition"—overly idealistic because it would *not* have considered animality precisely as human and precisely as constituted by praxis. Indeed, early on the same page, Anderson, partially quoting Sartre, states, "Thus, all praxis 'fundamentally or indirectly tends to produce man—even if it in fact realizes his destruction.' " (Anderson's quote, translation, and reference, *RL*, 73). Praxis, either individual or through groups, produces not a part of human nature but human nature itself, precisely as it is human.

41. Bowman and Stone, "Making the Human," 113.

42. Bell, 255.

43. See Michel Foucault, *The Archeology of Knowledge*, trans. A. M. Sheridan-Smith (New York: Harper and Row, 1976), 126–31. Of course, I am only focusing on one aspect of this brilliant work.

44. See my commentary on *Critique*, 14–17, 90–91, 135–37 and passim.

45. Elizabeth A. Bowman and Robert V. Stone, "Sartre's Morality and History: A First Look at the Notes for the Unpublished 1965 Cornell Lectures," in *Sartre Alive*, eds. Ronald Aronson and Adrian van den Hoven (Detroit: Wayne State University Press, 1991), 63.

46. See commentary on *Critique*, 108–35.

47. I am indebted to Elizabeth A. Bowman for suggesting this qualification.

48. I am interpreting a small part of a long footnote on exigency and value in the first book of Sartre's *Critique*, 247–50, n. 75.

49. On the other hand, Anderson again gives us a neo-Aristotelian interpretation of need. He writes:

Because *man* with needs satisfied is "given," "imposed" on us, as our ultimate norm and end, we neither need, nor can we find, any reason for valuing this goal other than the fact that our needs require it. I believe that this is what Sartre means when he cites another statement of Marx's, "need is its own reason for its satisfaction." (Anderson, *Two Ethics*, 156–57, giving the reference *RL*, 97 [*Rome lecture*])

50. Anderson, *Two Ethics*, 156, author's italics.

51. Bowman and Stone remark:

If it would be mistaken to ask whether the infanticides are *justified*—because this presupposes some transhistorical moral principle valid in advance of any action, and Sartre persistently denies there are such—we can still ask just how he proposes to account concretely for this normative element in the example. For him, the infanticides were a "revolt" against the present in the name of a yet-to-be-constructed "human future" for all newborns . . . "*yes* [Sartre interprets their act as meaning] *human life is an absolute value*, but only as the possibility of realizing in itself and for (and by) others, *integral humanity*." ("Making the Human," 113)

52. Thomas C. Anderson is continually scandalized by Sartre's attempt to adopt a moral perspective from the viewpoint of the oppressed. The oppressed, he persistently observes, are no more enlightened about their future than anyone else, and on Sartre's own admission they are frequently duped, but this is not the point. It is the struggle that is always moral, because this struggle is against needs in the sustained milieu of a constituted scarcity for which we are responsible. It is always moral to attempt to rescue a drowning person, whatever that person may later do with his or her life. See Anderson, ibid., particularly 186, in which Anderson summarizes his objections against what he deems is Sartre's excessive indulgence to the oppressed.

53. See Søren Kierkegaard, *Concluding Unscientific Postscript*, trans. David F. Swenson and Walter Lowrie (Princeton: Princeton University Press, 1941), 182–93, particularly 186. Kierkegaard does not explicitly make the claim that I attribute to him, but I think I give the gist of his remarks.

PART TWO

In Search of Good Faith

CHAPTER 1

On the Possibility of Good Faith

The usual approach to Sartre's notion of good faith is to consider it either as a subtle form of bad faith or as an unstable form of freedom that ends in bad faith. The general view is that, in *Being and Nothingness*, Sartre presents bad faith as the fundamental ontological condition of freedom. It is, of course, frequently pointed out that Sartre does allude to the possibility of a recovery from bad faith to authenticity, and it would thus seem that, if a genuine antithesis to bad faith exists, it is to be found in the concept of authenticity rather than in the concept of good faith.

In the context of *Being and Nothingness*, however, I believe that it can be misleading to refer to authenticity as a possible antithesis to bad faith. In this work Sartre accepts a clear distinction between the ontological and ethical realms; he describes bad faith as an ontological characteristic of consciousness but he refers to authenticity as an aspect of man's ethical life.[1] (For this reason, Sartre objects to Heidegger introducing the concept of authenticity in the ontology of *Being and Time*.)[2] Of course, there may be no ontological antithesis to bad faith; and, in the abstract it may be possible to show how both an authentic and inauthentic life can be based upon the sole ontological structure of bad faith. Nevertheless, I do not believe that this is the actual description of freedom given in *Being and Nothingness*. Rather, I shall try to show that Sartre's view of freedom implies two fundamentally diverse ontological modes of freedom: one that he calls "bad faith" and the other that he hesitates to name but, at times, calls "good faith." For the purposes of this chapter, it should be kept in mind that no particular claims are being made concerning the relations between bad faith and inauthenticity or good faith and authenticity.

Granting the distinction between good faith and authenticity, the use of the term "good faith" as an antithesis to bad faith still seems questionable. It is clear that Sartre is unhappy with the term; for in ordinary usage, the term "good faith" frequently designates precisely those qualities of faith that Sartre wishes to identify with what he calls "bad faith." For example, the term "good faith" seems to imply sincerity, but Sartre unequivocally proclaims sincerity to be an ideal of bad faith. Further, and perhaps even more importantly, the term "good faith" draws attention to an aspect of the commonly accepted notion of faith itself that Sartre again sees as an aspect of bad faith, namely, the will to believe.[3] Indeed, in *Being and Nothingness*, there is, I think, an implicit rethinking of the notion of faith, such that sincerity and the will to believe are seen to be reflective aberrations of faith that are characteristic of bad faith.[4]

One final note on terminology: following Sartre, I shall use terms such as "self," "freedom," "project," "good faith," and "bad faith" as nouns. But these nouns should not be taken substantively; Sartre does not regard the human being as a substance. Rather, these terms should be taken as a shorthand way of referring to the facts that each human act can be viewed in many ways and that each act has relations to past and future acts.

In describing the relation of our acts to each other, Sartre compares them to the lines of a portrait (*BN* 469–70). To elaborate on this analogy, we can say that the lines of a portrait are related to the whole portrait as each human act is related to its fundamental project, or self. That is, as each line being drawn both stands alone and yet is part of the portrait (gestalt) that is coming into being, so too, each human act both stands alone and yet is part of the nonsubstantive gestalt called "project," or "self."

Continuing with the analogy, we can say that as the lines of a portrait have two degrees of freedom in relation to the entire portrait being drawn, each human act has two degrees of freedom in relation to its fundamental project or self. The less important degree is that there is a small amount of indeterminacy in where and how the lines of the portrait can be drawn and still result in the same portrait; similarly, we have a small degree of freedom in deciding how we will act while retaining our project, or chosen self. More importantly, however, the degree of the artist's freedom extends to the fact that he can change his mind about the kind of portrait he wishes to draw. But here we must be careful how we develop the analogy. We should not imagine our artist free to throw his canvas away or free to erase the lines he has drawn, but we can imagine that he is able to change the entire character of his portrait by one properly placed line. For example, our artist might suddenly become winsome and change an almost completed, serious looking portrait of George Washington by giving him a Mona-Lisa-like smile. In a similar way, for Sartre, although we have only one life to live and cannot change our past, our real freedom is that we are free to perform acts that give new meanings to our past and open new possibilities for our future.

To continue one step further with the analogy, I understand the terms *good faith* and *bad faith* to refer to the twofold relation the artist can have to his portrait and to the twofold relation we can have to our fundamental projects. I consider the artist in good faith to be aware that, although he must complete the portrait he has begun (for we must imagine him to have only one canvas), he is still always free to give his portrait a new meaning. I consider the artist in bad faith to see his task merely to represent as accurately as possible the features of George Washington once again. Similarly, I will attempt to show in this paper that, for Sartre, good and bad faith are two different ways of relating ourselves to our chosen ideals; they are the two ways for a person to be free.

I

In general, my thesis is that, for Sartre, good and bad faith are radically diverse ways of believing in our freedom; they are the two fundamentally diverse ontological modes in which our freedom can appear. We can have different attitudes toward our freedom, because our freedom is always in question. We never face our freedom as a thing to be known apodictically; rather, we live our freedom as the elusive being of our consciousness. Our attitudes toward our freedom—or more correctly, our freedom's toward itself, since our freedom is our being—are thus attitudes of faith or belief.

We believe in our freedom in the way that we believe that someone is our friend. We may be mistaken in believing, for example, that Peter is our friend. We may even be responsible for this mistake; for we may merely have chosen to believe although we had no evidence to support our belief. Even if there is evidence and our belief is a ''critical'' belief, we are still responsible, for it is our belief. Thus, we do not face the evidence of our belief in someone's friendship in the way we face the evidence that a lamp is on the table. The evidence for belief does not convince; it can only persuade.

But if our freedom is our very being, how can we be in a position of having to believe in it? We cannot escape our freedom; we are condemned to be free. Surely then we must *know* that we are free. It is of course true that we are aware that we are free; but our freedom is not an essence. There is nothing *there* to be known. Further, for Sartre, freedom would not be freedom if it could not freely relate to itself. Freedom requires that it freely determine its own beliefs about itself. Thus, what is most distinctive in the human being is how it believes in its own freedom.

For Sartre, we first use our freedom *to forge for ourselves the implicit criteria of the truths of our beliefs.* In the chapter "Bad Faith" in part 1 of *Being and Nothingness,* Sartre distinguishes a good- and a bad-faith way that freedom believes in itself. Unfortunately, later in the same chapter, he seems to take back with the left what he has given with the right and the result is that what he has indeed given is overlooked. The passage is in the crucial section "The 'Faith' of Bad Faith." The title of the section gives the clue to the whole distinction between good and bad faith. For if there is a distinctive "faith" of bad faith, this implies that there is a distinctive "faith" of good faith. The passage reads:

Bad faith does not hold the norms and criteria of truth as they are accepted by the critical thought of good faith. What it decides first, in fact, is the nature of truth. With bad faith a truth appears, a method of thinking, a type of being which is like that of objects; the ontological characteristic of the world of bad faith with which the subject suddenly surrounds himself is this: that here being is what it is not, and is not what it is. Consequently a peculiar type of evidence appears: *non-persuasive* evidence. Bad faith apprehends evidence but it is resigned in advance to not being fulfilled by this evidence, to not being persuaded and transformed into good faith. It makes itself humble and modest; it is not ignorant, it says, that faith is decision and that after each intuition, it must decide and *will what it is.* Thus bad faith in its primitive project and in its coming into the world decides on the exact nature of its requirements. It stands forth in the firm resolution *not to demand too much,* to count itself satisfied when it is barely persuaded, to force itself in decisions to adhere to uncertain truths. This original project of bad faith is a decision in bad faith on the nature of faith. (BN 68)

Here Sartre clearly distinguishes good faith from bad faith as fundamentally different attitudes toward faith itself. "Bad faith apprehends evidence but it is resigned in advance to not being fulfilled by this evidence, to not being persuaded and transformed into good faith.'' However "unstable" bad faith is, it is still a project to remain in bad faith. Also, by implication, good faith is a "willingness" to be persuaded by evidence. Simply stated, good faith would seem to be a project of being spontaneously willing to be critical and open and bad faith a project of being spontaneously uncritical and closed.

Unfortunately, in the following paragraphs, Sartre seems to eradicate this seemingly clear distinction. He says, ''The ideal of good faith (to believe what one believes) is like that of sincerity (to be what one is) an ideal of being in itself.'' That is, the *ideal* of good faith is in bad faith. But I believe a clue to understanding these remarks is to realize that they are part of Sartre's answer to the question of how bad faith is possible. What I think Sartre is saying is that *bad faith is possible because it projects for itself an impossible ideal of good faith.* I shall thus argue that two notions of good faith are working in *Being and Nothingness*: one, the "commonsense" notion that faith *should* reach the ideal of an unwavering belief; the other, a rethinking of the notion of faith, or belief, that is so radical that, I think, Sartre hesitates to call it "faith."[5] The commonsense notion will be referred to as the "ideal of good faith" and the rethinking of faith as "good faith." At times, for emphasis, I will italicize the term *ideal*.

For Sartre, the commonsense notion of the *ideal* of good faith is impossible, because it implies that consciousness acts like a blind force. Rather, consciousness is intentional: it is spontaneously an awareness of something other than itself. Further, this intentionality is also an awareness, and thus consciousness is reflexive to itself in the same act by which it goes outside of itself.[6] Consequently, Sartre sees everything within consciousness to be impregnated with the character of consciousness as an awareness: Every belief is an awareness of itself as belief, and as an awareness of itself, it carries within itself the necessity for being more than mere belief. Every belief is an attitude toward belief; every belief questions itself.[7]

Good and bad faith are both projects that imply an awareness of the impossibility of perfect, or simple, belief; but they face and use the impossible ideal of faith differently.

Bad faith takes the impossible *ideal* of faith as its conception of "good faith." That is, bad faith is a project of believing that good faith is impossible. Since good faith is conceived to be impossible, bad faith is free to believe that anything goes in the realm of faith. Thus bad faith is a project of undermining all critical attitudes by justifying all uncritical attitudes. Bad faith removes for itself the foundation by which it could recognize itself as uncritical and judge itself as "bad." Bad faith is thus more than the mere cynical awareness that it has honestly chosen to exist as bad faith. Bad faith believes in itself; but what it believes in is not what it is. Bad faith believes that good faith has been *given* to it as impossible; bad faith is in fact a *project of believing* that good faith is impossible. Bad faith thus misses itself and it is indeed a project of missing itself. Bad faith can accomplish its self-deception because the ideal of a perfectly justified faith is in fact given to consciousness; bad faith merely uncritically assumes that this *ideal* of faith is good faith.[8] For example, I am aware that I can never achieve a *perfectly* justified belief in my ability to be courageous. Nevertheless, in bad faith I project the ideal of a perfectly justified belief as the goal of a good-faith belief in my courage. Since this *ideal* of good faith is impossible, I am now free to believe whatever I wish about my courage. "My inability to *believe* that I am courageous," Sartre says, "will not discourage me since every belief involves not quite believing" (*BN,* 69).

On the other hand, good faith does not accept the ideal of faith as the goal of faith. The project of good faith carries within it the critical awareness that the ideal of faith is in bad faith. Good faith itself can only be described as the project of freedom initially recognizing and accepting itself. Because of the nature of consciousness as an awareness, good faith accepts that everything within consciousness is *in question* and it sees this condition as the source of its freedom and responsibility. In particular, good faith is aware that, although all beliefs are in question, they are not all in question in the same way. There is a radical difference between a belief that carries a critical awareness of itself and one that is aimed at eliminating this awareness. Good faith is an original project of accepting responsibility for one's attitudes toward one's self. It is a fundamental project of being watchful, and it is also an awareness of the impossibility of maintaining a state of watchfulness. Thus good faith does not take itself as an ideal; it does not require the impossible of itself—it recognizes that to require the impossible is a bad-faith way of requiring nothing of itself.

To return to our example of courage: In good faith I am aware that I can never achieve a perfectly justified belief about my ability to be courageous, but I do not use this impossibility as an excuse for adopting uncritical attitudes toward my courage. I must have some attitude toward my courage: Indifference, seeming objectivity, active belief or active disbelief are all attitudes for which I am responsible. In good faith I accept responsibility for my attitude, and I at least attempt to adopt the critical attitude that I perceive is most suited for the situation.

There may, in fact, be no best attitude toward my courage, but this does not mean that any attitude is as good as any other. An attitude that would attempt to ignore my past behavior, for example, would be uncritical. I have a past, and while I am free to adopt a particular attitude toward my past, I am not free to undo the facts of my past. I can reinterpret the slate; I cannot wipe it clean. Further, my past may make clear to me my present project and reveal the place of courage within this project. To consider the simplest cases: I may realize that I have been courageous in the past and that my acts of courage have been acts of being faithful to my project. I now see that the question of whether I will be brave in the future is the same as the question of whether I will remain faithful to my project. On the other hand, I may have been cowardly in the past, and I may now see that my project is to live a secure, peaceful, and quiet life. Thus, I *may* see that a single act of bravery requires me to adopt a new lifestyle—it *may* require this but it does not have to because the individual himself determines the value of his actions in relation to his project.

In good faith I am willing to make a critical attempt to understand the value that my acts have in relation to my fundamental project. True, I have adopted my project and I am responsible for maintaining it. Further, I am *aware* of both my project and the value I have given my acts in relation to my project. Nevertheless, on the prereflective level, I do not *understand* either my project or my acts with the type of clarity characteristic of apodictic knowledge; my project and the value of my acts within my project are not present to me as things to be known. I do not contemplate my freedom from above but I am encompassed by the very freedom that I would know. My reflections are themselves within the project of my freedom; even my apparent objective reflections on myself are in question. Thus, my prereflective awareness of myself is more similar to the structure of belief than to the structure of (apodictic) knowledge. Good faith, however, does not use the fundamental ambiguity of this situation as an excuse for adopting uncritical attitudes toward itself.

In good faith we also aim at attaining more than a speculative, critical knowledge of our freedom. We discover the meaning of our freedom in action and being. Our fundamental project is not a program laid out by a type of immanent, transcendental ego; it is not an internal contest that may or may not have some relation to our bodies and to the world. Rather, our fundamental project is the way we *attempt* "to exist" our bodies within the world and before others.[9] Our freedom is more than an internal decision and less than the successful completion of some act. Our freedom is the intentional unfolding of our act and our ability to alter the direction of this unfolding. Our freedom can be described as our ability to maintain or to alter the vector of our existence, and good faith can be seen as the awareness that we are responsible either for maintaining or for altering the direction of our fundamental project.

Good faith also confronts me with the free way I have chosen to see my freedom. I am responsible for the way I see my ability to change. I am responsible for keeping the possibility for change remote from me or bringing it close to me. My acts either confirm me in my project or tend to bring me on the other side of my project onto a new project. In good faith I view my freedom to be more than my deliberations about my actions taken in isolation: "When I deliberate," Sartre says, "the chips are down" (*BN* 451). All my deliberations are within the context of my project and I do not face the real issue of freedom until I confront the possibility of changing my project. In good faith I am aware that I can consistently perform certain acts only by altering my fundamental project: "doubtless I *could have* done otherwise, but *at what price?* . . . it becomes evident that the act could not have been modified without at the same time supposing a fundamental modification of my original choice of myself" (*BN,* 464). Still, we must keep in mind that whatever new choice we make of ourself this choice must be some modification of our past: "A converted atheist is not simply a believer; he is a believer who has made past within himself the project of being an atheist" (*BN* 466–7).

A change in a fundamental project can be said to be a "conversion" insofar as it redirects our past; but it does not have to involve a "will to believe." And, when it does, it is because the change is itself a bad-faith project. True, a person generally does not change his mode of existence merely as the result of logical arguments. It is our free project that gives our reasons their particular weight and compelling force, and thus the reasons within a project can never of themselves lead outside a project. Nevertheless, a change in project does not have to result from an irrational leap, or a blind will to believe. Good faith, I think, tries to avoid two extremes in its attitude toward its freedom and its ability to change its fundamental project. It views freedom as more than a blind force following the direction of an intellect and less than a will acting in accordance with its own arbitrary goals. Reason has an ambiguous relation to freedom, but this ambiguity does not have to be uncritical. It is only when freedom chooses to be uncritical and in bad faith that it deceives itself that it must follow one of two extremes: it should act only where there are clear reasons or it should make an irrational leap.

But good faith is aware that these alternatives do not reflect its true condition. Between the clarity of apodictic evidence and the darkness of the leap there is the persuasive voice of critical reason, a reason that does not demand a best in order to have a better, a reason that calls for an open, questioning commitment to life.

Our freedom is also our temporality, and good faith implies an open critical view of our particular relation to objective time. In objective time, I see myself standing at the now, with my past as actions that have been, and my future as actions that are not yet. But this view of time is itself modified by a temporality in which my present is my particular *presence* to things, my past, the immediate context of all my actions and, in a very special way, my body, and my future, the immediate direction of my intentional acts. Again, the relation between temporality and time is seen, in good faith, to be ambiguous, or to use Sartre's term, it is seen to be *in question*. Here again good faith tries to avoid two extremes, extremes that are themselves aspects of a traditional realism and idealism: The temporality of our free project is more than a mere horizon revealing for us the facts of our past and the possibilities of our future, and it is less than a creative force providing us with a new past and a new future. The unity of our temporality is more than the psychological unity resulting from a mind or brain remembering past events and speculating about future ones, and less than the unity of a spirit for whom the past, present, and future exist simultaneously in a now.

The ambiguous unity of our temporality is, in turn, itself an aspect of the situational context of our freedom. For example, a person's decision to play basketball may have arisen partly because he happened to be tall, but it is also true that the spontaneous importance he gave to his tallness was itself due to his willingness to consider seriously the possibility of playing basketball. Further, because of his concrete relations to others, his tallness was never a brute given and his decision to play ball was never a translucent meaning. Still, he was responsible both for his decision to play basketball and for the way he now carries his past, youthful tallness within him. He will never be able to attain certain knowledge about the relation of his tallness to his decision to play basketball, not because of ignorance but because the relation itself is ambiguous. He will never be able to know himself objectively. Still, if he is in good faith, and if the need arises, he will seek to know the significance of his tallness as clearly as possible. He will listen to reason and logic, even though he is aware that he is responsible for the direction from which and the manner in which he listens. He will listen because his good faith is itself the openness in which he can listen to reason.

To sum up this preliminary discussion: Good and bad faith both imply the awareness that the ideal of a perfect, or simple, faith is impossible. But they face and use this awareness differently. Bad faith makes this impossible ideal of faith to be its ideal of good faith. This ideal is, of course, impossible, and thus bad faith is free to believe that anything goes in the realm of faith. The *ideal* of good faith is thus the conception of good faith that bad faith forges for itself. By altering for itself the meaning of faith, bad faith achieves the status of faith, i.e., it truly believes in itself, and it is not mere cynicism, the mere awareness that it has honestly decided to be in bad faith. Finally, bad faith turns the fleeting, but primordial awakenings of anguish away from its freedom and toward impossible attempts to judge itself objectively. Bad faith pronounces a judgment on its isolated acts but not on its bad faith. Its own sincerity is an aspect of its bad faith, for by the same act that bad faith denounces itself, it raises itself above the self that it has denounced. Sincerity is thus an impossible ideal, for the *awareness* of being sincere takes one beyond that very sincerity.[10] "In short, this is the origin of all the anguish of a 'bad conscience,' that is, the consciousness of bad faith which has for its ideal a self-judgment—i.e., taking toward oneself the point of view of the Other" (*BN*, 528).

On the other hand, a good-faith action does not aim at being perfectly justified. A mark, or sign, of the critical awareness characteristic of good faith is that it recognizes its possibility of falling into bad faith. Good faith does not so much judge itself as "good" as it recognizes the ever present danger of giving up the task of freedom. But good faith is aware of itself and its very project is not to miss itself. It sees that its own belief is in question but it accepts this condition as the situation of freedom. Also, good faith does not attempt to see its freedom as a mere question of willpower. It recognizes its freedom to be a more fundamental project, or gestalt: "'. . . the will, far from being the unique or at least the privileged manifestation of freedom, actually—like every event of the for-itself—must presuppose the foundation of an original freedom in order to be able to constitute itself as will" (*BN*, 443).

Indeed, good and bad faith can be seen as two different ways of relating our will to our original, fundamental project. Before we attempt to describe this relationship we should not overlook Sartre's own general, but important, distinction between good and bad faith:

> The very project of flight reveals to bad faith an inner disintegration in the heart of being, and it is this disintegration which bad faith wishes to be. In

truth, the two immediate attitudes which we can take in the face of our being are conditioned by the very nature of this being and its immediate relation with the in-itself. Good faith seeks to flee the inner disintegration of my being in the direction of the in-itself which it should be and is not. Bad faith seeks to flee the in-itself by means of the inner disintegration of my being. But it denies this very disintegration as it denies that it is itself bad faith. (*BN, 70*)

My interpretation of this passage is that good and bad faith are the two ways we have of facing our freedom. In good faith, we accept our obligation of determining our being. We do this both by continually tending in the direction of the self that we have chosen to become and by accepting our ability to change the type of self that we would become. In bad faith, however, we attempt to see the self as the fixed origin of our freedom. We thus believe that our only choices are either to resign ourselves in bitterness to the individual selves that nature has given us or to attempt to use our will power to escape from these selves. Thus good and bad faith confront freedom differently: Good faith uses freedom to create its essence by tending in the direction of its freely chosen self; bad faith uses freedom to escape the very essence and self that it has chosen for itself.

II

In *Being and Nothingness,* the chapter "Bad Faith" serves two main purposes: It reveals the being of consciousness to be freedom and negation by showing that we are capable of denying our fundamental freedom; and it lays the foundation for Sartre's "existential psychoanalysis" by introducing the concept of bad faith in relation to the Freudian notion of the unconscious. Indeed, the full implications of the chapter, "Bad Faith" in part 1 are not revealed until the chapter, "Existential Psychoanalysis" in part 4.

For Sartre, the attempts to flee freedom and to hide from anguish are prereflective projects of freedom. These attempts give rise to deep-rooted psychic aberrations, such as inferiority complexes. The common characteristic of these aberrations is the presence within consciousness of the unique phenomenon that Freud correctly recognized but incorrectly tried to describe and explain by the device of repression. The phenomenon, as distinct from its explanation, can be said to be a deep-rooted, relatively successful, attempt to hide from ourselves, or to lie to ourselves. Sartre recognizes the phenomenon; he maintains, however, that it is to be explained not by the semi-automatic device of repression, but by our fundamental bad-faith projects.

But at times do we not all try to lie to ourselves by attempting to hide from our freedom? Are we not then all in bad faith? Yes and no. There is a basic difference between the transitory, or secondary, states of consciousness in which we try to lie to ourselves and the fundamental project of hiding from our freedom. In this later case Sartre seems to agree with Freud on the importance of analysis; he suggests that the purpose of existential analysis is to lead us out of the bad-faith condition of hiding from our freedom just as the purpose of psychoanalysis is to lead us out of the state of repression. A particular example may clarify this point: Consider an individual suffering from kleptomania. The individual steals and claims neither the desire nor the need for the stolen goods. The individual who wishes to be helped also claims a willingness and an intention to stop stealing. But every decision to stop stealing is ineffectual. At this stage I think that both Sartre and Freud would agree that the person needs analysis.

The Freudian approach would be to help the patient recognize that kleptomania is merely a symptom of an early experience that has been repressed. The analysis is thus aimed at helping the patient face up to this hidden experience. The Sartrean approach, on the other hand, would be to help the patient admit that he has chosen to become a kleptomaniac. But how can this be? The person claims that he does not know why he is stealing. Sartre's answer would be that the patient has actually succeeded in convincing himself that he did not choose to become a kleptomaniac. He has (successfully) lied to himself.[11] How did this happen? One day he stole. Of course, he recognized that one theft did not mean that he was a kleptomaniac. But how many thefts are needed to become a kleptomaniac? No one really knows. And clearly he did not need what he stole. Perhaps after all he is a kleptomaniac? By continuing in his behavior, he forges for himself the evidence to believe in his own kleptomania. Why does he do this? In general, he does it to escape his freedom by choosing to believe that nature has given him a role to play. A kleptomaniac knows who he is. Also, it is a cheap and easy way of achieving notoriety. After all, how many kleptomaniacs are there in the world? A kleptomaniac is in bad faith because he has used his freedom to escape his freedom, but his attempts are not completely successful. At times he awakens in anguish to his attempts to flee his freedom.

There is some interpretation in this simplified example, but I believe that it reflects the way that Sartre sees his relation to Freud. Sartre's own example is that of an inferiority complex. He says: "This inferiority which I struggle against and which nevertheless I recognize, this I have chosen from the start" (*BN*, 459), and some pages later:

> It should be observed first of all that the choice of total ends although totally free is not necessarily nor even frequently made in joy. We must not confuse the necessity of choosing with the will to power. The choice can be effected in resignation or uneasiness; it can be a flight; it can be in bad faith . . . to choose inferiority does not mean to be sweetly contented with an *aurea mediocritas*, it is to produce and to assume the rebellion and despair which constitute the revelation of this inferiority. . . . (*BN*, 472).

This last quote draws attention to two aspects of Sartre's view of freedom that are often overlooked. First, there is the implied relation of joy to the original project of freedom, or good faith; second, there is the clear statement that the choice of oneself can be in bad faith. In fact, throughout *Being and Nothingness*, Sartre says that we *frequently* flee anguish in bad faith, not that we are always in bad faith.

Sartre's entire discussion of the inferiority complex is, I believe, important for the distinction between good and bad faith. Admittedly, we have to learn about good faith indirectly through the project of bad faith. The person who has chosen to live the prereflective project of an inferiority complex has chosen a bad-faith relation to the very being of consciousness. His very will emerges as a will in bad faith not because he wills "bad objects" but because the relation of his will to his original project is one of bad faith. His will is the very means of constituting the self-deception that brings about the inferiority complex itself; it is originally the means of creating the psychic evidence by which it can believe in itself as a "will to power." That is, the will attempts to appear as a will to power within a given essence, but it is rather the means of creating the very essence from which it would seem to appear.

Thus, one possible interpretation of an inferiority complex is that, on the prereflective level, the person with an inferiority complex has a project to be superior. This project is in bad faith because he is afraid of committing himself to his own freedom; he fears failure but he does not relinquish his project of being superior. To retain his project, he creates the belief in himself as having an inferior nature—he would be superior, if nature had not cursed him, if circumstances had been more propitious. He thus disarms in advance the possibility of responsible failure. On the reflective level, his will now appears as a struggle against his inferior nature; he appears to himself as an unfortunate individual trying to use his willpower to rise above his condition, a condition that he himself has created.

There is thus a close relation between the way the will appears on the reflective level and the way freedom functions on the prereflective level. And it is precisely in this close relation that bad faith ''approaches'' the project of good faith. This approach must be understood to be on the ontological level and it lays the foundation for the possibility of what Sartre calls a ''conversion.'' It occurs because on the prereflective level freedom does not exist as a ''will.'' Sartre says: ''The will in fact is posited as a reflective decision in regard to certain ends'' (*BN,* 443). Thus the possibility exists for bad faith to escape its condition. True, everything within the gestalt of bad faith is in bad faith, but insofar as the project is on the prereflective level there is an original awareness of itself as a project of freedom. Thus, while the will is inactive, freedom tends to return to its prereflective state; and the project of bad faith ''approaches'' the project of good faith insofar as it approaches the original condition of freedom.[12]

> Whereas in the form of reflective consciousness the will constitutes in bad faith false psychic objects as motives, on the other hand in the capacity of a non-reflective and non-thetic self-consciousness, it is consciousness (of) being in bad faith and consequently (of) the fundamental project pursued by the for-itself. (*BN,* 473)

But what then is the relation of will to a freedom in good faith? Clearly it does not create false psychic objects for itself. *It does not emerge as a will to power within an essence that it has originally created.* It manifests itself rather as the acknowledged means of creating an essence. The will thus emerges not as a means to hide freedom, but as the joyous acceptance of freedom and as a means of creating the definiteness of being from the indefiniteness of being from the indefiniteness of freedom.

> The one who realizes in anguish his condition as being *thrown* into a responsibility which extends to his very abandonment has no longer either remorse or regret or excuse; he is no longer anything but a freedom which perfectly reveals itself and whose being resides in this revelation. But as we have pointed out in the beginning of this work, most of the time we flee anguish in bad faith. (*BN,* 556)

III

The human being, Sartre says, is the passion to be God. But, for Sartre, God is an impossible ideal. This impossible ideal of a for-itself that is also an in-itself haunts the very being of consciousness; however, I believe it does so, for Sartre, in different ways. In bad faith, this impossible ideal is projected as if it should be the ideal of the for-itself. The for-itself, however, implicitly recognizes the ideal to be impossible; and thus the human being stands free to forge its own uncritical attitudes for truth, its own evidence for belief. Good faith also manifests itself as the failure to be the ideal of a for-itself that is also an in-itself, but here this failure is accepted as merely the human condition.[13]

This view gives a clue to interpreting Sartre's diverse ways of speaking about the "failure" of the human being; specifically, I believe it gives a perspective on the chapter "The Concrete Relation to Others." In this chapter, Sartre claims that all our relations with others "fail"; yet he hints that there is a difference in the mode of this failure:

> Masochism therefore is on principle a failure. This should not surprise us if we realize that masochism is a "vice" and that vice is, on principle, the love of failure. But this is not the place to describe the structures peculiar to vice. It is sufficient here to point out that masochism is a perpetual effort to annihilate the subject's subjectivity by causing it to be assimilated by the Other; this effort is accompanied by the exhausting and delicious consciousness of failure so that finally it is the failure itself which the subject ultimately seeks as his principal goal. (*BN*, 379)

Throughout *Being and Nothingness*, there is, I believe, the consistent hint that the love of "failure" is different from the acceptance of failure as the condition for the human being to be conscious. Consciousness, for Sartre, requires an ontological "distance" between awareness and the non-thetic object of awareness. To attain a goal and to be conscious of attaining it is already to surpass it. Bad faith projects the impossible ideal of attaining absolute oneness with one's ideals as the true goal of consciousness, but bad faith is aware that this goal is impossible. It confronts itself with ultimate failure in order to use this failure as an excuse for its own attempts to hide from freedom. Good faith would not want to achieve its goals at the price of not being aware of them; it accepts the fact that the human condition is to be always beyond itself.

IV

Sartre seems to me to be on the right track in his descriptions of freedom as a project in either good or bad faith. The real issue of freedom does not concern the freedom of our deliberations but our fundamental attitude toward our freedom itself. To be free means to be able to open or to close the door of freedom itself; it means to face our freedom or to try to hide from it. In the concrete, our freedom is the way we believe in ourself, and this belief is either a good- or bad-faith project, a project that gives the context for all our deliberations, reflections, and attitudes.

I have, however, a qualification and a reservation concerning Sartre's general view of freedom: My qualification is that I think that our freedom is more accurately described as "growing" into projects, or gestalts, rather than as initially adopting them. My reservation is that I doubt the advisability of *beginning* a description of freedom abstracted from its relation to others. While I believe that both my qualification and reservation challenge certain aspects of Sartre's fundamental ontology, I also suspect that they can be retained by emphasizing and interpreting other aspects.

In regard to my qualification: In *Being and Nothingness*, Sartre's view of freedom results, to a great extent, both from a particular interpretation of the phenomenological method and from a certain methodological procedure. First, Sartre interprets the phenomenological method in such a way that being-in-itself is revealed to be act, and freedom the negation of this act. This dichotomy makes it difficult to see growth as real, and from this perspective—and only from this perspective—can Sartre be said to have an absolute view of freedom. In general, however, freedom, for Sartre, is situational. For example, a mother takes a child to the opera and the child must relate to this event; the child will be forever one-who-has-been-taken-to-the-opera. Clearly, then, the absoluteness of Sartrean freedom does not consist in its independence from the given; rather, it seems to consist in the ability of consciousness to assume the given within the free project of consciousness thereby altering the given into *this* given. Returning to our example: The child is completely free to alter the event of being taken to the opera into either a dragging or a joyous accompaniment. The phenomenological perspective adopted in the introduction of *Being and Nothingness* leaves little room for a child learning about or achieving its freedom. Nevertheless, Sartre's actual description of freedom can be interpreted to show how this is possible.

Sartre repeatedly describes freedom as that which makes everything in consciousness to be *in question*.[14] Following this lead, can we not say that initially the child learns the meaning of its actions and the degree of its freedom? At first the child is not sure whether she is being dragged to the opera or whether, despite being taken by others, she is also happy to go. The Sartre of *Being and Nothingness* would perhaps object that no human event is neutral; initially the child's freedom alters the given so that the child is really learning about its own initial project, or gestalt, of freedom. But granting the reciprocity between freedom and the given, does it follow that initially all our free actions are within a clearly defined gestalt? I would prefer to interpret Sartre's claim, that freedom puts everything that is within consciousness to be in question, to imply that the very fact that freedom is a project can itself be in question. Thus initially our actions are neither totally divorced from a project, nor clearly contained within a project; our early actions imply and tend towards more than one project. Given a mature project; we can then look back and see that, in a sense, our project was always there in our earliest actions.

I think the man of good faith can be viewed as one who sees that he is responsible for inducing in himself his present, mature project of freedom. Here, I think, Sartre would fear that we have fallen back to the Aristotelian notion of potency and ultimately to a substantive view of human nature. But I doubt if the acceptance of growth requires the traditional acceptance of potency and substance, particularly as understood by Sartre.

Returning to my reservation concerning Sartre's procedure: In *Being and Nothingness*, Sartre makes it very clear that he considers consciousness to be a "moment," or "aspect" of the synthetic totality, being-in-the-world. Further, there is no doubt that, for Sartre, the factual, contingent existence of other persons gives rise to internal, necessary relations in each consciousness. Thus, what guides the study of *Being and Nothingness* is the synthetic totality consciousness-in-the-world-before-others and not a form of Cartesian dualism.

Further, Sartre is aware that to *consider* an aspect, for example, color, apart from its totality, for example, colored chair, does not mean that the aspect can *exist* apart from the totality. Nevertheless, I suspect that Sartre's use of abstraction contributes substantively to his ontology, and that there is thus a tension in *Being and Nothingness* between the synthetic totality guiding the study and the descriptions of the abstract moments, or aspects, of the totality.[15] In particular, the fact that consciousness can be described abstractly apart from its relations to others, even though it cannot exist concretely as such, leads Sartre to the view that, in a certain sense, consciousness *ought* to be independent of its relations to other persons; in the abstract, the intentionality of each consciousness should be directed innocently to a world unfettered by the freedom of others. This view of consciousness affects both Sartre's explicit description of bad faith and his implied view of good faith: bad faith is *self*-deception and while the other may be the occasion for our adopting a particular form of self-deception, he does not formally lead us into it; and good faith is an original project of facing our freedom, a project that is completely under our control.

I also suspect that Sartre's own procedure of beginning a description of freedom abstracted from a relation to others will lead to difficulties in developing his own distinction between the ontological and the ethical. On the one hand, *Being and Nothingness* seems to start us off in the right direction: good and bad faith are not described as moral categories. Good faith is our realization of anguish; bad faith is our flight from anguish. Good faith is our acceptance of the challenge of freedom; bad faith is our delight in the failure of meeting this challenge; good faith is joyousness, bad faith is seriousness. On the other hand, good and bad faith are also distinguished by the way we relate to our responsibility; and from this perspective they indeed seem to be moral, or ethical, categories. I think an answer to this dilemma that is consistent with the ontology of *Being and Nothingness* is to distinguish a pre-reflective, ontological sense of responsibility from a reflective, ethical notion of responsibility. But it is not immediately clear either how this distinction can be consistently developed or how useful it will be. Still, I suspect that the general distinction between the ontological modes of good and bad faith on the one hand, and the ethical categories of authenticity and inauthenticity on the other hand will prove to be fruitful.

Regardless, however, of the question of whether an ethics can be based upon the ontology of *Being and Nothingness*, and despite what I have called my qualification and reservation, it is not clear that any other method and procedure than the ones that Sartre actually adopted could have given us the vision to see how the will is related to a more fundamental freedom and how this fundamental freedom is a (good- or bad-faith) belief in the selfness we each choose. Further, although it is perhaps true that Sartre minimizes, for the sake of the clarity of this vision, the influence that others have on our freedom, it does not thereby follow that our freedom is merely subjective and arbitrary. If in this paper I have been speaking of freedom as a way of believing in ourselves, it must not be forgotten that, in the concrete, freedom, for Sartre, is the very intentionality that makes us a being-in-the-world.

We hear a great deal about the one sentence in *Being and Nothingness*, ''Man is a useless passion,'' but not enough about the grand and noble purpose that the book as a whole gives to human freedom. If man is a useless passion, so is the search for knowledge in general and the pursuit of philosophy in particular; for, according to Sartre, the human being is itself an outline of the solution to the problem of being.[16]

> My ultimate and intial project—for these are but one—is, as we shall see, always the outline of a solution of the problem of being . . . It is the very way in which I entrust myself to the inanimate, in which I abandon myself to my body . . . which causes the appearance of both my body and the inanimate world with their respective value. (*BN,* 463)

Notes

1. See Jean-Paul Sartre, *Being and Nothingness*, trans. Hazel Barnes (New York: Philosophical Library, 1956) 70 n. 9, 412 n. 14. Hereafter this work will be referred to, in references, as *BN*. See also my *Commentary on Jean-Paul Sartre's "Being and Nothingness"* (New York: Harper & Row, 1974) pp. 89–90. Hereafter this work will be referred to as *Commentary*. Reprinted: University of Chicago Press, 1980.

2. See *BN,* 564.

3. It might seem appropriate to eliminate the term ''good faith'' in favor of such a term as Karl Popper's term ''conjecture.'' Although I think that there is some similarity between what Popper calls ''conjecture'' and what I call ''good faith,'' I think it undesirable to adopt his terminology, or one similar to it, since the purpose of this study is to see if in *Being and Nothingness*, there exists a viable antithesis to bad faith. Also it does not seem appropriate to speak about our fundamental attitudes toward ourself and others as ''conjectures.'' Attitudes of critical conjecture would seem to presuppose a project of being critical.

4. This rethinking begins from the traditional distinction between knowledge and faith: knowledge is an intuition of apodictic evidence; faith, a commitment based on probable evidence. Sartre proceeds to show that the traditional view presupposes a more ontological status for knowledge and belief: knowledge is the being of the prereflective *cogito* insofar as it makes brute existence into a world; thus conceptual knowledge that merely recognizes things in a world is a secondary phenomenon occurring on the level of reflection (cf., *BN,* 171–180; *Commentary* 131–147). Similarly with faith, or belief: Faith is the very being of the prereflective *cogito* in so far as the prereflective *cogito* itself is a fundamental free project of believing in itself. Thus, for Sartre belief and freedom are not a mere property but the very being of the pre-reflective *cogito*. This way of speaking about the prereflective *cogito* perhaps already involves some interpretation of Sartre's texts, and hopefully what follows will justify this interpretation. Textually, I think the basis for this view is to be found in reading the chapter ''Bad Faith'' together with the chapter ''Immediate Structures of the For-Itself.''

5. In the interest of space, I have not considered all the seemingly contradictory ways that Sartre speaks of good faith. I think that the distinction I will make between the *ideal* of good faith and good faith clarifies most, but not all, of the confusion. To some extent, the ambiguity is necessitated by the need to use the term "faith," while rethinking the structure of faith. In this regard it is important to keep in mind that the chapter "Bad Faith" is not an independent tract on the nature of faith. See opening paragraphs of the second part of this paper.

Ronald E. Santoni, in a detailed analysis of this and many of the other articles in this second part, has taken issue with some aspects of my distinction between the ideal of faith and faith. I received Santoni's book too late to incorporate some of his criticisms, and in either case this task would have necessitated writing a different book from the one I present here. See Ronald E. Santoni, *Bad Faith, Good Faith, and Authenticity in Sartre's Early Philosophy* (Philadelphia: Temple University Press, 1995).

6. See *BN*, l–liv, 73–79 and 150–170, and the respective places in my *Commentary*. Reflexivity is not a self-reflection in the sense of a positional reflection on the self. Hazel Barnes is well aware of the status of Sartre's *"consciousness (de) soi"* (see *BN*, liv), but her decision to translate this expression as "self-consciousness" may be the basis for the general misunderstanding that Sartre claims consciousness to be a thetic self-consciousness. I think that a more accurate, although more awkward, translation of Sartre's phrase is (self-) consciousness.

7. See *BN*, 75–76.

8. For the use of the term "self-deception" as a translation of *mauvaise foi*, see Walter Kaufmann, *Existentialism from Dostoevsky to Sartre*, 2nd ed. (New York: New American Library, 1975), 280. In general, however, I prefer the more literal translation "bad faith," because I maintain that there is a distinctive "faith" to good faith.

9. Sartre says that in describing our prereflective relation to our body, it is best to use the verb "to exist" transitively. See *BN*, 329.

10. See *BN*, 62–66. Even on the level of prereflective cogito, sincerity is a bad-faith ideal. Our commonsense way of speaking hides the fact that, unlike the *being* of things, the being of consciousness is never one with itself. Our spontaneity is not like a burst of steam. It is always an awareness and always beyond itself. Nevertheless, it *may* be possible to rehabilitate the notion of sincerity by describing it as (1) a vow to remain faithful to one's present project, (2) a critical conjecture that, at present, one cannot foresee any reason to change one's project, and (3) a critical conjecture about the meaning of one's present project.

11. *Cf.*, *BN*, 67–70; *Commentary*, 86–91.

12. This interpretation of the relation of the will to freedom is perhaps a clue to understanding the confusing footnote at the conclusion of the chapter "Bad Faith."

13. This ontological "failure" can be described as the constant sliding of our ideal self from our pursuing-self. In our most spontaneous reflections, we never attain the self that we would be. This "elsewhereness" of our selfness from our self is what Sartre calls, "nothingness." For a comprehensive discussion of Sartre's understanding of nothingness, see *Commentary*, 53–77.

14. My interpretation of the phrase, "in question" has, no doubt, influenced my entire distinction between good and bad faith.

15. I think that Sartre's use of abstraction follows, to a great extent, from his interpretation of and his solution to the problem of solipsism. The Sartre of *Being and Nothingness* can perhaps be imagined as one absorbed in reflection walking down a lonely road. Halfway down the road he is startled by footsteps. He stops and listens. No, he was mistaken. It was only the wind moving loose branches. Still, someone could have been there; he can always be seen by another. He never was, and never could be, really alone. Yet for a time he thought as one alone.

16. An early version of this paper was given as an invited paper at the International Society for Chinese and American Philosophy, held at Fairfield, June 1978. A revised version was completed under a N.E.H. summer grant, and was read by Calvin O. Schrag and William McBride; I have incorporated several of their suggestions.

CHAPTER 2

Good and Bad Faith:
Weak and Strong Notions

I will distinguish in this paper two notions, or senses, of good and bad faith, "weak and strong," and I will attempt to establish that both senses function in Sartre's *Being and Nothingness* and are implied in much of his other writings. I will begin with identifying the weak notions with what I call the "usual understanding" of these terms. Towards the end of the paper, however, it will become clear that, if one accepts the characterizations of the strong notions, the original weak notions become altered and are no longer exactly equivalent to the "usual understanding" of these terms. I believe that the usual understanding of good and bad faith appears contradictory because it confuses notes of the weak and strong notions, notes that this paper attempts to separate. Thus the procedure will be to begin with a description of what I term the usual understanding of good and bad faith and to gradually show how these weak notions, even in their confused sense, imply strong notions. Once the strong notions have been delineated, they will then be compared with what I hope will be a more precise understanding of the weak notions. My purpose in elaborating these distinctions is to show that a viable strong notion of good faith exists only when contrasted with a strong notion of bad faith.

I call the usual acceptance of Sartre's notion of bad faith "weak" because it has a wide extension. Bad faith is seen in this view as a necessary aspect of the human condition, specifically, as the unsuccessful way in which we all must cope with our freedom by assuming roles in society. Given this weak sense of bad faith, good faith seems to be, at best, a momentary awakening, a fleeting glimpse of the futile character of our condition, a glimpse that never fully and never for very long escapes the conditions of bad faith itself. Nevertheless, even these weak senses of good and bad faith are not vacuous; they describe, in Sartre's philosophy, definite features of the human condition, features which I will now sketch and which I will later contrast with those characteristic of strong notions of good and bad faith.

I

It seems clear that, for Sartre, we can never escape role-playing. He implies that, although we are free and responsible for the roles we play, our only option is to leave one role and enter another. True, once we realize that we have been playing a role and that we have passively accepted the way society sees and defines us, we may, in apparent good faith, react to this attempt of society to dominate our existence, and we may try to free ourselves from our acceptance of this domination, an acceptance that we now see as bad faith. But we will end in a new and different bad faith. Thus, in *Nausea*, the hero, Roquentin, gradually awakens from the slumbering acceptance of existence and from his own superficial attempts to give meaning to his life through travel and through the routine of writing a scholarly study of the Marquis de Rollebon. As an aspect of his awakening, the lives of his fellow citizens appear to him to be mannered, their voices hollow and their actions mechanical. He begins to see the bad-faith aspect of both their lives and his own, and he attempts to flee this vision. Towards the end of the book, Roquentin has a momentary intuition of the incredible gap between something and nothing; he faces the unconditional absurdity that anything should be. He further sees that this ''brute'' existence has been transformed into a world through human consciousness. His nausea is the realization that the world as a meaningful entity depends on the fact of human existence and freedom, facts which are themselves mere happenings. After this insight, Roquentin no longer seems to fit into society; he decides to write a novel in order to cope with his anguish, and, as Robert Denoon Cumming has noted, the book *Nausea* is itself the book that Roquentin decides to write at the end of the book.[1] But has Roquentin escaped bad faith? It would seem not. He has simply become a novelist and assumed a new role within the bad-faith society that he is condemning by his act of writing. Still, something did happen to him and his new life is not exactly the same as his former. Roquentin did not merely denounce himself for his bad faith; he changed his way of life. Nevertheless, insofar as his new life was also another role, Roquentin's good faith, in the final analysis, seems to have had very little significance for him.

This interpretation of the weak notions of good and bad faith can be supported by an analysis of the technical notion of bad faith introduced by Sartre in part 1 of *Being and Nothingness*. In the context of part 1, the chapter on bad faith attempts to show that both negative statements as well as the absence and lack we find within the world originate from the nature of human consciousness as a ''negative activity.'' One of the aspects of this negative activity is our ability to question freely the meaning of our existence including the issue itself of whether we are free. When we do so question, the ambiguity which results from this questioning can lead to anxiety and nausea. Further, according to Sartre, we can and frequently do flee from this anxiety, and this flight takes one of the several forms of lying to ourselves, or deceiving ourselves, about our freedom.

There have been many attempts to explain how self-deception is possible and even a few attempts to show that it is impossible, but it would seem clear that, at the very least, we sometimes misunderstand the meaning of our behavior. For Sartre, self-deception and bad faith are the same, and, in what I call the weak sense of these terms, we can say that we cannot escape self-deception, or bad faith, because we go from one self-deception to another. Indeed in this context, Sartre sees sincerity itself to be a sign of bad faith. For example, we may sincerely admit to ourselves and to others that we are lazy. Our sincerity appears as honesty, but it is an honesty that points away from our laziness and calls attention to our virtue of honesty. This apparent honesty is a subtle way of letting our laziness remain intact. It is a way of praising ourselves for our apparent self-knowledge. We see our sincerity as an ideal position from which we objectively judge our vices. What we do not admit is that our sincerity is also open to question because it is only a partial view of ourselves.[2] Further, if we were truly honest about our condition we would attempt to change it rather than condemn ourselves for vices that we are retaining. In relation to the meaning of our behavior, it is our actions and not our abstract judgments about ourselves that are the best criteria for honesty. But, if it is true that our attempts to judge ourselves sincerely are in bad faith, it would seem that all self-knowledge is tainted with self-deception. Consequently, even our lucid understanding of ourselves points merely to the nonobjectivity of our self-knowledge and to our awareness that there is no neutral position from which to examine our behavior. Again, in the weak sense, our good faith is only a fleeting realization that we cannot escape bad faith itself.

Our universal bad-faith condition can also be understood as calling attention to the way we continually "use up" our freedom by our actions and decisions. For Sartre, we can, loosely speaking, be said to have an essence insofar as we have a past, and the longer we live the more of a past we have. We are always free to redirect our lives and discover new meanings in our past, and no matter how great the "weight" of our past, we can always perform actions that are "out of character" and that are conversions to a new character. Nevertheless, we cannot escape the decisions we have made in the past; we cannot escape either the way or the extent to which we have used up our freedom. Also, we cannot avoid the way others see and objectify us. For example, for Sartre, the anti-Semite "overdetermines" the Jew. The Jew, however, cannot escape the overdetermination; he is free only to react to it authentically or inauthentically.[3] Finally, this weak, universal sense of bad faith seems to be implied by Sartre's claim that man is a useless passion, and that we must act in anguish, abandonment, and despair. Again accepting this universal, weak sense of bad faith, our good faith seems to be merely the Sisyphus-like struggle in which we are momentarily aware of the absurdity of our condition.

II

Although I believe there is validity to the usual interpretation of Sartre's notion of bad faith, I think that it misses the essential direction of his thought. Throughout much of Sartre's writings I believe that these weak notions point to and imply strong, limiting notions of both good and bad faith which I think it would be useful to introduce by an analogy.

There is, I think, a legitimate but "weak" sense in which we can say that we are all crazy, or insane. If we momentarily picture the meaning of our individual actions in relation to the world's activity they must at times appear to us to be futile if not ridiculous and crazy. Particularly those of us who are engaged in the academic professions must sometimes wonder about the meaning of our lives in the face of so much of the world's poverty, so much of the constant preparation for war and so much waste of human energy and resources. In the face of such insanity who can claim to be sane? Still, there are people who have a different and more specific type of insanity; there are people who suffer from so-called diseases such as schizophrenia and melancholia. They suffer from their insanity in a way in which we do not suffer from ours. We can of course say that there is no sense in trying to help them since we will be merely delivering them into another type of insanity. But this reasoning is sophistical. They have a right to live a more human existence even if this existence is itself from a different perspective a very crazy kind of existence. There is thus a strong, limiting notion of insanity and opposed to this notion there is a viable concept of sanity. Analogously, I believe that many of Sartre's writings refer to a strong, limiting notion of bad faith in relation to which there is implied a viable notion of good faith.

Before turning our attention to *Being and Nothingness*, I would like to illustrate how I see the strong notions of good and bad faith functioning in Sartre's *Anti-Semite and the Jew*. In portraying the anti-Semite, Sartre shows him to be a man who is afraid both of himself and of truth. He is afraid of himself because he is free, and he is afraid of truth because truth can be known only indefinitely. To hide from his fear, he fixes upon the Jew as a clear symbol of an evil that must be overcome in order to allow good to occur within the world. Once evil, symbolized by the Jew, is removed, the anti-Semite believes that the positive principle of good works automatically within the world. Sartre says:

> How can one choose to reason falsely? It is because of a longing for impenetrability. The rational man groans as he gropes for the truth. . . . But there are people who are attracted by the durability of a stone. . . . What frightens them is not the content of truth, of which they have no conception, but the form itself of truth, that thing of indefinite approximation. (*Anti-Semite and the Jew*, 18–19)

> A man who finds it entirely natural to denounce other men cannot have our conception of humanity; he does not see even those whom he aids in the same light as we do. His generosity, his kindness are not like our kindness, our generosity. You cannot confine passion to one sphere. (*Anti-Semite and the Jew*, 21–22)

> Anti-Semitism is thus seen to be at bottom a form of Manichaeism. It explains the course of the world by the struggle of the principle of Good with the principle of Evil. . . . Therefore Good consists above all in the destruction of Evil. Underneath the bitterness of the anti-Semite is concealed the optimistic belief that harmony will be re-established of itself, once Evil is eliminated. (*Anti-Semite and the Jew*, 40–43)

I believe that these quotes make it clear that Sartre is describing a specific type of consciousness. In the context of this paper, the anti-Semite is in bad faith in a very specific and strong sense of the term, otherwise, there would be no reason for Sartre to single him out for condemnation. Implicit, however, in this very condemnation of the anti-Semite is the realization that others can avoid a Manichaean outlook and practice good faith, also in a strong sense of that term.

Returning now to *Being and Nothingness*, I think that strong notions of good and bad faith are also implicit throughout Sartre's descriptive ontology. In this respect, I think that the chapter "Bad Faith" should be read as providing the foundation for describing two different ways in which consciousness can appear as a belief structure. By referring to consciousness as a belief structure, I am suggesting that Sartre sees belief as an intrinsic aspect of awareness. But I do not think it either necessary or fruitful to elaborate this claim here.[4] Nevertheless, at least the following should be noted: belief is not distinguished from knowledge merely by a relation to an object; that is, for Sartre the intentional structure of consciousness requires that the *act* of believing be distinguished from the *act* of knowing. The point that I wish to make now is that I think this belief structure is itself further distinguished by Sartre into two basic types. The intentional structure of a bad-faith belief is fundamentally different from the intentional structure of a good-faith belief; that is, persons in bad faith are distinguished not only by *what* they believe but by the *way* they believe.

I think that Sartre lays the foundation for the description of good and bad faith as two fundamentally different ways of believing in the chapter "Bad Faith" in *Being and Nothingness*.

> Bad faith does not hold the norms and criteria of truth as they are accepted by the critical thought of good faith. What it decides first, in fact, is the nature of truth. With bad faith a truth appears, a method of thinking, a type of being which is like that of objects. . . . Consequently a peculiar type of evidence appears; non-persuasive evidence. . . . Thus bad faith in its primitive project and in its coming into the world decides on the exact nature of its requirements. It stands forth in the firm resolution *not to demand too much*, to count itself satisfied when it is barely persuaded, to force itself in decisions to adhere to uncertain truths. This original project of bad faith is a decision in bad faith on the nature of faith. (*BN*, 68)

I take the last sentence of the above quote to be crucial. "This original project of bad faith is a decision in bad faith on the nature of faith." Good and bad faith are thus distinguished not by their relation to objects, but by their relation to faith itself. Abstracting from the problem of what is meant by describing good and bad faith as "decisions," and turning our attention merely to how they are distinguished as beliefs, we see that in a very simple sense good faith is a critical faith and bad faith an uncritical faith. The uncritical aspect of bad faith consists in the way it "views" the nature of faith or belief itself. One consequence of this is that bad faith does not recognize its own uncritical stance because its global view includes an "appropriate" view of criteria. Of course, all belief is based on probable evidence and there are no a priori criteria to measure the critical claims of this evidence. A bad-faith consciousness, in the strong sense of the term, must, I think, be pictured as one that alters the nature of evidence for its own purposes. This device can succeed and not collapse into a mere cynical awareness of cheating because the evidence for belief is indeed ambiguous: belief can never be totally justified.[5] Indeed, Sartre suggests that the person in bad faith, in the strong sense of this term, uses the ambiguity in the nature of belief for his own purposes. If there are no absolute ideals, then there are no absolute criteria and the person in bad faith is free to believe that anything goes in the realm of belief. The person in bad faith does not explicate this attitude; rather he turns his mind away from the glimpses of his condition. Ironically, this individual is usually the type of person who seems to need absolute ideals, and since these are lacking in the world he both creates them where he needs them and believes that they were really there for him to find.

Within the context of *Being and Nothingness*, the full sense of the strong notion of bad faith is, I think, not elaborated until the section, "Existential Psychoanalysis," in part 4. Indeed, I think that it is crucial to read Sartre's chapter on bad faith in conjunction with all of part 4. Here it becomes clear to what extent Sartre's view of consciousness must be understood in relation to Freud's view. In opposition to Freud, Sartre claims that we choose our neurosis. Here again, I think that it is useful to distinguish a weak and strong sense of "neurosis." Although we all have some psychic aberrations, I understand Sartre in this section to be concerned mainly with a definite, limiting notion of a neurosis as a deep, self-deception. Thus speaking of an inferiority complex Sartre says: "This inferiority which I struggle against in which nevertheless I recognize, this I have chosen from the start" (*BN*, 459). A simple example may illustrate how I think this "choice" might occur: Imagine that a child has studied and then failed his first examination in mathematics. This failure could be a crucial experience for the child; he may have to face the possibility that in the future even his best efforts in mathematics as well as in other areas may result in failure. Of course, this one failure gives little evidence for his chances of performing successfully in the future; but for the child this evidence may appear sufficient to justify rejecting future efforts with their possibilities of failure. In fact, there is some evidence to show that through no fault of his own either nature or circumstances caused him to perform poorly in mathematics. But if this is the case, then why study? If the child "reasons" in this way he will of course fail future examinations, thereby generating the needed evidence to believe that through no fault of his own he lacks ability in mathematics. In later life it may be useful or necessary for him to learn mathematics and he may now use his "will power" to conquer his "lack of ability" in mathematics. Here, Sartre agrees with Freud that the individual who thus struggles with himself is not attacking the right problems and even if he does succeed in conquering his "inability" to learn mathematics another psychic aberration will occur until he confronts the early experience he is avoiding. Of course, for Freud, the early experience this individual refuses to face is not directly related to mathematics; for Sartre, on the contrary, the early experience is precisely his "choice" to believe uncritically in his own lack of ability in mathematics. Indeed, for Sartre, this inferiority complex may be a device for hiding a desire to be superior. An extreme fear of failure could cover a desire to achieve and, in this interpretation, the inferiority complex is self-deceptive in its very project. The child implicitly desires to perform successfully but fearing failure creates the evidence that he would have been able to succeed if circumstances and nature had not been against him. He can thus retain the simultaneous belief in his superior abilities and his justification for not even attempting to perform in accordance with these abilities. Further, if at some later time he should "sincerely" claim to desire to conquer his inferiority complex, in this case his mental block in mathematics, without admitting his original flight from effort and fear of failure, his "sincerity" is in bad faith, in the strong sense of that term.

III

I would like to conclude this sketch by trying to make the strong notions of good and bad faith somewhat clearer. Towards the end, I will briefly compare the strong notions with the revised senses of the weak notions alluded to at the beginning of this paper.

It is clear that we cannot at every moment question the roles we play in society and the meaning of our existence. The possibility for questioning is always there, and this is sufficient for making us responsible for continuing in the roles we have chosen. We must choose to play roles but everything depends on how we are placed in reference to our roles. If we accept our roles as given to us by nature or society, whereas in fact we have chosen them, then we live in bad faith, in the strong sense of that term. In this case, we do not face what Sartre calls our "fundamental choice," rather we view our freedom to concern merely our deliberations about actions within our role. This freedom, however, is deceptive; it limits us to the relatively minor choices within our present role and thus hides our responsibility for choosing the role itself. Sartre says that when we deliberate "the chips are down," and he means that generally our deliberations keep our larger lifestyle fixed, as when a professor of philosophy deliberates about what textbook to use, and never questions his role in society as a professor. For Sartre, this "freedom" is uninteresting and, for the most part, predictable. But if our professor of philosophy were to decide to make his way in the world as a painter, this "choice," or conversion, would represent a real use of freedom. In this instance, the deliberations that preceded the conversion might later make the conversion reasonable but they could never fully account for it because, before the change, all deliberations were colored by the former life-style. In such a case there is a genuine leap. But the above description has to be qualified. Leaps are rare and it would thus seem that we would seldom be in a position to exercise our real freedom. This is not completely true. Sartre's point I think is that glimpses of the possibility of a radical change surface now and then from beneath our everyday choices. The professor of philosophy, who is deliberating about what textbook to use, will at times realize that this everyday choice is also a way of choosing to continue his life-style as a college professor, and this choice to continue his role is interesting and significant. To try to make our description clearer here, we can attempt to visualize our professor continuing his life-style in either a good- or bad-faith way. This portrait, however, will be based on a supposition: we must assume that anyone living a relatively comfortable life will have glimpses of a larger social context in which he can see his own life-style as a "role" and visualize real alternative possibilities for himself. Given this supposition, the professor, in good faith, will *at times* allow himself to hold and reflect upon these fleeting glimpses that his life-style is a role that can be changed. For it may happen that social conditions would cause the continuing in such a role to be unreasonable. The professor, in bad faith, should be visualized as one whose habitual way of life turns him from facing these glimpses of the larger context which would reveal his life-style as a role. Further, and this is the precise difference between good and bad faith, the professor living in bad faith can continue in his life-style because he has an altered notion of belief that itself hides from him his uncritical life-style. This uncritical stance, however, seems to go against the natural tendency of consciousness to question itself, and thus, according to Sartre, the individual living in bad faith will experience moments of anxiety.

In the strong sense of these terms, good and bad faith thus appear as two different ways of coping with the ambiguity that is inherent in every act of belief. Good faith accepts ambiguity and does not use it as an excuse for being uncritical; bad faith uses ambiguity for its own purposes of justifying its uncritical attitudes. One way of understanding how this uncritical stance can be sustained is to visualize a bad-faith attitude as projecting an impossible ideal of good faith. If the *ideal* of good faith is seen as impossible to attain, then bad faith is free to disregard the uncritical aspect of its own belief. Indeed, bad faith can be thus understood as a belief that since real good faith is impossible bad faith is also impossible. That is, belief is simply belief and one belief is as good as another. To repeat, bad faith can sustain itself as a true belief because there are, in fact, no absolute or *a priori* criteria by which to classify beliefs as critical or uncritical. Still there is a world of difference between one who attempts to have reasonable beliefs and one who avoids the effort because there are no initial guarantees that reason will arrive at the truth. To belabor the point with one further example: A soldier may say that his role is to obey orders and that if everyone questioned superiors all the time there would be anarchy. But is it ever an issue of questioning all orders all the time or is this reasoning used as an excuse to relieve him of the burden of living with the possibility that he may have to question orders sometimes?

I think that the same strong notions of good and bad faith can be seen in Sartre's *Nausea*. It is clear to me that Roquentin does not, at the end of the novel, return to the same bad faith that he was living in at the beginning of the novel. At first, he was hiding from his freedom, and living a life characterized by a strong sense of bad faith. At the end of the book, he does indeed return to a role, as we must all do, but I believe that there is a basic difference. Now he is no longer hiding from his freedom; rather he has consciously chosen a role, a role that like all others does not give a perfect solution to the danger of hiding from responsibility. There is no role that, of itself, gives meaning to life.[6]

But a life of good faith, in the strong sense, is one that attempts to better a world laden with roles determined by others. The first step to accomplish this is to realize that the roles of society are not fixed by nature, and this is what Roquentin realizes at the end of the novel. The mirror that his writing presents to himself and to the world is not a conclusion but a beginning from which change is possible. But the world is laden with an archeology of meanings, and Roquentin must be prepared for a continual awakening to the extent to which he still views aspects of life as natural when in fact they are merely roles determined by society. Nevertheless, it is his conversion to good faith that prepares him to recognize this latent "bad faith."[7] Further, I believe that it is this strong sense of good faith that has allowed Sartre to recognize that aspects of his early views were in bad faith. For example, Sartre apparently later realized that his descriptions of freedom in *Being and Nothingness* assumed a certain openness as natural to society when in fact it merely reflected his own relatively comfortable, cosmopolitan life. Thus he sees a progression from bad faith to good faith in the views on freedom expressed first in *Being and Nothingness* and later in such works as *Genet*, and in the *Critique of Dialectical Reason*. This progression, however, follows directly from the strong notion of good faith implied in *Being and Nothingness*.

I think that the weak and strong senses of good and bad faith are related. The weak sense of bad faith calls attention to the tendency and danger to flee from the ambiguity that results from the fact that so much of our existence is based on belief. Bad faith, in the weak sense, thus calls attention to the possibility of bad faith, in the strong sense. Clearly, however, one can live in bad faith, in the weak sense, while also living in good faith, in the strong sense.

But we may still question the suitableness of calling the general human condition "bad faith," even in a weak sense of this term. The question of suitableness is indeed an open question; the term, however, does point to a particular aspect of the life that we live in our present society. Society makes it very difficult for the average person to question the meaning of life and the values of role-playing. We are not here concerned with the obvious benefits that we derive from society. The issue is the ease with which present society can alter human consciousness and role-playing so that it seems natural to do what is clearly wrong. That the Third Reich happened confronts philosophy with a fact that cannot be ignored, namely, that, in the concrete, there is inherent in today's society a tendency to buy security at any price and to believe that this purchase is reasonable. The issue is not whether human nature is corrupt, but whether the average individual will make the effort needed to live a free life. When society makes it difficult for individuals to follow their own consciousness, it seems to be a historical fact that few will do so. If this tendency in human nature is called "bad faith," it is done, I believe, as a warning that society itself must be open and encourage questioning if the average person is to avoid living a life of bad faith, in the strong sense of the term.

I realize that in mentioning the social dimension I have already altered my original model, and it is clear to me that this dimension is needed for the full picture of good and bad faith. Indeed, within the context of Sartre's philosophy, a further, and I think useful, distinction would have to be made between good and bad faith and authenticity and inauthenticity to complete the picture. Thus the present descriptions must be taken as abstract. They describe, for the most part, partial aspects of two basic ways in which a person, in a generally open society, can manifest his beliefs and freedom. For even in an open society a free life is a task that some in good faith embrace and others in bad faith flee.

Notes

1. *Cf. The Philosophy of Jean-Paul Sartre*, edited and introduced by Robert Denoon Cumming (New York: Random House, 1965), 14.

2. Also, our so-called sincerity often hides the fact that we choose the vices that we admit to. Thus, in *The Flies*, trans. Stuart Gilbert (New York: Alfred Knopf), 92, Sartre writes:

> "Electra: Note her words, Philebus. That's a rule of the game. People will beg you to condemn them, but you must be sure to judge them only on the sins they own to; their other evil deeds are no one's business, and they wouldn't thank you for detecting them."

3. See Jean-Paul Sartre, *Anti-Semite and the Jew*, trans. George J. Becker (New York: Schocken Books, 1948), 79–141. (All further references will be to this edition.) Sartre does not appear concerned to develop consistently the distinction between authenticity and inauthenticity on the one hand and good and bad faith on the other hand. Still I suspect that his views can be shown to be consistent. In *Being and Nothingness* he clearly states that authenticity and inauthenticity are moral categories and, as such, do not belong in a descriptive ontology as does the phenomenon of bad faith. In *Anti-Semite and the Jew*, however, Sartre seems to clearly portray the anti-Semite as in bad faith and as reprehensible. Further, the question of authenticity does not arise in reference to the anti-Semite but in relation to the Jew. The bad faith of the anti-Semite creates the situation in which the Jew must now respond either authentically or inauthentically. I think Sartre's point is that objectively the consciousness of the anti-Semite is a wrongly directed, global and pre-reflective orientation to the world; nevertheless, it will always be an open question to what extent the

anti-Semite is responsible for his condition. Thus regardless of the guilt of the anti-Semite, his pre-reflective bad-faith condition creates the situation in which the Jew, on the reflective and thus the moral level, must respond either authentically or inauthentically.

4. What I am suggesting is that belief, for Sartre, is consciousness itself as viewed from a certain aspect. In particular, belief refers to the relation, within the pre-reflective cogito, of the non-thetic self to its ideal selfhood. That is, our "project" is a belief structure. Still I think that Sartre's view of good and bad faith has significance independent of this ontology. Cf Jean-Paul Sartre, *Being and Nothingness*, trans. Hazel Barnes (New York: Philosophical Library, 1956), pp. 47–105. See also my *Commentary on Jean-Paul Sartre's "Being and Nothingness,"* (New York: Harper & Row, 1974; Reprinted with a new introduction; Chicago: University of Chicago Press, 1980), 78–110.

5. It is frequently stated that Sartre has given us an excellent description of self-deception, but has not shown us how it is possible. But I think that Sartre has shown us how at least some deep self-deception can occur. Indeed, as I hope will become apparent, I see bad faith, in the strong sense, as a specific type of deep-rooted self-deception. The point that is overlooked, even by Fingarette's generally sympathetic treatment, (Herbert Fingarette, *Self-Deception*. New York: 1969) is that Sartre's paradoxical way of describing consciousness is not due to his inordinate love of colorful language, but is rather meant to point to a paradoxical aspect of consciousness itself. Briefly, for Sartre, every belief in p implies a nonbelief in p. That is, we can never so believe in p that we entirely eliminate the attitude of not believing in p; further, it is only by an effort, that is characteristic of bad faith, that we maintain a seeming unwavering belief in p. Thus to *begin* an analysis of self-deception by describing it simply as a simultaneous belief in p and *not-p*, is to impose a simplicity and homogeneity to consciousness that may make self-deception impossible to explain philosophically.

6. In the concrete, one always determines the meaning of a life with a role but the role does not, of itself, give meaning to a life.

7. That is, "bad faith" in the *new*, weak sense referred to in the beginning of this article.

CHAPTER 3

Sartre: On Action and Value

A central concern of Sartre's ethics is the specification of the relation between moral laws and human actions. Sartre rejected the absolute a priori status of the universal over the singular, of law over what is regulated by law, and of value over human actions. On the other hand, he was too much of a realist not to see that our spontaneous actions encounter structures in the world. For Sartre, the world is indeed clarified by universals, controlled by laws and guided by values. These structures, however, are dependent upon either the fundamental fact of our existence or upon the way we act in the world. The world is our world. All of Sartre's major philosophical writings, as well as his sui generis works, such as his books on Genet and Flaubert, attempt to reveal the ways in which our presence and actions bring into existence a world with structure and value. Specifically, a careful reading of *Being and Nothingness* will show that Sartre does not hold that we merely overlay structure and value onto a world that is otherwise absurd.[1] Values and structures are true objective aspects of the world, but, to repeat, they arise only from the presence and the action of the human reality.

Value arises in the world, because we can question what it means for us to be human. The ability to question the nature of our being implies that consciousness is originally a unique type of matter, namely, one that is not identical with itself. Sartre calls this lack of identity of consciousness with itself a "nihilation" or "nothingness." Value and structure arise in the world because nothingness occurred in matter, altering it into a world.

Value implies the relation of a temporally incomplete stage of a phenomenon to its completed totality. Without the totality, the event would not be a stage. "Thus lack is appearance on the ground of a totality" (*BN*, 88). The appearance of totality in the world does not arise from a

113

mere projection of human, reflective consciousness onto matter, but rather, from the fact that human beings exist within the world. Things are totalities and the world is the totality of all totalities because human consciousness is a self seeking to be a self as a totality. The self as a totality is the ultimate possibility and value of my free praxis. "Thus my ultimate and total possibility, as the original integration of all my particular possibles, and the world as the totality which comes to existence by my upsurge into being are two strictly correlative notions" (*BN*, 461).

The primary totality that human consciousness introduces into matter is the self: I am not now the self that I would be. Consciousness, for Sartre, is represented by this entire sentence and not merely by the first "I." The second "I" is not merely a concept in the mind of the first "I." I do not exist at some moment in time and contemplate the self that I wish to be as an object existing in some abstract future. "If human reality were limited to the being of the 'I think,' it would have only the truth of an instant" (*BN*, 84–85). For Sartre, however, the identity of the human reality over time arises from the fact that it is a being-in-the-world. But this union of consciousness with its situation is always in question. If a mother takes a child to the opera, the child may alter the taking into a dragging, and the child's later hatred of the opera may then be seen as caused by the mother's dragging. Or, to take another example, if I am born into a family of moderate income, whose general value is that its children should be successful in the world, I prereflectively encounter the value of the "successful self." Whether I choose to fulfill my role, or to be relatively indifferent to success or to be a dropout, the self that I seek to be is not the same as the self that I would seek if I were born rich or poor. A rich person may adopt poverty as a role, but the poor live it as the condition of their humanity. In each case, however, the total self that I seek gives value to my actions.

Consciousness is thus a self-seeking-to-be-a-self-as-a-totality. Just as the full moon is already present in the crescent moon as the sought for totality, so too the self as a totality is present to the self. The presence, however, of what we may here call the ideal self to the self is both more intimate to and different from that of the presence of the full moon to the crescent moon. The full moon is present to the crescent moon insofar as it gives meaning to the moon as a phase. It is only in imagination that we picture the full moon drawing to it the phases of the moon. There is no true efficient or final causality in this external relation. Further, the full moon is a completed totality; the full moon can indeed be realized.

The ideal self is, however, present to the self as a detotalized totality; that is, the ideal self constantly recedes as I approach it. To be more accurate, the ideal self is a detotalized totality insofar as it includes in its ideal both the possibility that I will be more than I am, and the question that I might be different than I now am. In this respect, value is the surpassing of all my surpassings in two senses.

First, I seek to surpass the self that I would like to be in the future. For example, if I seek success, I seek also to be beyond the struggle for success. Likewise, the true revolutionary already seeks a self that is both an awareness of the revolution and beyond the struggles of the revolution. Second, value is the negation of all my surpassings in the sense that I am free to question the entire complex of a self-seeking-to-be-an-ideal-self. Sartre's philosophy implies that this second sense in which value can be the surpassing of all my surpassings can again be taken in two senses.

The first is the more ordinary sense in which Sartre speaks about changing our original project. The revolutionary can become a reactionary; he can renounce all his former values. For Sartre, this is one of the more interesting senses of freedom. Sartre is not concerned about those deliberations that occur within our project, but rather with our possibility of changing projects. Although conversions are possible, they are rare because they require so much effort on our part. We can indeed change. "But *at what price*?" (*BN*, 454)

Sartre, however, implies that there is another more radical sense in which value is the surpassing of all our surpassings. Here we approach the limits of language, because this value does not exist until the very praxis that aims at establishing it exists. This new surpassing cannot occur in the way that a conversion occurs, because the condition for its possibility does not exist in the world. In a conversion, the revolutionary, for example, can become a reactionary, because the possibility of being a reactionary already exists in the world. But, in this last sense of value, action is aimed at establishing a new humanity, of which the very possibility does not yet exist in the world. The initial actions are thus aimed at establishing the conditions for its possibility. This last comment can be understood in both a local and worldwide context.

In a local context, it seems clear that the initial acts of revolt, for example, are not aimed at a clear idea of a freedom to be attained. On the one hand, the prototype of this freedom cannot exist in their oppressors, and, on the other hand, those revolting have before them no other clear example. In both the French and Russian revolutions, there were writings and examples of peoples in other countries, but, in the concrete, there was no practical way in which those revolting could interiorize these examples. This does not mean that the only path of those revolting was to become oppressors themselves, but it does mean that this path was the more natural one for them to follow. As a true surpassing, however, the revolutionary action must aim at a freedom other than that of the oppressors. Initially, this does seem to have been accomplished both in the American and Russian revolutions, regardless of later relapses into old models.

Thus every local revolution faces an ambiguous situation, because it must deal with established, powerful nations. To truly alter the kind of pirmading of humanity that we now have, with the rich and powerful on top, we would need a series of successful revolutions, not necessarily bloody, that would alter our concrete image of humanity worldwide. What would seem to make this change feasible is that we know what to avoid, even if we are not clear what we wish to put in practice. Also, it would seem that radical changes of this type have already occurred in history; our practical concept of humanity is not that of the Egyptians, nor even of the Greeks. (These last remarks are admittedly an interpretation of the direction of Sartre's thought.)

Sartre has no need of a theory of human action, since action is the human reality itself as it follows through its intentional structure.[2] The intentional being of consciousness is free, and thus the actions needed to establish the conditions for the possibility of a new humanity may never appear: the French, American and Russian revolutions may never have occurred. We could be living in a history in which the very possibility of revolution may never have occurred. On the other hand, we could be living in a history in which revolutions had been more successful than they actually have been. For better or worse, we collectively have the history that we deserve. History is the result of real victories over oppression and real defeats under oppressors. For Sartre, not only is the Hegelian optimism unwarranted, but we must also reject the belief that dialectical materialism will, of itself, produce a new and better humanity.

It is clear that, for Sartre, possibles do not exist in a Leibnizian realm of eternal possibilities; rather, the possibility of being is itself established by action. "Thus the possible of Leibniz remains eternally an abstract possible whereas for us the possible appears only by possibilizing itself. . . ." (*BN*, 469)

We are now in a position to see why in *Being and Nothingness* Sartre entitled his section on values, "The For Itself and the Being of Value" (*BN*, 84). It is important not to read through the term "being" as mere philosophical verbiage. In a sense, Sartre's work on phenomenological ontology is an attempt to rehabilitate the term "being" for philosophy. By focusing attention on the being of value, we begin to see that value is surpassing of all surpassing in the second of the above senses, namely, that value *might* establish new conditions for the possibility of being. For Sartre, the drama of human life dissolves into an epiphenomenon unless value and action are seen to be different aspects of what it means to be human. The only way for the human reality to free itself from the great chain of being is to accept that value, as the truth and meaning of being, arises only from action. "My ultimate and initial project—for these are but one—is, as we shall see, always the outline of a solution of the problem of being" (*BN*, 461).

Our individual and social solutions to the problem of being are not academic. Our solutions to the problem of being are the concrete way we each attempt to define humanity through our actions. These actions forge our freedom. We are free, but we can use our freedom to create the a priori conditions that will in turn limit our freedom or the freedom of others, as is done in colonialism and racism, for example; or we can attempt to establish the conditions for the possibility of ourselves and others expanding our freedom.

There is, however, an evolution in Sartre's thought on the ways our free actions establish a priori values in the world. In *Being and Nothingness*, the notion of value is related to what Sartre there called the free project. "The free project is fundamental, for it is my being" (*BN*, 479). This, and other comments like this, have occasioned some commentators to speak of Sartre's notion of freedom as absolute. But this claim is ambiguous; there is no other freedom, for Sartre, except human freedom, and to be human is to be situated. We speak of human freedom as being limited only because we first conceive of the freedom of an angel or God. With this caveat in mind, it is nevertheless true that Sartre grew to appreciate the difference between a historical situation and a local environment, and in this respect, there is a development in Sartre's thought from *Being and Nothingness* to the *Critique of Dialectical Reason*.

In *Being and Nothingness*, Sartre recognized that the freedom of the oppressed was not the same as the freedom of the oppressor. This difference in freedom could not, however, be one of degree, for such a view would imply an Aristotelian conception of the human body as potentiality. Rather, for Sartre, the difference is that the value of the oppressor's freedom is the limit of the freedom of the oppressed. "Because *I am a Jew* I shall be deprived—in certain societies—of certain possibilities, etc. . . . . What is going to be the result of this for the situation? We must recognize that we have just encountered a *real* limit to our freedom—that is, a way of being which is imposed on us without our freedom being its foundation'' (*BN*, 524).

Sartre is here beginning to qualify the notion of situation. Every free act is situational, and, in this respect, the situation does not limit freedom. I must have a specific body, and I have no choice in the body I am born with. In the abstract, freedom is different, but not limited by situations. Social situations present a complication, because here the other's freedom aims at limiting us. In *Being and Nothingness*, Sartre still sees the Jew as having a choice. Anti-Semitism is a situation that the Jew could reject. The Jew could reject being a Jew, and thus not adopt the limitations imposed by the anti-Semite. Clearly this solution is not satisfactory; in renouncing his Jewishness, the Jew may also be renouncing his sociality.

What ''ought'' the Jew to do? *Being and Nothingness* is an ontology, and it does not consider the question of ''ought.'' In *Anti-Semite and the Jew*, Sartre reexamines the issue and no longer feels constrained to limit himself to an ontology. The ethical issue is raised; the authentic Jew should choose to be a Jew in the face of anti-Semitism. Sartre recognized that this solution is also unsatisfactory, because while it may seem to save the Jew as an individual, it leaves the social structure of anti-Semitism untouched. ''Thus the choice of authenticity appears to be a *moral* decision, bringing certainty to the Jew on the ethical level but in no way serving as a solution on the social or political level: the situation of the Jew is such that everything he does turns against him.''[3]

For Sartre, the Jew confronts a Manichean notion of freedom. Sartre interprets the doctrines of Manes as claiming that both good and evil are positive forces. If one conceives of evil as a positive force rather than as the privation of good, then evil can be attacked directly. The reason that wars make the meaning of life simple is that, for a time, the enemy is an evil that is also a positive being. Destroy the enemy and the good of victory is secured. It is a truism that this good is not the good of peace, and after a war the proper attitude is to turn attention to the ambiguous and unending task of building the peace. There are some people and some nations, however, that long for the clarity of war. They see the world in terms of good and evil forces. Sartre calls this a Manichean outlook, because good is seen as a force that will of itself overflow the world, once evil is eliminated. A society that believes that its evils are caused by a criminal class or by another nation sees its only task as the elimination of the so-called criminal class or threatening nation. The anti-Semite, as a modern Manichaen, sees the Jew as others see a so-called criminal class or apparent threatening nation, that is, as the personification of evil. All the ills of society result from the presence of the Jew, and thus the task of creating good in society is the same as that of eliminating the Jew. For Sartre, the anti-Semite, by making value to be the elimination of evil, attempts to flee the burden of establishing value in the world.

In the present situation, the authentic Jew must confront the Manichaeism of the Anti-Semite by insisting on the specificity of his or her Jewishness. Practically speaking, this frequently means that the Jew will be isolated from the non Jewish members of a community. It also means that the Jewishness is itself falsely limited, because it is defined in relation to black and white morality of the anti-Semite.

Anti-Semitism is a worldwide situation, and thus the Jew cannot be truly authentic until the historical situation is altered so that Jewishness is more than a response to the threat of Jewish elimination. Sartre recommends a concrete liberalism. ''This means, then, that the Jew—and likewise the Arabs and Negroes—from the moment they participate in the national enterprise, have a right in that enterprise; they are citizens. But they have these rights *as* Jews, Negroes or Arabs—that is, as concrete persons'' (*Anti-Semite*, 146).

Some years later, in his study *Saint Genet, Actor and Martyr*, Sartre again recognized that his earlier solution was incomplete. The tragedy in the situation in which the freedom of some attempts to limit the freedom of others was not really examined. Genet, who everyone saw as a thief, becomes the thief everyone needs. Genet becomes a thief, because he seeks to be the authentically social person. Genet accepts that others need him to be subhuman in order that they may be ''human.'' Society also requires that the subhuman appears to be so from nature. Genet thus chooses to be explicitly conscious both of the choice of limiting himself and of making this limitation to appear as something created by nature. ''To live is now to watch himself live. It is to acquire a deeper understanding of his condition every single instance as a whole and in its detail, in order to assume it unreservedly, whatever it may be. He takes his bearings every second.''[4] The world tries to make Genet into a small evil precisely in order to justify its own small ambitions, but Genet throws back at the world an invented evil that devours their petty goods. ''Although he may occasionally relapse into resentment, in the manner of very young children who momentarily regress to an earlier stage of their development, nevertheless, the fact remains that he invented the willing of Evil for Evil's sake. And not only evil for its own sake, but evil in itself.'' (*Genet*, 158) Genet now has a new value, the surpassing of all value precisely as value is being. ''Genet derealizes himself, he plays the role of a fake Genet who is the duke of his phantasms'' (*Genet*, 365).

Genet's poetry plays on the ambiguous tie between value and being. Value both is and is not being, for value is the surpassing of being. As we have seen, in the ultimate sense of this surpassing, the value of the self-that-I-might-be does not yet exist in reality as a prototype; the very conditions for the possibility of this value have to be established by action. This value is thus precarious; the very conditions for its possibility may never be realized. It is in this sense that value is nonbeing. This non-being is not a mere emptiness. A square circle cannot be; it has no value. But, while a radically new self is not yet possible, it may become possible. Here we are back to the second, more radical notion of surpassing that was mentioned earlier. The gap between what might be possible and what is possible is bridged by being as action. For example, this revolution is not yet possible and it may never become possible. But it may become possible if the proper actions create the conditions for its possibility. That is, certain objective conditions have to occur before a revolution is possible, and even then it may never be actualized. Thus people who are isolated have to be brought together; they have to experience their inhuman condition as caused by other humans, and they have to be willing to die rather than endure their oppression or hunger. But they may loose heart and prefer to hold on to whatever existence they have; or they can be defeated before they are ready. But even in weakness and defeat, some value has been created in the world for others to see.

In relation to Genet, however, value is more ambiguous. Genet is not a revolutionary in the usual sense of the term. The world made his innocent, childhood act of taking into a theft, and the world made the orphan into a thief. Genet does not choose to revolt. On the contrary, the world of adults is the world he wishes to enter. He wants to be accepted, but the road is closed. He has been judged to be unworthy. For Genet, his unworthiness is not something to surpass, but something to realize. He has been produced by the adults Manichean outlook, but this outlook was ambiguous. The adults did not want to change their lives; they possessed a justified humanity, and their only problem was how to hold on to it. Their ultimate value was how to exist unchallenged, but this value was a contradiction. They needed Genet to hate; they required evil. But this requirement was again ambiguous. On the one hand, they recognized Genet and every thief to be no real threat to their position; at most a thief was a nuisance. On the other hand, they had a faint glimpse that Genet and others like him could revolt. Genet was both helpless and the potential cause of their society's dissolution. For the most part, the adults of his French, democratic society hide from their own fear of the world's unworthy revolting. Indeed, they hide from the very image of subhumanity that they created. It is this subhumanity, this ultimate unworthiness, that Genet realizes so that the world may face its own need for evil. He does it not as a revolutionary but as a poet.

In the language of his poetry, Genet uses the ambiguous tie between being and value in order to put value in nonbeing as such. That is, Genet makes the very unworthiness of entering the world to be the very value he will realize in the world. But Genet is authentic; he does not take the easy Manichean way to evil. Evil, for Genet, is not a positive force; evil is a negation, a negation held in being by Genet's poetry. "From these examples, the reader will have grasped the true function of the verb *to be*: since it must derealize the Ney into the Yea, must transform the fact into a value and the real into an appearance, its frozen movement reproduces the dizzying and annihilating apparition of beauty. In fact, it *is* this apparition itself in the realm of language" (*Genet*, 399).

The ideal self that Genet attempts to realize is of a humanity unworthy by its very essence to enter society. But it is this very evil that the society needs and demands for its continuation. Genet takes as his value the very negation of being that came to him from his being called a thief. Genet will not simply play the role of a thief, he will be thiefhood. And more than this: For those who have created Genet to be a thief the ultimate evil is the nonexistence of God. And Genet creates this nonexistence. All the characters which the world recognizes as evil are seen to result necessarily from a hierarchy leading down to the God-Who-Is-Not, that is, up to Genet. "He reconstructs that real on every page of his books in such a way as to produce for himself proof of his own existence of God, that is, of his own existence" (*Genet*, 469). Genet thus demystifies the Manichean outlook of the adults, who pretend that they are forced against their will to punish him, when, in fact, they need him and have created him.

Sartre's study of Genet brings to light another aspect of the situation in its relation to action and value. We cannot invent values by reflection. We discover values in the world, and interiorize them as our own. This interiorization allows us to adopt an attitude toward the world's values. But, if the values we discover in the world are in bad faith, if they

attempt to establish a priori limits to our freedom, then our interiorization of these values will always be tragic. If we interiorize the generally
accepted social values as something to be avoided, then we isolate ourselves from our fellow humans. If we accept these bad-faith social structures, however, we grant that the humanity of some requires the subhumanity of others. The American negroes were put in this situation by
slavery. Here as elsewhere, the only proper remedy is a change in the
social structure such that each individual accepts the challenge of creating good. Socially and politically, we must be willing to gamble. The
basis for our social structure is a Manichean worldview that requires
the belief in an absolute evil, which we attempt to eliminate in order
that good may occur. Our bad faith is that we require this absolute evil
for our existence.

Although Genet chose evil for evil's sake, his project must be distinguished from the more traditional choice of evil in the form of good.
The anti-Semite projects an essential evil onto the Jew; the elimination
of this essential evil now becomes the good that draws the anti-Semite's
actions. The anti-Semite is in bad faith; he wishes to limit his own
freedom by limiting the freedom of the Jew. Genet's situation, and analogously that of many criminals and ''insane'' people, is more tragic
than that of the Jew. Genet sees himself in the world as the evil the
world needs. Genet chooses sociality over isolated bitterness.

In the *Critique of Dialectical Reason*, the situation becomes even
more complex because Sartre is no longer concerned only with what
happens to individuals in oppressive situations, but with the historical
practice of oppression. Oppressive actions alter language, institutions
and machines. The world as the *practico-inert* acquires an inertia and
an intentionality of its own. But the force of the practico-inert would
vanish, if human beings were not sustaining and furthering its power by
new oppressive practices. The liberal democracies could not operate in
the face of naked oppression. The relation between practice and value
is therefore mystified. ''Value . . . is both the revealing of *my praxis* in
its free development in so far as it posits itself within immanence, and
the revealing of a future signification as an inertia which necessarily
refers back to my freedom.''[5]

For example, we are taught that actions have value insofar as actions
are examples of a moral law. If I save the life of a drowning person, the
value of my praxis is given by the law that claims that it is moral to
endanger one's life to save another. Law appears as reason personified,
and actions appear not to be rational unless they are in harmony with
law. What is hidden is that the entire complex, action-related-to-law, is

a result of our own actions as these attempt to solve for us what it means to act morally in a situation.

In the same long footnote just referred to, Sartre examines a particular form of humanism in order to show how this mystification can arise. In the humanism advocated by the anarcho-syndicalist, a division between skilled and unskilled labor arose because universal machines, such as the lathe, required skilled labor, and it seemed natural to advocate a difference of value between skilled and unskilled work. To be fully human was to be skilled. The unskilled were not responsible for being born unskilled and were thus to be treated justly in a humanism that recognized a diversity of human talent. This hierarchy appeared as the human condition itself. On the other hand, it was the machine that required human beings to be skilled. From this perspective, this humanism could have been transcended, because these types of skills reflected the ''needs'' of machines. The owners of the factories could lack these ''skills'' and still be fully human. But a further mystification made this transcendence historically impossible. It appeared that *my* nature required me to be skilled. I was thus both born unskilled and responsible for being unskilled. This mystification of the origin of value was itself, however, the result of historical actions, or what Sartre calls ''praxes.''[6]

For example, the praxis of colonialism shows that our history operated within a division between the civilized and the uncivilized that is similar to the earlier division between the skilled and unskilled. Given this division, value, in the form of ethics, now attempts to transcend the division; for example, ethics requires that the colonized should be treated justly. Such a mystified value, however, never questions the morality of the division itself, namely, whether colonization is a justified praxis.

If value is mystified, it is because we have made it to be so. This claim cannot be made outside of history, but rather within history, by aligning ourselves, as intellectuals, with the underprivileged members of society. For Sartre, it is clear that we have, at present, the means to feed and clothe the majority, if not all, of humanity. We do not do so because we sustain in existence a scarcity that gives us the very condition for the possibility of our history. ''*Scarcity* is a fundamental relation of *our* history and a contingent determination of our univocal relation to materiality'' (*Critique*, 125). This remark has confused many of Sartre's critics, because they have not understood how a relation can be both contingent and fundamental. But Sartre is here consistent with the phenomenological outlook of *Being and Nothingness* and with what I have called his attempt to deconstruct the hierarchy of being. For example, the existence of human consciousness is contingent, but given its existence, consciousness establishes necessary relations. Sartre calls these relations "contingent-necessary-contingent" relations. Necessity is thus an internal relation existing between two facts, neither of which have to be. In a similar way, because of our free actions, social and historical relations can become necessary. A world characterized by colonialism, a world in which there are doors to keep people out, a world in which a child's drawings are graded, is a world in which we have made scarcity to be the a priori necessary condition of human actions.

We have made the world to be ours through our presence in the universe and through our actions. Through our presence we have given the natural world its unity, and by our praxis we have given the world its history. Who is this we? For Sartre, the social order is a pyramid, sustained in existence by the praxes of oppression. The higher we are on the pyramid the more we oppress others. Still, Sartre sees a great difference in whether we chose to sustain and further our privileged position or try to rectify it. There is thus a relatively clear direction for our future praxis. This direction can be seen by aligning ourselves with the most underprivileged members of society. We must always, for Sartre, support their attempts to acquire political power and economic wealth; where they are too weak to fight for themselves, we must help them to do so. It is their actions more than our own that will determine the conditions for a new humanity. We may, on the contrary, attempt to prevent their efforts. The tragedy is that we may succeed.

Notes

1. See in particular Jean-Paul Sartre, *Being and Nothingness*, trans. Hazel E. Barnes (New York: Philosophical Library, 1956), 171–218. In the references in this article, this work will be cited as *BN*. Also see Joseph S. Catalano, *Commentary on Jean-Paul Sartre's "Being and Nothingness,"* New York, Harper-Row, 1974; reprinted Chicago, University of Chicago Press, 1980, 132–147.

2. Sartre does not develop a Cartesian dualism in *Being and Nothingness*. The terms *for-itself* and *in-itself* are heuristic. They have no specific meaning, but, on each level of the discussion, the term *for-itself* points to the more conscious or intentional aspect of either the human reality or the world. There is not merely a union of consciousness with a body; consciousness is not embodied. The human body *is* consciousness; it is matter as constantly being surpassed. Action and reflection are two different modes of consciousness and comprehension. We think with our eyes and hands as well as with our minds.

3. Jean-Paul Sartre, *Anti-Semite and Jew*, trans. George J. Becker (New York: Schocken Books, 1948) 136–137. In the references in this article, this work will be hereafter cited as *Anti-Semite*.

4. Jean-Paul Sartre, *Saint Genet, Actor and Martyr*, trans. Bernard Frechtman (New York, George Braziller, 1963), 55. In the references in this article, this work will be hereafter cited as *Genet*.

5. Jean-Paul Sartre, *Critique of Dialectical Reason*, trans. Alan Sheridan-Smith (London, Verso, 1976), 247–251 n.1. In the references in this article, this work will be hereafter cited as *Critique*. See also Joseph S. Catalano, *Commentary on Jean-Paul Sartre's "Critique of Dialectical Reason,"* (Chicago, University of Chicago Press, 1986) 140–141.

6. For a discussion of the way value is related to the self in Sartre's study of Flaubert, see Hazel E Barnes, "Sartre's Concept of the Self," *Review of Existential Psychology & Psychiatry*, vol. 17, n.1. (Sartre Issue)

CHAPTER 4

Successfully Lying to Oneself: A Sartrean Perspective

Sartre rejects the Freudian unconscious and views consciousness as translucent. How then can he claim that we deceive ourselves? It would seem that any lie to ourselves would have to disintegrate beneath the clear light of awareness, and to degenerate into cynicism.[1] But, I think that Sartre is right; we do deceive ourselves, and, I believe that he has presented a generally viable description of how self-deception occurs.

The text in question is the chapter "Bad Faith" in part 1 of *Being and Nothingness*.[2] Two things should be noted about the placing of this chapter in the context of the book. First, logically, it depends on the chapter before it, "The Origin of Negation, and second, its full significance is not developed until the section "Existential Psychoanalysis" in chapter 2 of part 4. Textually, the significance of this claim reduces to the fact that *Being and Nothingness* is not a collection of essays, but a book, with a unified structure. This fact is seldom fully appreciated. There is a specific logic to the book as a whole; it proceeds from the abstract to the concrete in such a way that the concrete is more than an instance of the abstract. True, the work is a phenomenological ontology, and as such, it aims at descriptions rather than syllogistic deductions. But the descriptions work within a very tightly controlled methodology.

To be precise, Sartre, in *Being and Nothingness*, never says more than is needed to make the specific point in question. This logic is so geared that the phenomenological descriptions pivots about the chapter on the body in part 3, chapter 2. It is there that we discover that the consciousness is not merely embodied, but that it *is* an organic body. And, more to the point of the present discussion, in part 4, the notions of con-

sciousness as prereflective and translucent are qualified by distinguishing between conceptualizing our awareness of an object and our nonthetic apprehension of an "object." I consider this qualification crucial
for understanding how it is possible to lie successfully to oneself, and I
will return to consider it throughout this paper.

Sartre's text introduces two sets of terminologies, one relating to bad
faith, the other to self-deception. The relation of the two sets of terms
is somewhat ambiguous. The term "bad faith" is the more Sartrean
term, and it appears to be more general than the term "self-deception."
The way the chapter unfolds self-deception is used to explain how bad
faith can occur, but the possibility exists that some forms of bad faith
are not self-deceptions. I believe that this possibility is developed in
works after *Being and Nothingness*, where the social dimension of bad
faith is examined, for example, in *Saint Genet: Actor and Martyr*.[3] I
think, however, that it is safe to claim that, in the chapter on bad faith,
there is a practical identity of bad faith with self-deception.

The chapter opens by referring us back to the earlier chapter on nothingness. Sartre begins: "The human being is not only the being by
whom *negatites* are disclosed in the world; he is also the one who can
take negative attitudes with respect to himself." (*BN*, 47). In the first
chapter, "The Origin of Nothingness," Sartre had, in a very general
way, agreed with Heidegger that the fact of making negative judgments
needs an ontological foundation, and that this foundation is the human
reality.[4] For the purpose of understanding Sartre's view of self-deception, it is important to understand why Sartre describes consciousness
as a nothingness, but it is irrelevant whether he was fair to Heidegger.

"A Nothing about Which Something Can Be Said"[5]

Admittedly, the notion of nothingness strikes one as mystifying. Why
speak about consciousness is such a strange way? Actually, I believe
that Sartre's intention is to unmystify our notion of consciousness. We
tend, since Aristotle, to see consciousness as fitting in with a natural
hierarchy of things: minerals, plants, animals and humans. This hierarchy does indeed place the human reality on top, but only insofar as it
possesses added faculties not possessed by the things below. We *are*
animals, except that we can also reason. There is thus a natural ordering
among things. But what could have established such an ordering? Only
a being or beings beyond Nature. Plato's Other World thus haunts the
Aristotelian world of natures.

Further, to conceive of consciousness as one force among other forces in nature is to claim a perspective on nature as a whole. We mirror nature; that is, we are born into a natural hierarchy of beings, and our intellect acts as a perfect mirror, reflecting back to us nature as it is in itself. Whatever part the active intellect has in the Aristotelian tradition, the distinctive union of knower and known terminates in the passive intellect. The Kantian intellect is, of course, active, but its activity is also natural; the categories not only constitute nature, they are also produced "by nature" and ultimately by God.

Consciousness, for Sartre, is said to be a nihilation in the sense that its active quality is not homogenous with any so-called "force" of nature. Indeed, the nothingness of consciousness constitutes the forces of nature, not merely conceptually, but ontologically. But the notion of self-deception does not require developing how, for Sartre, consciousness can give rise to an objective differentiation and order among things. The point is that a distinctive lack of identity is introduced into consciousness that provides the condition for the possibility of self-deception.

One of the most striking things about Sartre's notion of being is that he maintains that the principle of identity is synthetic. A is A; a tree is a tree. True, Sartre claims, but this identity is constituted by its relation to consciousness.[6] Consciousness is consciousness. False, Sartre claims, for who or what could constitute its identity over time? Who or what could hold it in existence? God? Perhaps, if he existed, but, I believe, that a proper Sartrean answer is that not even God could create a knowing being that would *be* a knowing being; it would always have to be at a distance from itself to be aware of itself. Without this lack of identity, knowledge would collapse into an in-itself of a mechanical force.

Of course, Sartre is not simply denying the logical principle of identity; he is rather drawing our attention to two kinds of reality, conscious and nonconscious. A dualism? Perhaps, but not of the Cartesian type. There is only matter, although for matter to be aware it must lack coincidence with itself. It is indeed possible to reformulate the principle of identity so that it captures this division between a matter that can be aware of itself from matter that simply is. We can say that a consciousness not identical with itself *is* a consciousness not identical with itself. But, for Sartre, the paradoxical way of speaking has the advantage of reminding us of the distinctiveness of conscious matter. Sartre retains the paradox by always keeping together the "is" and "is not," when referring to the human reality. "Yet there is no doubt that I *am* in a sense a cafe waiter—otherwise could I not just as well call myself a diplomat or a reporter? But if I am one, this can not be in the mode of being in-itself. I am a waiter in the mode of *being what I am not"* (*BN*, 60).

I take Sartre's point to be that the very condition for the possibility of not being a waiter is created simultaneously with the fact of being a waiter; and, in relation to other things of the world—tables, chairs, etc.—it is this negative condition that characterizes the human reality. The reference here is not merely to my future possibilities and to the fact that I can change my occupation, but rather, to the ever present possibility of changing, even while I am acting in a chosen role. This waiter who is pleasantly serving me my coffee can suddenly storm out of the cafe, proclaiming "No more of *this!"* hopefully after he serves me my hot coffee.

Briefly, bad faith is an attempt to hide both from the responsibility of choosing and sustaining our present lifestyle and from the ever present possibility of changing our lifestyle. Also, I consider, along with Sartre, that the interesting cases of lying to oneself are related to our attempts to hide from our responsibility for our lives; in the concrete, the specific manifestations of these self-deceptions are determined by the social situation in ways that can only be hinted at in this paper. But the important point to keep in mind throughout this discussion is that real negations are not simply created by the individual without any foundation in one's real life. The individual confronts circumstances that limit his or her choices and condition his or her real possibilities. This waiter cannot realistically consider becoming the president of France, but he is still a waiter in the sense of not being one, for he can assume other roles in society. This point is relevant for our discussion, for while I shall maintain that the self-deceiver can fudge evidence for his self-deceptive beliefs, it does not follow that anything can serve as evidence.

Nothingness, for Sartre, is thus that distinctive characteristic of human consciousness by which it continually lacks coincidence with itself. The self is constantly seeking to be the self-that-it-would-be. This is not an infinite regress, but an activity of negating that my self is ever present in the world as a table is present. This applies to every aspect of the human reality precisely as it is human. I am indeed, for example, a male; I was born such. Nevertheless, precisely as I am human, my maleness is always in question; I am never a male in the sense that a table is a table. My biological constitution does not characterize the meaning of my being a male. If I choose to be celibate, homosexual, or heterosexual; if I choose to be passionate, indifferent, or rational, in relation to my maleness, I determine, in each case, the meaning of my maleness precisely as it is a human characteristic. We are not concerned here merely with different conceptualizations about the body, but with the different ways the body "exists itself," to use a Sartrean phrase. In each case of maleness, the walk, the gestures, the talk are all affected, and a good existential psychoanalyst could, in theory, see manifestations of one's sexuality in every aspect of one's life.

But the same nothingness that allows us to structure the meaning of our selfhood prevents this constitution from being a once in a lifetime effort. If I am heterosexual, I am also not identified with my heterosexuality. The principle of identity fails to hold. My maleness is indeed a structure, a web of behavior that I constitute in order to enter into it, and as such, it is relatively stable. But I have not only constituted my maleness by my past behavior, I also now hold this structure in existence. Further, as a constituted structure, it can be undone by the same efforts that constituted it. It is thus always in question. I always face the possibility of having a different relation to my biological maleness; or to be more exact, I can always reconstitute the structure of my maleness, for my biological maleness is never an in-itself, which is then accidentally modified by my behavior or conceptualizations. We are here on the level of being.

In the above sense, the term "nothingness" indicates an "elsewhereness" of consciousness; that is, even as I am engaged in my customary mode of maleness, the possibility of change always exists. This is my anguish, which I can never lose, but which I can attempt to hide from by deceiving myself about my condition. I can claim to *be* heterosexual as a biological constitution; I can attempt to hide from the choice of my sexuality. The condition for this possibility exists, because to be free is to have a free relation with our freedom itself. That is, we never face our freedom as a thing; it is the nothingness of consciousness, the elsewhereness of our awareness. I seldom directly face the possibility of changing, but this possibility exists in my everyday behavior. No matter how much I claim that I never had any desire to be a homosexual, this possibility is clearly a viable structure for me; it is my heterosexuality precisely as it can be other than it is even as it is what it is.

Bad faith is simply one of the manifestations of the nothingness of consciousness. Of itself, negation, in a Sartrean context is not necessarily "negative" in the ordinary sense of the term. Freedom may be a burden, but it is also what distinguishes us from the rest of the things of the world. In this sense, negation is something "positive." Nevertheless, for Sartre, the character of freedom as negation is particularly evident in our attempts to hide from our own freedom and limit unduly the freedom of others. Indeed, to be precise, our first awareness of ourselves is already affected by the way others see us. "My consciousness is not restricted to *envisioning* a *negatite*. It constitutes itself in its own flesh as the nihilation of a possibility which another human reality projects as its possibility. . . . it is as a Not that the slave first apprehends the master, or that the prisoner who is trying to escape sees the guard who is watching him" (*BN* 47). The point is that the practical limits of our freedom arise, to a great extent, from the way others see us. The slaves sees himself in the eyes of his master as having a subhumanity. It is this image that he naturally interiorizes and makes his own, even as he may demand to be treated "more humanly."

I have tried to show in these introductory remarks that, given the Sartrean conception of consciousness, the condition for the possibility of self-deception is already established. The two aspects of a Sartrean notion of consciousness that make self-deception possible are the lack of coincidence of the self with its own selfhood, and the fact that to be aware does not necessarily imply that we have thematized or conceptualized that of which we are aware. I will try to develop both aspects so that hopefully the condition for the possibility of lying to oneself is made evident. I am thus only aiming at describing a very abstract state of lying to oneself without bringing into discussion the social conditions that make this lie to ourself rather than some other to be possible. Here I think that I follow Sartre's own procedure.

Translucency and Objectification

In beginning his analysis of bad faith, Sartre says, somewhat indifferently, "Frequently, this is identified with falsehood" (BN, 48). In the context of the section, "Existential Psychoanalysis," in chapter 2 of part 4 of *Being and Nothingness*, it is clear that one of the advantages of portraying bad faith as a lie to oneself is that it enables Sartre to give an alternative to the Freudian explanation of neurosis and psychosis. I shall come to this shortly. For the present, let us follow Sartre in distinguishing a lie in general from lying to oneself. "The ideal description of the liar would be a cynical consciousness, affirming truth within himself, denying it in his words, and denying that negation as such" (*BN*, 48). Sartre's example makes the meaning of this last phrase clear. The ideal liar not only denies what he believes to be true in words, but he denies that his words are lies. "I'd never want to deceive you! This is true! I swear it!'' (*BN,* 48). This ideal cynical lie presents no special problem. Even a substantive notion of the self could handle it, without recourse to splitting the psyche. There is, however, one important point to note. This liar does not succeed in deceiving himself, and the evidence is that his ''secondary behavior'' is not in line with his lie. That is, once the immediate situation involving the lie is absent, the liar acts in accord with his true convictions.

Lying to oneself, however, is a more difficult phenomenon to explain. It is clear that we can attempt to lie to ourself, but can we succeed? Can we believe our own lies to ourselves, so that our own secondary behavior is determined by our lies? I think that such lies are a part of our experience, and further, I see the Sartrean explanation of why they occur and how they are possible as generally viable. ·

Sartre sets the stage by admitting that the Freudian explanation makes lying to oneself easy to understand. Granting some sort of division between the id and the ego, one can claim that a ''truth'' lies hidden in the id that is not known by the ego. I may believe that I suffer from claustrophobia or that I have an inferiority complex. But I am deceived. My real problem, according to Freud, results from some early traumatic experience, probably sexual, that my fragile ego could not handle. This problem remains repressed in the unconscious. Since I have no privileged access to my unconscious, I am as the ''other'' in relation to the id; I can easily be deceived. Sartre objects to this Freudian view on the grounds that it divides consciousness, and that the phenomenon of resistance is impossible to comprehend. How can I resist the analyst questions when they are getting to the truth, if I do not consciously know the truth?

Sartre returns to discuss Freud, and gives a much more sympathetic study in the section on existential psychoanalysis, and in his later works. What he says at this point about Freud, however, seems valid enough, and it does help focus the issue of how we can lie to ourselves successfully. Sartre's rejection of Freud, however, confronts us with the problem of understanding how we believe our lies to ourself. If we reject the unconscious and claim that consciousness is translucent, how can we deceive ourselves?

Part of the paradox is solved by clarifying exactly what Sartre means by calling consciousness ''translucent.'' Primarily the term is meant to be a rejection of the Cartesian thesis that ideas are the immediate object of knowledge. There is, on the prereflective level, no mediation between knowing and that which is known. I perceive red, not my sensation of red. I perceive Peter coming towards me, not my image of Peter. This rejection of mediation also implies that nothing can be perfectly hidden from consciousness. To be conscious, for Sartre, is to be aware. But, and this is crucial, *this awareness does not have to be a thetic comprehension.* Sartre's claim that consciousness is translucent does not imply that we always have a correct understanding of that of which we are aware, whether this be our own internal states or external objects. Translucency does not guarantee that I will always correctly conceptualize that of which I am aware. For example, I perceive Peter coming toward me; but I am shocked; it is not Peter. A Sartrean explanation would note that I perceived what was there at that distance from me, namely a Peterlike object. In this particular case I conceptualized the perception of this object erroneously, a state of affairs that could not be corrected if consciousness was always mediated.

I do not mean to imply that our prereflective understanding is always of something indistinct, but only that it does not have to be distinct. Whether distinct or indistinct, on the prereflective level there is no mediation. I am having a conversation with Peter and now I have a clear prereflective awareness that this is Peter with whom I am talking. I do not first know my concept or impression of Peter and compare this with some external object. On the other hand, there is also no mediation, when my prereflective awareness is indistinct. I perceive an indefinite thing in the mist, and it is still true that consciousness is translucently aware of this indefinite thing. I am not aware of an indefinite perception but my perception is of an indefinite thing.

The important thing to note is that the translucency of consciousness does not guarantee either that something is clearly present in consciousness or that what is in consciousness is correctly conceptualized by us. In relation to Sartre's text, I think that the entire section "Existential Psychoanalysis" would be meaningless, if translucency implied that what is translucently present to consciousness is *always* clearly and correctly conceptualized by us.

Translucency, for Sartre is a natural byproduct of intentionality, and, as such, it is indebted to Husserl. Sartre, however breaks from Husserl by insisting that intentionality reaches not merely the structure of a thing but its existence. Here, again translucency must be understood correctly. For, while existence is not a noumenal quality, it is also not a structure. Existence, for Sartre, is that quality that makes a thing to be *there* independently of me. In human existence, this quality is the elsewhereness of consciousness that allows it at any time to become other than it is; it is Peter's friendly voice as it is here and now also capable of denouncing me.

The above discussion implies that we have to be careful when using the term "object" or "objective" in relation to prereflective awareness. First, as already indicated, we do not conceptualize or thematize everything of which we are immediately aware. Second, the fact that something is objective in the sense that it is the intentional object of consciousness does not imply that the objectification, if conceptualized, will be done correctly or unbiasedly. This distinction is particularly relevant in relation to our understanding of ourselves and the others understanding of us. We can have an "objective" understanding of ourselves in the sense of knowing ourselves as an intentional object, but this understanding may not be "objective" in the sense of "unbiased."[7] I will attempt to bring out the interplay of these two meanings. Specifically, I will attempt to show we can be in error about our own states of consciousness, when nothing is hidden from consciousness. I will then examine how we can lie to ourselves successfully.

Translucency and the Ego

The answer to the question of how we can misunderstand the states of our own consciousness is found in Sartre view of consciousness as expressed in his early work, *The Transcendence of the Ego*: we encounter our ego *first* as a structure in the world and we then interiorize this structure. Consequently, Sartre notes: "*My I*, in effect, is *no more certain for consciousness than the I of other men*. It is only more intimate."[8] Unlike Gabriel Marcel, for example, Sartre insists that we do not have an inner core of our being that the other cannot taint and which is accessible to us in a privileged introspection. Rather, for Sartre, the self is always vulnerable. I know my self as the other knows me. I am not in a privileged position when I attempt to understand myself. True, I have a more intimate awareness of myself but not a more objective one, in the sense of an unbiased view.

Thus, while Sartre rejects both Freud's dynamic unconscious and Husserl's transcendental ego, it does not follow that we always have a clear understanding of our behavior and our own self. There is, for Sartre, no unconscious in the sense of a force that acts on us with apparent motivations of its own. Nor is there a transcendental ego in the sense of an a priori structure of consciousness that predetermines the unity of beliefs and perceptions. All the unity and structure of consciousness comes from that of which we are aware. Nevertheless, this unity of the self, or what Sartre calls the "project" can be understood on many levels, for it is affected by the way others see us and the way we interiorize their perception of us.

This project refers to neither a noumenal self nor to a totality existing apart from our individual acts. Sartre writes: "Thus if I am rowing on the river, I am nothing—either here or in any other world—save this concrete project of rowing. But this project itself inasmuch as it is the totality of my being, expresses my original choice in particular circumstances; it is nothing other than the choice of myself as a totality in these circumstances" (*BN*, 564). On the ontological level, there is only this concrete act of rowing; but this act is oriented in the world in a special way. If one could properly interpret my bodily movements, the way I am related to fatigue, whether I complain or not about the effort of rowing, how I look at others in the boat or look at the sea about me, one would understand the meaning I am giving to my existence. But this meaning arises from a complex web of relations; it is myself in the midst of the world before others. None of this proves that we always lie successfully to ourselves about the meaning of our acts. We may, at times, be fairly on the mark; we may be mistaken in good faith. But the fact that the I is a transcendent object in the world, the fact that I do not have a privileged knowledge of my states of consciousness does establish the condition for the possibility of lying successfully to oneself.

This point is crucial and it is worth attempting to restate. On the ontological level, my consciousness is the act I am performing at this time. But this act is very distinctive; it exists in the world differently than the way a table exists. A table simply is what it is; but the act of rowing, for example, is what-it-is and is not what-it-is. This act of rowing *is* my selfhood. At this moment of history, I am this act of rowing. But this act is something that occurs over time, and I am this temporality. My project is nothing else than the way I sustain in existence a certain kind of behavior over time. I am now moving the oars in the water in this way: I really don't want to be doing this rowing; I want rather to impress my companion. I am smiling a smile that is not a smile, rowing with a strained effortlessness, in the face of the other's ambiguous admiration. This game is usually understood as such by both parties; I know the meaning of my effort and I see that the admiration of the other is for my effort to impress and not for my ability at the oars. But this game is acceptable to both of us.

But the situation can be otherwise. I can be here and now deceiving myself about the meaning of my project; or, to be more accurate, a particular human act can be self-deceptive. For example, I am living a false idea of manliness that makes me believe that I am rowing easily and that the other is admiring my rowing. As my body moves over time, I think that I experience a smoothness of my muscles that is simply not there. I believe in my ability, just as I believe in the other's admiration. This self-deception is possible, because my I is my interiorization of the way I see myself in the world before others. I see a sparkle in the other's eye that I *choose* to interpret as admiration for my ability at the oars, but which any unbiased observer would recognize as admiration for my effort to impress my companion.

To an unbiased observer, my rowing exhibits a tension that is my effort to sustain an effortlessness that is not present. For me this tension is understood as my effort at rowing. There is, for me, no strain in my smile; there exists, for me, only what I consider to be the natural effort of rowing, and the smile appropriate to such natural exertion. Thus tension is indeed present in a successful self-deception, but it is nothing else than the self-deceptive act itself.[9]

In the chapter, "Bad Faith," Sartre has not rejected the insight gained from his earlier work, *The Transcendence of the Ego*. Since I do not have a privileged comprehension of my self, only a more intimate awareness, I can fudge evidence about myself. The value of both my intimate awareness and the other's objective awareness of me are not given as apodictic. I can make the value of my intimate awareness to count for more than the other's objective understanding of me. Needless to say, I do this by making my intimate awareness to be the true objective one. This is always possible, since the other may indeed be the one in bad faith.

Does this mean that anything can count as evidence? Yes and no. A person in good faith seeks critical evidence for beliefs. I believe in good faith that I acted honestly, and I give you my reasons. Let us assume that you are also in good faith, and you see that I bypassed certain important considerations. In good faith, I may indeed admit that I acted precipitously, if not consciously dishonestly. I am at least willing to change or modify my beliefs about myself in the face of new evidence. In bad faith, however, almost anything can count as evidence, although even here we have to be realistic and see the manufactured evidence as at least relating to the belief. For example, what is the evidence for a justified belief in anti-Semitism or that the poor are naturally lazy? There is none; that is, there is no unbiased evidence. And yet there are anti-Semites, and people who live in fear and hatred of the poor. These people give reasons for their beliefs, but if every claim is proved wrong, the belief remains as strong as before. Even in bad faith, however, these claims must be apparently relevant qualities about people; for example, that they are too clever.

It is not merely the objects that one believes in that differ in good and bad faith, but it is the faiths, or beliefs, themselves that differ. The distinction between a critical and an uncritical belief may appear to be one of degree, but we are involved with two radically different attitudes toward the evidence of one's beliefs.

Bad Faith and the Ideal of Faith

The "mechanism" that allows a good and bad faith form of belief can be described partly as follows: The fact that belief is always a question of degree of evidence points to the possibility of a truly justified belief. An ideal of belief emerges, not necessarily explicitly, but as a question that can always be asked about belief. This "ideal belief" would be one that is so justified that we would never have to reevaluate our belief. This ideal is, of course, impossible to achieve, but it can still be taken as the ideal of what a justified belief should be like. It is the *ideal of a perfectly justified belief that bad faith takes as the ideal of good faith; that is, bad faith has a bad-faith view of good faith.*[10] Sartre writes: "The ideal of good faith (to believe what one believes) is, like that of sincerity (to be what one is), an ideal of being-in-itself. Every belief is a belief that falls short; one never wholly believes what one believes. Consequently the primitive project of bad faith is only the utilization of this self-destruction of the fact of consciousness" (*BN*, 69).[11] For bad faith, good faith should be perfectly justified. But no faith is capable of such justification. Therefore, for *bad faith*, any evidence is as good as any other, and "a peculiar type of evidence appears; *non-persuasive* evidence." (*BN*, 68)

The uncritical evidence of bad faith is thus seen by the person in bad faith to be as valid as the critical evidence of good faith. Further, bad faith can maintain itself in being without conceptualizing its bad faith, since it sees itself as at least desiring an ideal of faith. The ideal that bad faith seeks is itself in bad faith; it is an attempt to flee the burden of a self seeking to become a selfhood.

Is this attempt to flee freedom successful? Yes and No. Yes, in the sense that the person in bad faith can successfully use freedom against itself, forging an essence that then appears to arise from "nature." For example, a child may study for his or her first mathematics examination and fail. The significance of this one failure is clearly ambiguous, but *this* child chooses not to face a world that might condemn her best efforts in mathematics. The child chooses to see her failure as arising from a natural inability to do mathematics, and thus genuine efforts in the future are seen as useless. The subsequent failures resulting from this project confirm the child in the project itself and provide the needed evidence to believe even more firmly in her ''nature.'' In this respect, the child's flight from freedom has been successful. But, the tension of a self at odds with itself is present. It may appear as a feigned interest in literature precisely as this is opposed to mathematics and in cavalier remarks about mathematics and science. The self-deception *is* these strained attitudes. This self-deceiver, however, comprehends this strain as the natural attitude a lover of literature has towards mathematics. This misjudgment is not a mere mistake, but the way the self-deception is maintained.

Sartre summarizes the main difference between good and bad faith, when he writes: ''Bad faith does not hold the norms and criteria of truth as they are accepted by the critical thought of good faith'' (*BN*, 68). The characteristic of good faith is that it recognizes, either implicitly or explicitly, *that the ideal of faith is in bad faith.*[12] Belief cannot avoid its essential ambiguity; belief is a question of degree and cannot be guided in its critical sense by any supposed ideal of belief. How does this good-faith rejection of the need for an ideal of faith manifest itself? It is seen in the fact that good faith always confronts the evidence first, or at least is willing to examine the evidence of its beliefs. The fact that there is no absolute norm does not prevent one in good faith from seeing that there can be a critical difference between having more or less evidence about belief.

A controversial example from Sartre's own life illustrates, I believe, the nature of good faith. Sartre at first defended Russian communism. Between 1952 and 1953, in a series of articles for *Les Temps Modernes*, that later became incorporated into *The Communist and the Peace*, Sartre defended his belief in communism, even in the face of communist repression both in Russia and in France. His line of defence is interesting. The question was not some elitist notion of freedom. The French worker, he notes, ''wants liberation. But her freedom doesn't resemble yours; and I think that she would gladly do without the freedom of expression of which such fine use is made in the *Salle Gaveau* if she were freed from the throbbing rhythm of the machine.''[13] Sartre also drew attention to the fact that he had never supported the dogmatism of dialectical materialism, that he always defended the right of everyone to speak. The oppression against the elitist members of the society was not to be condoned; but, if the lives of the common people were improving, then the oppression could be temporally tolerated.

When Russia invaded Hungary in 1956, Sartre again wrote a series of three articles in *Les Temps Modernes* that was to become the *Ghost of Stalin*. Now the situation is changed. Whatever socialism may become in the future, the invasion of Poland showed that Russian socialism had lost its roots with the people. The invasion could not be justified, since "nothing is served by arresting the free development of a country by force; it is up to it to overcome its contradictions."[14] Oppression was here not merely directed against the intelligentsia, but also against the common person, and such a socialism is hopelessly lost. Sartre rejected Russian socialism.

One can quarrel with Sartre's early defence of Russian communism. Perhaps he should have seen what was coming sooner. But it is clear that his belief in the practical viability of international socialism, spearheaded by Russia, was based on his assessment of evidence. When, for him, the evidence changed, his belief changed.

Bad faith, on the contrary, does not really change in the face of new evidence, because it is not really about evidence. Bad faith aims at a stability of beliefs that evidence cannot provide. It is thus more a belief in belief itself rather than a belief arising from evidence. What makes it "bad" and self-deceptive is that it sees itself as of the same type as a belief that arises from evidence. Our self-deceptive rower chooses to see his strain as evidence for his ability to row well. Let us imagine that his companion points to the meaning of his effort, by remarking, "Why don't you take it a little easier?" Our self-deceiver can respond in several ways. He could suddenly see himself as he appears before others, and become a less "serious" and more honest person. But there can be a great deal at stake in his view of himself, and our self-deceiver may rather choose to interpret the remark as referring to his companion's desire to be rowed more gently. Or, if this interpretation is obviously not the case, for even self-deception needs the appearance of evidence, then the person may indeed recognize a certain unnaturalness in his rowing. But this is interpreted as a minor misunderstanding rather than a project to deceive himself about the meaning of his behavior. He tells his companion that he slept poorly last night, and that he must be more tired than he realized. Later that day, when driving home, his companion notices the same kind of strain to attain an effortless driving that is simply not there. Nothing has changed. The evidence of a few hours ago counts as nothing.

Self-Deception as Neurosis and Prejudice

There are two important areas of life where bad faith manifests itself as a self-deception: the first in many deep-rooted prejudices, the other in many neuroses and in some psychoses. In both cases a web of evidence is created in order to justify a belief that is contrary to the real state of affairs. This evidence is sufficient to convince the subject. A few examples, may illustrate how this occurs.

In the *Anti-Semite and Jew*, Sartre makes it very clear that the anti-Semite is in bad faith because he has determined in advance to hate the race of Jews. Objectively, it is clear that no evidence has brought him to this conviction. If one disproves every bit of evidence that he presents to support his anti-Semitism, the belief remains just as strong as before.[15] The anti-Semite believes, however, that he has evidence. The other has just tricked him; tomorrow he will remember the real reasons that justify his belief. Or he may claim that the arguments of his opponents merely prove that individual Jews may escape the general contamination of the race. But this he admits. Each Jew, however, must prove to be the exception.

The anti-Semite believes that his belief is justified. He perceives himself as a misunderstood crusader. This race, the Jews, has become historically tainted, and the race of Jews is at the core of all the essential evils of our society. Sartre sees anti-Semitism, correctly, I believe, as a contemporary form of Manichaeism. For the Christian heretic, Manes, evil and good are equal co-principles in the formation of the world. Evil is thus a positive force preventing the manifestation of good. The Manichean believes that the elimination of evil allows good to happen of itself. After evil is eliminated, there will come a time for cooperating with the forces of good. The Manichean has deceived himself, because it is the hatred of evil that is loved. The time for good will never come. When anti-Semitism is no longer popular, other forms of racism will take its place.

The anti-Semite does indeed experience tension; the tension is nothing other than the self-deceptive belief about the Jew. This tension is the hatred that needs no reason but itself. The anti-Semite chooses to see his hatred as a crusade against evil. He holds this hatred in existence so that evidence is seen always on the horizon. He is indeed aware of his effort at maintaining his hate, but he conceptualizes this effort as the energy that should go into hating a natural evil.

There may of course be times when one has to concentrate on the elimination of evil, but the person in good faith recognizes that this is temporary and that the task of doing good, of altering the world for the better, is never brought about by simply eliminating an evil. It is this ambiguous task of doing good that the person in self-deception flees. The person in bad faith, the racist, for example, does not have to face the task of determining who he is and what he will become, since his basic goal in life is given by his hatred.

Many forms of neurosis and psychosis exhibit the same form of self-deception. An inferiority complex, for example, can prevent someone from attempting to attain goals that he would otherwise seek. But it is frequently this very lack of effort that the subject initially seeks to justify, while retaining the goal. An inferiority complex can thus be a project to be superior. For example, this individual wishes to be different, to be noticed, to be exceptional. But success in such a project is always in question. If one wants to be a writer, a lifetime of effort may not lead to recognition. In good faith, one seeks to enjoy the writing, attempts to get published, makes the efforts, and lives the gamble that recognition, in the present state of our society, may never come, even if it is deserved. For our person in bad faith, however, this risk is too great; but this individual does not wish to abandon the project of being superior. He believes that he would be superior, if nature had not cursed him with an "inferiority complex." He cannot work, because he sees his efforts to be doomed in advance. He claims that he needs self-confidence. But this individual does not need self confidence; he is lazy. His neurosis is the "intelligent" choice of believing in his superiority and being able to be lazy at the same time. Again the tension is misunderstood. His effort at sustaining the self-deceptive project of superiority is conceptualized as his struggle against an inferior nature.

But how can one deceive oneself about one's project in life? Sartre's answer is to remind us that prereflective awareness is nonthetic. "But if the fundamental project is fully experienced by the subject and hence wholly conscious, that certainly does not mean that it must by the same token be *known* by him; quite the contrary" (*BN*, 570). The "quite the contrary" is important. Reflection is not privileged. To repeat, we have an intimate awareness of ourselves, but not necessarily an objective understanding, in the sense of unbiased. We learn about ourselves objectively only through others. The issue is complex because both we and the other may be in either good or bad faith. If we are both in good faith, our objective understanding attempts to be unbiased. Thus in good faith we are open to balance our intimate awareness of ourselves with the way the other interprets the meaning of our behavior. In bad faith the value is given almost exclusively to our intimate awareness. In bad faith, our reflections work within our bad-faith project, so that when we reflect upon ourselves we see the value of our intimate understanding as automatically providing us with a view of the way we appear before others. In bad faith, we consider that if others do not recognize what we see to be our true objectivity, then there is something wrong with their perception of us. Since our reflections are in bad faith, we may need "help" to get out of our self-deceptive condition, assuming that we have a willingness to do so.

Evidence to justify one's self-deceptive belief is generated differently, in different cases. In kleptomania, for example, a person may steal something that they do not need. They chose not to pay attention to what they are doing. At first they cannot succeed. They know what they are doing; there is too much effort, too much explicit awareness of oneself in the process. But one chooses not to think very much about the strange object in one's pocket or how it got there. The self that took the object is out there in the world, moving arms and legs, but it is not the real self. Next time the effort needed to take the unneeded object is easier. Finally, it becomes habitual, and a stage is reached where one does not know that one is taking objects. The distraction has become perfect. One is now a "kleptomaniac." But why would anyone want *to be* a kleptomaniac? Again, it could be a bad-faith project to be "superior." The individual wants to be different, and to guarantee his exceptional status in society. How many kleptomaniacs are there in the world? Besides, one always has a built-in excuse for failure: great things would happen, if only I didn't have this "illness."

Suppose that the kleptomaniac now wishes to be cured of his cursed affliction. The "existential analyst" asks him why he *wants* to be a kleptomaniac. It is here that the existential approach is different from the Freudian. The existential approach recognizes the translucency of consciousness; the neurosis does not point to some hidden truth; it is itself the problem. *Only it is not conceptualized correctly by the individual, and this misjudgment is chosen and sustained.* The person, of course, denies that he has chosen to be a kleptomaniac; indeed, he has tried to stop himself, and he is coming here for help. The existential analyst must now bring the person back to those early years to face the steps by which kleptomania was chosen as a bad-faith way of defining his existence. Practically speaking, the person cannot do this on his own, for all his reflections are within his bad-faith project.

R.D. Laing pushes this insight to cover psychosis. A child brought up among parents that make it known that he is unwanted, may, particularly if he has no friends, find the real world unbearable. There are only a certain number of options. The child might find the strength to hate his parents. But more likely he sees his objective self as unwanted. His intimate awareness of himself is of someone desirable. But what is the value of this awareness when weighed against the objective value of himself that he sees in the eyes and behavior of his parents? Here good faith might lead to suicide. But, in this tragic situation, bad faith can be a blessing. His intimate knowledge, his private world, is for him the real world of value. All children love to daydream, and the child gradually gives himself to the evidence that his private world is the world of value, and thus the real world. A point is reached when a gestalt is formed. The child believes in his world and becomes "insane." This insanity is a way out of an impossible situation, and it would not work unless the child completely believed in the product of his own creation. Laing's therapy consists in treating the now insane adult as someone who made an intelligent choice in a tragic situation.

On Waiters and Flirts

Sartre's own examples in the chapter "Bad Faith" can now be handled easily. He says, "Let us consider this waiter in the cafe" (*BN*, 59). There are waiters and waiters. Some people are waiters because the pay and hours are good. The job doesn't mean that much to them. But others define themselves by their job so that they encounter the rights and duties of their task as some greater-than-human structure that they must obey. Indeed, it is this that they seek. *This* waiter makes his role to be his salvation. He would enter any job in the same manner. If he were a soldier, he would push the button that would unleash the bomb, without a second thought or moment of hesitation or qualm of consciousness. The job, for this individual, defines the man, and humans are not made to question their roles in society. Freedom to such an individual is seen as dangerous. Freedom is wild, chaotic; he will bridle his, even if the other does not do so. "He applies himself to chaining his movements as if they were mechanisms; he gives himself the quickness and rapidity of things" (*BN*, 59). Of course he knows what he is doing. He is playing at the role of being a waiter. But he accepts the role as that which should define him so as to remove from him all responsibility. This is his self-deception. He knows that he is play acting, and that he can never perfectly achieve the essence of being a waiter. But this play acting is all that anyone can expect from him. Society wants him thus, and he accepts society's demands. "There are indeed many precautions to imprison a man in what he is, as if we lived in perpetual fear that he might escape from it, that he might break away and suddenly elude his condition'' (*BN*, 59). There may indeed have to be roles in society, but every individual is free to question the meaning of a role. There are times when a soldier must say no to shooting, and there are times when a waiter must say no to serving. But *our* waiter has chosen his job precisely in order to avoid the responsibility of questioning his role in society. He deceives himself into believing that one should aim at being a waiter as a pure function that does not critique itself. The tension of sustaining this self-deception is nothing other than the overly tense way he waits on his customers.

In the same way, Sartre's example of flirting should be interpreted as referring to a woman for whom flirting is a way of life. Any woman can flirt now and then, and be aware of what she is doing. But for this woman flirting is a way of defining her relations with both sexes. This holding of hands is never, as a human act, a mere contact of body with body; it is always meaningful. But what is the meaning? Is the closeness of bodies essential to the conversation? This flirt has managed to believe that the conversation is the human event. Her body is getting closer to the other, but this awareness is kept on the horizon of consciousness. She does not see the touching of flesh upon flesh as a delineated object in the world. She has an intimate awareness of herself as wanting this conversation. She believes that this is what she wants, and is surprised when the conversation ceases. She can succeed, because it is indeed true that this meeting *could be* about a conversation, and that the holding of hand *could be* accidental to the event. Two people could be so engrossed in conversation that they are not aware of their bodies touching. This possibility becomes for this woman the true state of affairs. If her friends call her a flirt, then they do not see things as they really are; that is, as she sees them. She can't help it if her body moves thus and thus. There was probably a time when she was explicitly aware of what she was doing, but gradually a gestalt was formed, a pattern of behavior, that, while now sustained, has nevertheless a momentum of itself. She sustains this momentum by choosing to see her flirtation as the natural effort that a woman experiences when talking to a man.

Conclusion

Following Sartre, I see two distinct attitudes that we can have toward the evidence of our beliefs: a good-faith attitude and a bad-faith attitude. In the concrete, the attitudes, the evidence and belief are one and the same; there is no common ontological characteristic of belief shared by these two modes. Ontologically, good and bad faith are two radically different kinds of things; the same name of "belief" is used, since they both have something to do with evidence. A good-faith belief is actually based on specific evidence, while a bad-faith belief does not need this or any other specific evidence. Thus, while both good and bad faith can be said to be a nothingness and a lack of identity of a self with its selfhood, ontologically, this nothingness and lack is different in each case. In good faith, I attempt to achieve a critical understanding of the way I appear before others and the way I have interiorized this objectivity. If people consistently tell me that I am rude to strangers, then I am willing to try to see myself as such. I may not succeed in getting a perfect knowledge about myself, but I can achieve an increasingly better understanding of the objective meaning of my behavior. In bad faith, and specifically, in self-deception, I have no real interest in altering my understanding about myself, since my belief is aimed at sustaining a certain attitude whatever the cost. I have chosen to see myself as incapable of change, for it is change that I fear. I wish to see myself in the world as a table is in the world, having a stable unalterable essence. I achieve this attitude by restructuring for myself the very nature of belief. A belief emerges that has no necessary relation to any specific evidence. This belief attempts to bridge the gap between itself and a critical belief by viewing the ideal of belief to be impossible to achievement. Since no belief can be *perfectly* justified, bad faith appears to itself as a justified belief. Thus a person in bad faith can hide from conceptualizing its bad faith as "bad" and as self-deceptive.

This substantive way of referring to belief is convenient, but it can be misleading. There is no structure of belief over and above the person acting. The critical attitude of good faith, and the self-deceptive attitude of bad faith are the individual existing here and now in the world before others. The self-deceptive rower is the tension of an awkward body that attempts to appear naturally capable of rowing well. The self-deceptive rower experiences this tension as the natural effort of rowing, but others see that most of the effort is going to the creation of an ease-of-rowing that is simply not present. Is this self hidden from this self-deceiver? Yes and no. Yes, in the sense that he manages to conceptualize his tension as the natural effort that appears when rowing vigorously. No, in the sense that he does indeed experience a tension that is not normally present in a properly coordinated act of rowing. But this tensed act of rowing *is* the self-deceiver; it is a self maintaining itself in a self-deception as it keeps from itself the possibility of change.

Notes

1. This article originated as a reply to Ronald E. Santoni's paper, "The Cynicism of Sartre's 'Bad Faith,' given at the December, 1987 meeting of the Eastern APA. Santoni has since developed his views in a recent book. See above p. 96 n5.

2. Jean-Paul Sartre, *Being and Nothingness*, trans. Hazel E. Barnes New York: Philosophical Library, 1956, pp. 47–70. In the references in this article, this work will be cited as *BN*.

3. Jean-Paul Sartre, *Saint Genet: Actor and Martyr*, trans. Bernard Frechtman (New York: George Braziller, 1963). For a brief study of Sartre's study of Genet from the perspective of an authentic attempt to cope with an environment of bad faith, see my *Commentary on Jean-Paul Sartre's 'Critique of Dialectical Reason Vol. I, Theory of Practical Ensembles*. Chicago, University of Chicago Press, 1986. pp. 36–37; 113–114.

4. For a detailed study of this chapter, see my *Commentary on Jean-Paul Sartre's 'Being and Nothingness,'* New York, Harper-Row, 1974; reprinted Chicago, University of Chicago Press, 1980.

5. This paraphrase of Wittgenstein is taken from the title of Kathleen Wider's interesting paper, "A Nothing about which Something can be said: Sartre and Wittgenstein on the Self," forthcoming in *Sartre Alive*, edited by Ronald Aronson and Adrian van den Hoven, Detroit, Wayne State University Press, 1991, 324.

6. I believe that this interpretation is supported by reading the chapter, "The Origin of Nothingness" together with the very difficult chapter 3 of part 2, "Transcendence." Nevertheless, it is not crucial to my thesis; for what is absolutely clear in *Being and Nothingness* is that the principle of identity does not apply to consciousness. Or, if it does apply, it does so as a constituted phenomenon. Consciousness as a lack of identity of a self with its own selfhood is examined in some detail by Sartre in chapter 1 of part 2, "The Immediate Structures of the For-itself." A fuller understanding of how self-deception is possible would have to take into consideration the distinct way the self is a presence to itself, the way it forms its own possibilities, and the way it attempts to achieve its own selfhood. I have only touched upon these here. Further, in self-deception, the temporality of consciousness is different from one on good faith. In good faith, we recognize the past to be sustained in existence by us; in bad faith, we attempt to disown responsibility for the past of our present. "Now the meaning of the past is strictly dependent on my present project. This certainly does not mean that I can make the meaning of my previous acts vary in any way I please; quite the contrary, it means that the fundamental project which I am decides absolutely the meaning which the past which I have to be can have for me and for others" (*BN*, 498). In self-deception, we deceive ourselves into believing that the past that we sustain is rather an in-itself, something given by nature or accident.

7. I am grateful to a reader for this distinction.

8. Jean-Paul Sartre, *The Transcendence of the Ego*, translated and annotated with an introduction by Forrest Williams and Robert Kirkpatrick, (New York: Farrar, Straus and Girous, The Noonday Press, 1957), 104.

9. I am indebted to another reader for criticisms that led me to bring out this aspect of self-deception.

10. See above, 80–82.

11. I do not think that Sartre's claim that sincerity is in bad faith presents a special problem for two reasons. First, we do use the term in Sartre's sense, and second, this use is clearly in bad faith. The sincerity spoken of refers to seeing our way of live not as something chosen, but as given by nature. The person who admits that he is lazy, but does nothing about it is in bad faith. He expects people to take him as he is, but this is not to mean that he is chosen his bad faith. Further, such a person is very particular about the "faults" he picks; he will let us know his faults, and he will not thank us for mentioning the faults that we see in him. One can always attempt to "rehabilitate" the meaning of sincerity. I myself have made such attempts in the works cited here. I believe all such attempts dubious in value. In the final analysis, I believe that we should not need the reflective and thematic assurance that is supposed to come with sincerity. Our actions should indicate our intentions. Of course, sincerity about one's past as past is not at issue here. I can, of course, admit that I *was* lazy.

12. I am convinced that there are two notions of both good and bad faith operating within *Being and Nothingness*. There is a general sense in which we are all in bad faith. I call this the weak notion, because of its wide extension. In Sartre's *Critique of Dialectical Reason*, it is clear that this pervasive bad faith is caused and sustained by group action; it is the concrete way we determine and hold on to our history. Briefly, we have created and sustained a hierarchal order in which some people are seen "by nature" to be on top. There are innuendos of this position in the chapter on bad faith, where Sartre refers to the way we see certain people as a Not. There is, however, a strong sense of bad faith, and self-deception is of this type. That is, despite the historical bad-faith structures, there are patterns of self-deception. Also, there can be a viable "good faith," even though the individual is in bad faith, in the weak sense of the term. For a recognition of the need to see bad faith as a social structure, see also, Robert V. Stone, "Sartre on Bad Faith and Authenticity contained in *The Philosophy of Jean-Paul Sartre*, edited by Paul A. Schlipp. La Salle, Ill.: Open Court Publishing Co., 1981, 245–56.

13. Jean-Paul Sartre. *The Communist and Peace with a Reply to Claude Lefort*. Trans. by Martha H. Fletcher and Philip R. Berk. New York: George Braziller, 1968. 228. For an analysis of this and the following work of Sartre see my commentary on Sartre's *Critique*, 24–31.

14. Jean-Paul Sartre, *The Ghost of Stalin*, trans. Martha H. Fletcher. (New

York: George Braziller, 1968). (Published in England as *The Spectre of Stalin*, trans. by Irene Clephane, [London: Hamish Hamilton, 1969].) 61.

15. Jean-Paul Sartre, *Anti-Semite and the Jew*, trans. George J. Becker, New York: Schocken Books, 1948. (Published in England as *Portrait of the Anti-Semite*, trans. by Eric de Mauny, London: Secker & Warburg, 1948.)

CHAPTER 5

Authenticity: A Sartrean Perspective[1]

The moral task, for Sartre, is ambiguous. On the one hand, the moral dimension points to the individual's freedom, but on the other hand, it also points to the institutional forces that the individual has to confront. Of course, in the abstract, there is no reason why our institutions could not be supportive of our freedom. For Sartre, however, our institutions are tainted, because their overall direction aims at producing a form of privacy that renders the individual socially and politically impotent, and at creating in us an other-directed behavior in which our true individuality is absorbed in the behavior of some anonymous "they."[2]

Our institutions maintain in existence a world of competition that we then interiorize as the natural human condition. But most of all our institutions are alienating, because they produce and sustain the very conditions of scarcity that other minor institutions then attempt to remedy.[3] We are thus involved in a mass self-deception. But this socially constituted bad faith is not necessarily the truth of an individual life. To determine the truth of a life requires that we look both at its local and its historical situation.

Introduction

If the task of living a moral life is ambiguous, the use of the term "authenticity," to describe that task, in a Sartrean context, seems not only ambiguous but wrong. To use the term "authenticity" seems to be taking up again the misguided task of developing an individualistic ethics indicated by the enigmatic footnote in the chapter on bad faith in *Being and Nothingness* and abandoned by Sartre in the unfinished *Notebooks for On Ethics.*[4] About this Sartrean "turn," the standard interpretation of scholars is that Sartre, in his later philosophy, discovered the significance of the social realm, probably under the influence of Merleau-Ponty, and gave up the attempt to develope an ethics of authenticity in favor of, what can loosely be called, an ethics of social praxis.

I find myself in a bit of a quandary in writing this paper, because on the one hand, I do not agree with an important part of this "traditional" interpretation, and, on the other hand, I do not wish to make much of the disagreement in this paper. Elsewhere, I have given a more textual analysis of Sartre's philosophy; here, however, I am concerned with developing certain notions regardless of whether, in the final analysis, they can be integrated with Sartre's own thought.

In what follows, therefore, I will not be concerned with developing a dialogue with Sartrean scholars. Nevertheless, I think that it might eliminate some misunderstandings if I give, in a preliminary way, the general outlook I am taking on Sartre's writings, and if I indicate briefly why I think that this perspective opens the way for a rehabilitated use of the term "authenticity," even in a Sartrean context.[5]

First, I should mention that I maintain that Sartre's philosophy had a social outlook from his earliest writings. What the later philosophy adds to the earlier is not a social perspective, but an *historical* one. Towards the end of this paper, I will give a brief explanation of the difference between the social and the historical. (Admittedly, this difference is itself an interpretation of Sartre's texts, and, if pushed, I would again say that I find the distinction viable, whether or not it is Sartrean.) The basic reason why I find Sartre to have always had a social outlook is that I take the early essay, *The Transcendence of the Ego*, to be crucial to his thought, and never to have been totally abandoned, although it is radically modified in the *Critique of Dialectical Reason* and in Sartre's study of Flaubert, *The Family Idiot*. As I will try to show, the lesson of the *Transcendence of the Ego* is that our intimate understanding of ourselves is radically altered by the way the other sees us. From this perspective, it is possible to reconstruct a continuity in Sartre's thought, with development, of course, and with even a "conversion" to the historical. This perspective and consequent reconstruction of Sartre's thought has, at least, two interesting consequences for me.

First, it reveals, albeit it from a limited perspective, a continuity in Sartre's writing from the *Transcendence* up to the *Critique* and including *The Family Idiot*. This last is important, because I think that it is wrong to dismiss Sartre's study of Flaubert as a bourgeois occupation, and to limit the moral concerns of Sartre's later philosophy to the context of the *Critique*. Second, and more important for the use of the term "authenticity," from the perspective of the *Transcendence of the Ego*, Sartre, for me, should never have attempted an ethics of recovery of being, or of the fundamental project. At first, he simply did not see the ethical significance of his own distinction between an intimate awareness of oneself and an objective one. For me, Sartre rediscovered the importance of this distinction hesitatingly in the *Anti-Semite and the Jew* and more explicitly in *Saint Genet, Actor and Martyr*. Thus, from my perspective, an ethics of recovery was never viable in a Sartrean context, and becomes explicitly rejected, as early as 1952, in Sartre's study of Genet. From this perspective, Sartre did not have to await his "conversion" to the historical, as announced in the *Search for a Method*, to abandon the hope of developing an ethics of authenticity. He had already abandoned *this* quest in the study of Genet.

Insofar as I see Sartre to have temporarily lost his bearings and to have thus become involved in the hopeless search for an ethics of a recovery of being, or of the fundamental project, *he* was obliged to reject the use of the term "authenticity." But, in the sense of a reconstruction of Sartre as mentioned, I think that the term is useful, because it does not involve me in the general task of trying to reconstruct a whole ethics. For me, the term retains something of its initial meaning of a recovery, but not a recovery of being, or the fundamental project, as such, but as a tendency and need for recovering what should be a good-faith view of the way others see us. Having said this, if the term still grates upon the ears of some Sartrean scholars, then I would have them accept it as my own and as resulting from my private use of Sartre. One final word on my use of Sartre. Having given my perspective, I will not in general qualify my remarks, except to indicate at times that I am making explicit a notion that is only implicit in Sartre's writings. This is particularly true of the notion of pure reflection that, for me, is still too close to Husserl in the work of 1939, *The Emotions*, but becomes less so by *Being and Nothingness*. In both cases, however, the notion is open for interpretation, and I have taken my liberties here. Those familiar with Sartre's texts will also note that the opening paragraph is itself a interpretation of Sartre that goes somewhat against the usual view. In particular, I am extrapolating the notion of bad faith from *Being and Nothingness* to the *practico-inert* of the *Critique of Dialectical Reason*. Sartre himself never does this, but I find it useful for my purpose of revealing what I see to be a degree of mystification in our social practices.[6]

Aside from the issue of an ethics of recovery, Sartre had other reasons to be shy of using the term ''authenticity.'' It is clear that Sartre would be opposed to a use of the term ''authenticity'' that referred either to being true to oneself or to a privileged reflection on death or to an insight into the nature of being. In all these senses, the term ''authenticity'' implies that we have had an original bond either with our own true self or with Nature or Being, and that we have been lead astray by the demands of the world. The implication is not only that we are united to a reality greater-than-ourselves, but that this union is beneficial to our human existence, precisely as it is human. For example, Buber says that beneath the objectifications of our relations with each other there exists in each of us a thou, which privileged moments reveal to the properly disposed mind, and Heidegger invites us to be open poetically to Being.

Sartre's view of authenticity could never mesh with such views of reality. Sartre is a naturalist and a materialist of the most radical kind, so radical that he considers that our present concepts of nature and matter still carry with them the supernatural remnents of both our Platonic and Judeo-Christian heritage. I view it as consistent with Sartre's philosophy to claim that we do have ties with being, with matter, to be precise, but that both our mechanistic and poetic ways of describing these ties cover an appeal to a transcendent consciousness that we pretend to have dismissed.[7]

We are also indeed bonded to each other; but again, the naturalistic way of describing these bonds, for example, to claim that mothers naturally love their children, is again to appeal to a benevolent Nature that hides the very God that science pretends to dismiss. The bond of a mother to a child is not of itself human in a positive moral sense. The bond is there, although it is morally neutral: it can be destructive as well as beneficial. Moreover, the issue is complicated, because the conditions for the possibility of loving and hating this child in this way would not exist unless it was both established by previous human action and now sustained by present actions. Thus, this woman's choice of how to love or hate her child is a choice of sustaining or attempting to alter the very conditions for the child's humanity: the woman, or man, who teaches a child how to compete for money is helping to sustain the social role of competition.

Making the Self

The background for my reconstruction of Sartre's thought on authenticity has its roots in one of his earliest writings, *The Transcendence of*

The Ego. This work both shows his indebtedness to Husserl and his separation from Husserl's philosophic program. Effectively Sartre maintains that *all* the unity of consciousness comes from outside consciousness, from that of which we are conscious. Sartre here gives a radical interpretation to Husserl's notion of intentionality to mean that our ego, or self, is an object that we discover in the world. We indeed have a more intimate awareness of our ego, our self, but not a more objective understanding of it. "My *I*, in effect, is *no more certain for consciousness than the I of other men*. It is only more intimate."[8] Further, there is no a priori guarantee that either our intimate awareness or the others more objective comprehension will be closer to the truth about us. "Peter's emotion is no more *certain* for Peter than for Paul. For Both of them, it belongs to the category of objects which can be called into question" (*Transcendence*, 95, Sartre's italics).

To claim that our ego is transcendent is thus to claim two things: First, it is to insist that we interiorize only what we have first encountered in the world. Thus what we call our character, or our self, is the product of the way we interiorize what is given to us in the world. Second, it is to claim that there is no a priori privileged perspective on what I call my self or ego. Much later in his career, in the *Critique of Dialectical Reason*, Sartre will refine this view in relation to language, but what he says there can be extended to the self.[9] A child, for example, acquires the first understanding of itself in the way the parents behave toward it. It sees, hopefully, a self that is loved. As the child matures, it gradually becomes aware of itself, for example, it understands itself as a *she* that is more than this self-that-is-loved. The child finds a will of its own. She discovers an intimate self that has thoughts, desires and possibilities not given by the parents. But the parents are also something more than one-who-loves-it. They also have their thoughts and purposes. Thus everyone has a private self. The child, however, denies that this objectivized private self is its private self: *its* thoughts and *its* desires are different from those of anyone else. The intimate self thus emerges. The intimate self is, however, a product of social interaction, and not a starting point.

The road from the *Transcendence of the Ego* to the *Critique of Dialectical Reason* was developed in *Being and Nothingness*. In that work, Sartre begins to detail his view of consciousness, by distinguishing between prereflective and reflective awareness.[10] For example, when we are engrossed in a conversation or in reading a book, we are taken up in the activity itself. We are not explicitly aware of ourself as reading; that is to say, our reading is not known as an object. Nevertheless, it does not follow that our act of reading is a blind, mechanical activity. For example, as I am now reading, I am not explicitly aware that I normally read to obtain information and that now I am reading for recreation. Clearly, if I were so aware, I could not read for pleasure. But my reading is still an awareness of reading.

The analysis of this simple phenomenon is very important for Sartre. On the one hand, it implies that the self is a product and not an a priori principle of activity. Second, it implies a priority of action over, what we might call, armchair reflection. It is when I am acting that I am most myself: the fact that I am one who reads now for recreation is also the fact that I normally read for knowledge. The self *is* nothing other than the specific way my act of reading is oriented to this page on the book. This orientation is thus both a product of my previous actions and, subsequently, a constituted principle of present action. This ambiguous status of the ''I'' is revealed when I am momentarily interrupted in an activity: I become aware that *I* have been reading, namely, the I-who-needs-relaxation, and indeed, *I* have been relaxing, forgetting my need to relax.[11]

There are thus two truths related to my reading. It is true that I am reading to relax. This truth relates to my ego. But this reading to relax points to a more originative truth: I read now to relax only because I normally read to acquire knowledge. In *Being and Nothingness*, this particular insight is not pushed into the social dimension. Where, for example, did I get the notion that one could make a living by reading other than as a recreation. What kind of society produces ''intellectuals?''

Abstracting for the present from this social aspect of consciousness, we can follow Sartre in *Being and Nothingness* and distinguish three states of consciousness: First, there is the prereflective consciousness, the one absorbed in activities: I am now reading to relax, absorbed in my reading and indeed I am relaxing. Second, there is the completely reflective consciousness, the consciousness that appears when we cease our activities and attempt to discover what our activities mean: I now reflect on what it means to read normally as a ''professional.'' Third, there is what Sartre calls perfect reflection, a momentary grasp of ourselves while not ceasing in the activity and not turning the activity into an object of study: I am now reading to relax but I suddenly become aware of how strange it is to read as a ''professional.'' What is this reading that I am doing?[12] *As a first, abstract, understanding of authenticity, we can say that the authentic person does not consistently distract herself from these moments of pure reflection.*

All these states of consciousness are, in Sartre's term, "translucent." Translucency is not a substantive notion; indeed, none of Sartre's terms are meant to be taken in a substantive sense. The term "translucency" points to the fact that there is no mediation between my awareness and the thing or person of which I am aware. Neither the ego nor a concept nor a perception intervene between my awareness and that of which I am aware. I am aware of red, not my sensation of red. But then is it not true that in reflecting upon myself, I am aware of myself and not of an idea of myself? True indeed. But this self of which I am aware is itself the product of my actions, and to be more precise, it appears as the ideal limit of my acts. By a difficult process that Sartre calls a radical conversion, that I will later touch upon, I can change the direction of my actions and thus alter the ideal limit to which my action tend. Ordinarily, however, even our so-called critical reflections remain within the limits that are given by ego; that is, our actions tend toward an ideal limit, that is frequently not spelled out, and our reflections on ourself operate within this limit. Thus, of itself, ordinary reflection does not give us a privileged insight into our self; reflection normally reveals the self we have determined to seek to be. Later, we will see that even pure reflection cannot always reveal the true direction of our actions to us.

For Sartre, the real distinctiveness of human consciousness is indicated by the term, "nothingness." This term is meant to point to a type of elsewhereness of our conscious states: we are never completely absorbed in an activity so that we are identical with it. There is always an oblique reference to a self, not as an object of thought, but as the possessor of the activity. We now see a different sense of "I." My absorbtion in reading this book, for example, is my personality; it is the special way this reading is my reading. "Thus from its first arising, consciousness by the pure nihilating movement of reflection makes itself *personal*; for what confers personal existence on a being is not the possession of an Ego—which is only the *sign* of the personality—but it is the fact that the being exists for itself as a presence to itself" (*BN*, 103, Sartre's italics).[13] Thus, again, the important point is that it is not necessary to reflect upon ourselves as an object in order to be aware of ourselves. To be absorbed in reading is to be aware of oneself as reading, although this self-awareness is not an object of our reflection. That is, all awareness is a nonthetic self-awareness.

The ability of consciousness to question itself, the elsewhereness of consciousness, the reflexivity of consciousness are all aspects of what Sartre calls the freedom of consciousness. Even as I am absorbed in reading a book for recreation, the possibility exists that I can become explicitly aware that the enterprise of reading only now and then for recreation indicates something about my general outlook on life. What is this quest for knowledge? Is it valid? This possibility of questioning the meaning of my activity, even while I am performing it, is the constant underside of my activity. It is my freedom; it is, as it were, my nausea. For Sartre, this implicit awareness that the entire gestalt in which we organize our life can be changed is not something from which we should hide. But we can attempt to hide from it, and indeed our gestalt can be to avoid the possibility of ever encountering our free self. This is what Sartre calls bad faith.

The Self in Bad Faith

For Sartre, the freedom of an adult appears, for the most part, as a gestalt. Our free acts are, as it were, like one of those portraits done by Matisse, in which just four or five lines give us an entire face.[14] Every line relates to every other, one change means an entirely new expression. In the same way, there is nothing but our actions, but each act is part of a whole and indicates the whole. There is one qualification to be made in this analogy of freedom with a portrait. In human life it is possible to create, in bad faith, a way of acting in which the purpose is to deceive ourselves about the general direction of our actions.

Good and bad faith are, in my view, each holistic views of the world. In bad faith, rules, laws, the greater-than-human, the existing social structure with all its major roles are all accepted as existing "by nature." The basic values and meaning of life appear to exist prior to all human action. Specifically, a pyramiding of human existence appears to exist by nature. The existence of those on top of the pyramid appears, in bad faith, to be justified by the mere fact of being on top; those at the bottom have to establish their right to exist in the eyes of the justified. In bad faith, a waiter, for example, sees his job as settling for him the meaning of life in advance of its living. He has his private life, of course; but he accepts uncritically the social role society has given to him.

> A grocer who dreams is offensive to the buyer, because such a grocer is not wholly a grocer. Society demands that he limit himself to his function as a grocer, just as the soldier at attention makes himself into a soldier-thing with a direct regard which does not see at all, which is no longer meant to seek, since it is the rule and not the interest of the moment which

determines the point he must fix his eyes on (the sight "fixed at ten paces") There are indeed many precautions to imprison a man in what he is, as if we lived in perpetual fear that he might escape from it, that he might break away and suddenly elude his condition." (*BN*, 59)

From another perspective, bad faith emerges as a self-deception aimed at hiding the very character of one's freedom from oneself.[15] The individual in bad faith creates the very pattern of behavior that then appears to come from nature. He creates a web of evidence that is taken as justifying the very belief that established the evidence. The anti-Semite has *his* evidence; it is his intimate awareness of the Jew. No one but other anti-Semites know the Jew as he does. For the anti-Semite, the value of his own intimate reflections outweighs all the critical evidence about Jews. Or, consider the person who always claims to be after some ideal, but does nothing to reach it. He sees the value of his actions to be condemned in advance, so there is no need for action. He seems to suffer from an inferiority complex. But this complex hides a duplicity. He wants to be superior, but fears failure or is lazy. He seeks failure, not the failure that comes from honest effort, but the failure that already exists in inaction.[16] It is this preordained failure that then becomes for him the very evidence to show him that he suffers from some disorder. In one of the few places that Sartre refers to vice, he speaks of it as "a love of failure" (*BN*, 379).

At first, the individual in bad faith is probably aware of attempting to deceive himself, but the thetic meaning of the action appears only obliquely and in moments of pure reflection. The individual inhibits these moments of pure reflection, by creating a secondary reflective *I* which is seen as superior to the action now being done. The individual who claims that he is lazy, but at least sincerely admits his fault to you, is also escaping this admission: He who knows that he is lazy is above and beyond his own laziness. He is not, however, beyond his laziness by future actions that might change him, but he is now both lazy and beyond his laziness. This individual may even attempt at times to conquer his laziness, just as a person with an inferiority complex may seek to acquire a more encouraging view of himself. But this is all part of the self-deception. For these "acts of the will" are simply another attempts to hide from the initial choice of having an ideal but not being willing to work toward it. "The will in fact is posited as a reflective decision in relation to certain ends. But it does not create these ends. It is rather a mode of being in relation to them: it decrees that the pursuit of these ends will be reflective and deliberative" (*BN*, 443). In bad faith, this deliberation is used to hide from rather than reveal the true intent of one's actions. I claim, for example, that I am trying to overcome my inferiority complex so that I may better act, but this attempt to cure myself is only another distraction from action.

Is the person in bad faith conscious of being in bad faith, and is the person responsible for being in bad faith? The answer to the first question is easier than the answer to the second. Bad faith is a prereflective condition and thus so-called armchair reflections on one's conditions, or what Sartre calls impure reflections, will not reveal one's state to oneself. The person in bad faith may be aware that he is not critical, but to be critical is seen as something in bad faith. It is the critical other who is wrong. Nevertheless, bad faith is a certain violence done to consciousness. The normal condition of believing, which is also to question what one believes, is treated as a temptation, as something to be repressed, or better not attended to: I believe that an intellectual life is a meaningful life, but it may also be true that only a more direct action is needed at this time. In bad faith, I reject this temptation to my normal belief about my role in society. The best way to avoid temptation is not to meet it head on, but to allow oneself to be distracted. Bad faith is thus a kind of self-induced sleep.

The fact remains, however, that in moments of pure reflection, when we are caught off our guard, we implicitly recognize our condition. But, these moments can become less and less. We can train ourselves so that we are never caught off our guard; our bad faith becomes a structure as familiar to us as our face. Further, to repeat, our freedom basically concerns our overall way of relating to the world, and not our deliberations within our project. "When I deliberate," Sartre says, "the chips are down" (BN, 451). Reflection, as we recall, is not privileged; we cannot adopt a neutral perspective on ourself. An emotional person reflects in an emotional manner. Change is indeed possible, but, Sartre says, "*at what price?*" (BN, 454, Sartre's italics). We can change only by somehow altering the basic way we orientate ourself, that is to say, orientate our body, to the world.

But assuming that we have what Sartre would call a bad-faith project, are we responsible for being in bad faith? Sartre never raises the issue as such in *Being and Nothingness*, because he sees his function there as merely describing phenomena. Clearly, the issue is complex. The possibility of being an anti-Semite or of having an inferiority complex is not invented by the individual. Although, on this abstract level, of what Sartre calls an ontology, it is not possible to impute responsibility to one in bad faith, *in the reflective sense of an awareness of an aware-*

ness of actually being in bad faith, it is still true that bad faith is objectively a flight from freedom.[17] Bad faith can also be understood to be an initial rejection of the ambiguity in the confrontation between freedoms. I reject the ambiguous task of learning whether the way I *think* you see me is the way you *do* see me. But the situation is far more complex than this. We have been assuming that the other is in good faith. That is, if you are in good faith, you will have a more or less objective view of me. You can tell me about this self of mine, and, assuming that I also am in good faith, I can attempt to modify my intimate awareness of myself with your more objective view of me. I will also recognize that there is no a priori guarantee that my understanding of your report about me is, in fact, the way you see me. I will have to make distinct efforts to comprehend your understanding of me.[18]

But suppose that you are in bad faith. Your objective view of me is tainted by your own bad faith. Suppose I do not have an inferiority complex and that you think that I do. If I interiorize your objectification of me, the situation can become tragic.

Authentically Confronting Bad Faith

I am thus distinguishing good- and bad-faith projects on the one hand from authenticity and authenticity on the other hand. Sartre never explicitly does this. For me, good and bad faith *first* refer to the individual's project about the nature of belief itself. Bad faith is a bad-faith attitude towards what constitutes the kind of evidence needed for a reasonable belief. In an extended sense, bad faith now means the social practices and institutions that maintain such beliefs and make it easy for an individual to interiorize bad faith as one's own. Thus racism is a bad-faith structure of a society, and practices like discriminating against housing for blacks in an all-white neighborhood make it possible for an individual to gradually interiorize a racist attitude towards blacks. For me, the primary, although not the exclusive issue of authenticity, as I am using the term, is how the black now responds to these racist attitudes.

It is possible to reconstruct an evolution in Sartre's understanding of what happens when one attempts to live an authentic life in the face of those who objectify you in bad faith, and from this perspective, we can see at least one good reason why a completed ethics was never forthcoming.[19] For example, anti-Semitism is a bad-faith situation created by those who see the Jew as having an essential inhumanity that no talents or good works can ever erase. The Jew, in this situation, is a scapegoat for those who do not want to face the ambiguity in their own human condition. Anti-Semitism is a role that not only defines one in relation to the world but also enables one to adopt very specific relations to other people. An entire world of friends and enemies arises naturally from the anti-Semitic attitude.

While Sartre specifically characterizes the anti-Semitic as an individual in bad faith, he never raises the issue of the anti-Semite's inauthenticity. Is a child brought up in a completely anti-Semitic environment responsible for being an anti-Semite? Anti-Semitism as a free project is objectively an attempt to hide from one's freedom and responsibility. Nevertheless, one never knows what the alternatives are for the individual anti-Semite. This child may be raised to see freedom as a danger and to see the Jews as threat to his security. Further, this particular anti-Semite did not establish the condition for the possibility of there being anti-Semites in the world. In the abstract, one can hate people with red hair, but, in the concrete, this self, one-hating-people-with-red-hair, does not exist in the world as a way of life to be interiorized.

Aside from the issue of responsibility, it is nevertheless true that anti-Semitism creates a limiting situation for the freedom of the Jew. This limit is not the ordinary constraints that arise from a situation. Indeed, properly speaking, a situation does not limit freedom. Freedom is, by its very nature, situational. There can be no situation without freedom and no freedom without a situation. If I am born short, it is difficult for me to be a good basketball player; but shortness as a hinderance arises only in relation to the purpose of putting a ball through a net high off the ground, and reciprocally the net is high only in relation to the possible heights of human organic existence.

This issue is different in regard to anti-Semitism or any other racist notion. Anti-Semitism is the project of making the Jew responsible for being born a Jew. Each individual Jew's soul is seen to be tainted at birth with an original sin for which each Jew is responsible. If a Jew does good, the essential evil is still there. If a Jew renounces his or her Jewishness, if a Jew is seemingly assimilated into a society, the Jewishness is still present. Anti-Semitism is a free project aimed at limiting the humanity of the Jew. ''We must recognize here that we have encountered a real limit to our freedom—that is, a way of being which is imposed on us without our freedom being its foundation'' (*BN*, 524). The anti-Semite attempts to inflict an inner prohibition into the psyche of the Jew. Can the Jew resist? Apparently forgetting what he has said in the *Transcendence of the Ego*, Sartre claims that the Jew can "disobey the prohibition, pay no attention to it, or, on the contrary, confer upon it a coercive value which it holds only because of the weight which I attach to it" (*BN*, 524).

In the *Anti-Semite and the Jew*, Sartre can be seen as carrying through much more consistently the early insight of the *Transcendence*: Jewishness is first a situation, before it is interiorized by the individual who sees himself to be a Jew. But what is the social significance of anti-Semitism? Anti-Semitism is seen as a specific manifestation of a contemporary Manichean outlook. For the Christian heretic Manes, the world results from the co-principles of good and evil. Good and evil are thus both eternal, positive forces, and the essential task in life is to eliminate evil in order that the force of good can act on the world. For the present day Manichean the general direction of moral action is clear and simple: one simply eliminates evil and good will happen of itself. To eliminate or constrain the Jew, the American Indian, the Black, the poor, the criminal class, the communist is the same, for the present day Manichean, as producing good in the world. ". . . now we touch on the domain of psychoanalysis. Manicheism conceals a deep-seated attraction toward evil. For the anti-Semite evil is his lot, his Job's portion. Those who come after will concern themselves with the good, if there is occasion. As for him, he is in the front rank of society, fighting with his back turned to the pure virtues that he defends."[20]

What should the Jew now do in the face of anti-Semitism? For Sartre, the authentic Jew affirms the specificity of his or her Jewishness. A false democracy forces the Jew to be like everyone else; in practice, this requirement forces the Jew to imitate those in power and to renounce his Jewishness in his public life. The authentic Jew must fight this assimilation and insist on the specificity of his Jewish heritage, even in his public life. Sartre admits, however, that the situation is tragic. In affirming his Jewishness, the Jew isolates himself from the general public community. Sartre advocates a concrete liberalism which will respect the specificity of each race, nationality and heritage of its citizens precisely as they are citizens.[21]

It is now possible to see Sartre further developing the tragedy that occurs from a Manichean outlook, in his study of Genet. The adopted child, Genet innocently takes something. For Genet's provincial community, this is not a mere act of theft, but the work of one born a thief. Society needs thieves and Genet is born for the role. Genet, however, wants nothing more than to be accepted by the adults of his community. He sees himself in the world as a thief; he knows in his heart that he is not one. But who is right? They, the adults, whose world he wishes to enter, must be right. Genet freely accepts the role given to him. But, he will not be a half-hearted thief; he will not simply be a manifestation of evil. Rather, Genet chooses to be the incarnate, essential evil the world needs but does not dare to face openly.

> In the case of Genet, as in that of untouchables, for example, the negroes of Virginia, we find the same injustice (the latter are grandsons of slaves, the former is an abandoned child), reinforced by the same magical concepts (the "inferior race," the "evil nature" of the negro, of the thief), and the same angry powerlessness that obliges them to adopt these concepts and turn them against their oppressors, in short the same passible revolt. . . . Genet's *dignity* is the demand for evil.[22]

Genet's way out of his tragic situation is to become a poet, but his poetry is the glorification of all evil as evil. But is this not what the world requires? The world requires that the inhumanity in the human condition be seen as arising from an essential evil that tempts man away from a natural condition of paradise. The criminals of the world provide that glorious function, and they make the task of the justified easy: eliminate us and your world will be perfect.

In his study of Genet, Sartre correctly carries the lesson of the *Transcendence of the Ego* to its logical conclusion. Genet cannot surpass the inner prohibition aimed at limiting his freedom. Genet is indeed free, although he is not free to enter society without either being a thief or being a confessed thief who is struggling to change. Genet's authenticity is the way he throws back at the world the very thiefhood it would have him accept. The world's thiefhood is ready made; there are crimes and there are laws and jails. But behind the laws and jails is society's Manichean need for evil, and the need to see oneself as the purger of that evil.

Authenticity and Collective Responsibility

In the *Critique of Dialectical Reason*, Sartre lays the foundation for introducing the strictly historical dimension into our actions. From our reconstructed notion of authenticity, the *Critique* can be seen to examine the question of our individual and collective responsibility for making the world to be the way it is. What I find particularly significant is what I see to be the implicit distinction between the social and historical dimensions of our lives.[23] In *Genet*, the situation in which Genet's freedom operated was examined mainly from the perspective of its local or regional determinations; for example, Genet's foster parents, the provincial community in which he lived.

In the *Critique*, Sartre distinguishes a simple social relation from a historical one. In a simple social relation, for example, a mother loving her child, there can be one-to-one reciprocity. Even here we must add that the reciprocity is constituted by the actions of the mother and child and is not a priori. But as a historical relation, the mother faces the child through the mediation of a third. For example, the mother, as a woman, has a historically determined role in society. In the concrete, her love for her child is affected by the mediation of the way society sees her womanhood. If the mother is poor or rich, the love for her child will also be affected by this mediation.

The love of a mother for a child thus operates within a complex system of mediations that Sartre examined, in the abstract in, *The Search for a Method*.[24] Sartre here breaks with both a pluralistic and a traditional Marxist interpretation of the relation of the individual to history. In the abstract, there is no a priori way of determining whether the regional or historical determinations will be decisive in an individual life. For example, the specific characteristic of the love of this woman for this child may arise more from the way both are related to a firstborn child than from economic or other historically pertinent considerations. But even if the historical situation is not crucial for this individual, it is still present, affecting every relation. For example, Genet was able to enter society on his own terms, because he chose to express his mirroring of the world's evil in poetry, and the role of a poet is an acceptable one, even in our Manichean society. But on the other hand, the distinctive character of Genet's poetry will never come to light by studying its historical dimension; here the crucial situation is his life as an orphan in a particular provincial community.

I think that it is thus very useful to make this distinction, between the regional and historical, that is implicit in Sartre's thought explicit, and to distinguish between the local and the more or less worldwide context of our lives. To rent an apartment or buy a house in an all-white community is to de facto participate in a worldwide network of owners and renters whose actions aim at segregation and oppression of the underprivileged segments of society. On the other hand, each individual act of renting or buying has its own specific truth apart from its historical truth.[25] One individual may live in such a neighborhood, enjoying its security but not its segregation. This individual may be fully aware that, in general, our society, by its calculated negligence, causes the very conditions of poverty and crime from which the "good" then flee. Thus, one can be forced to participate in an objective bad-faith historical structure, while individually attempting to be in good faith. In this context, the characteristic of being in good faith is that one gradually recognizes the degree to which one has been unknowingly participating in bad faith. *To be authentic is to attempt to do something about one's necessary participation in evil other than experiencing its tragedy.* (Sartre's distribution of newspapers and pamphlets as well as his participation in demonstrations were his own efforts to get beyond the self-deception of the intellectual's private experience of the tragic.) But even if one only experiences the tragedy in the situation, this is much more authentic than in acting in such a way that one defends and deepens the world's bad-faith social structures.

In his study of nineteenth-century bourgeois respectability in the *Critique*, Sartre shows how it is possible to sustain a bad-faith structure that has been received from the past. Respectability is a social organization that is both sustained by a loose organized action and interiorized by each member.[26] The bourgeoisie's appearance was one of a disciplined life: stiff shirts for men, corsets for the women. The individual bourgeois may indeed have believed this to be the truly cultured way one was supposed to behave in society. Nevertheless, the action itself aimed at something deeper.

The revolution of 1848 may, in part, have been ambiguous, but in the final analysis it concerned who was to run society, the workers or the bourgeoisie. The bourgeoisie had the law and justice on their side, but they benefited by this justice. The workers were indeed a potential threat; if they could be armed no force could stop them. But, as breakers of the law, the workers were seen as an unruly mass that needed to be disciplined. Massacres were justified to keep this wild segment of humanity in line. Further, for the bourgeoisie, the national workshops had failed because the workers were lazy. The self which the worker saw in the bourgeois eyes was a self that was essentially lazy, but which could at any time burst out in wild, erratic, uncivilized actions. For Sartre, the bourgeois humanism that led to this view is the reverse side of a racist Manicheism. The racist postulates the other as essentially inhuman, while admitting that a particular Jew or Black may have escaped a contaminated birth. The nineteenth-century capitalist admitted that the worker was human at birth, but saw him losing his or her humanity by freely choosing to work for wages. The worker was thus responsible for becoming something less than a self-made man.

Bourgeois respectability was aimed at masking the bad-faith humanism of the capitalist. The goal was to show that the bourgeois merited their position in society, and that this merit could be passed on to future generations. "Their right had to be based on a merit which was birth and on a birth which was merit, that is to say, on a non-acquired merit which would justify the class in maintaining them in their father's post (*Critique*, 773). Their disciplined life showed the unruly nature of the workers existence. An individual bourgeois may have indeed treated his workers humanly, but as a bourgeois he wore the same stiff shirts as every other bourgeois, and he could at any time show the superiority of his position.

The bourgeois's son is taught to see his father as the savior of the worker. The massacres were a necessary evil, and the father's intelligence and discipline allows for the livelihood of the worker. The son sees himself as the successor of the father. By a distinct, but difficult critical reflection, he could see himself oppressing the worker, but it is easier to go along with the image of himself as the successor of the father. Is the son responsible for his position? Practically speaking it will be impossible for him to stay neutral; the son's responsibility will depend upon whether he attempts to justify further his family position by new acts of oppressing the worker or abstain from these and thus weaken his privileged position.

To what extent was an individual bourgeois responsible for his position in society? He was responsible if he allowed himself to be defined by the rights and duties of the very society that kept him in his upper class. Second, he was responsible if he accepted the killings and subjection of the worker. Third, he was responsible if he aligned himself with active groups that aimed at sustaining his position in society. A bourgeois could identity with those elements of his own bourgeois class who accept responsibility for the massacres of their class and who oppose further oppression. Sartre, however, does not expect the authentic bourgeois to leave his class and become a worker.

In *Being and Nothingness*, Sartre showed how we lie to ourselves by adopting an uncritical attitude toward the nature of belief itself. Here, in the *Critique of Dialectical Reason*, he shows how self-deception can occur on a historical level. He reinterprets the phenomenon of other-directed behavior so that it is seen as arising a from hierarchical structure inherent in our institutions. Specifically, our institutions create an objective system of other-directed actions, which we each then interiorize and perform. There is the role of the doctor, lawyer, waiter, teacher, or engineer awaiting to be fulfilled by any person who is willing to do only what the function requires. One thus becomes a doctor not as oneself but as other than oneself; roles await one in society and are not to be questioned. Is providing basic medical aid to the poor more important than giving facelifts to the rich? The intern that actively asks this question will never become a doctor. As an individual, he may choose to help the underprivileged; but he is to allow others to choose as they wish. The medical system as a system can thus remains directed toward helping the rich more than the poor despite the fact that a doctor as a private individual may question the system. Precisely as a medical function, giving facelifts is seen to be just as medically valid as aiding in childbirth. The successful doctor is trained to see that his function is to practice the medicine he chooses to practice, and to leave the system alone. Besides, if this doctor doesn't give face lifts someone else will. *This* doctor thus give facelifts as if he were the other doctor who would do it, if he did not do it. The strangeness of the phenomenon of other-directed behavior is apparent in extreme cases. In Nazi Germany, companies knowingly competed for the manufacture of efficient ovens for the concentration camps. The manufacturers could say to themselves that their intention was merely the production of efficient ovens as ovens. In today's world, we can wonder how it is possible to enjoy the benefits of our computer age, even though most of the research is directed towards creating artificial intelligences that can destroy human life without direct human intentionality. How are we able to participated in a worldwide insanity, while attempting to keep our individual lives sane?

For Sartre, organized power groups working in symbiosis with institutions make it possible for us to concentrate on our personal life, while ignoring our historical condition. Privacy is thus a bad-faith ideal. The right of assembly is kept as an abstract right; the practical conditions for its possibility are not developed. Your political opinion should be your own; your private vote is sacred. The underprivileged thus never get a chance to become organized, and to discuss their common needs.

The Truth of a Life

In the concrete, the question of authenticity is complicated because, as was stated, the historical dimension of our actions may not always be the most significant. It may happen that here and now the local context is the determining one. A child raised in a middle class environment, may still be unloved or feel pressured to compete with other members of the family. In his study of Flaubert, which complements the *Critique of Dialectical Reason*, Sartre shows how the specificity of being bourgeois did not characterize Flaubert's specific challenge to living an authentic life.[27] Flaubert was expected by his parents to be at least as successful as his brother. Flaubert wanted to please his parents and yet he did not want to compete with his brother. Flaubert's constant fainting was a way out of his dilemma. He showed his parents a self that could not compete with his brother, because it was the self of a weak nature of which he was not responsible. In the abstract, this would have been a completely unauthentic project. But, in this case, Flaubert creates this weakness in himself in order to pursue a goal that he would not otherwise have been able to pursue and still keep the peace at home. Because he is physically weak and may faint at any time, he begins to write. His family would never have allowed him to pursue the ambiguous goal of becoming a writer, but it is allowed, since he is seen to be handicapped with a 'weak nature.' Flaubert could never play act this deception; it works because he also believes in his weak nature. What Sartre calls, Flaubert's early "wound," the pressure of competing with his brother and the choice of a weak body as an excuse of not competing, is never dissipated. Rather, Flaubert lives it on many different levels, in what Sartre now characterizes as a spiral existence. It is always present and it always points back to the original choice of a weak nature in order to write, but it takes on different significance in different stages of his life.

Although Flaubert may have found a way out of his personal problem he is still a bourgeois. He collects rent as other any other bourgeois. But he doesn't raise rents exorbitantly and he is decent to his tenants. Should Flaubert have revolted against his bourgeois life. In his own way he did. Practically speaking the issue of being a reformer was too far removed from him. He had his own problems and they were real. He rejected the image of the successful self that others wanted him to follow, and in practice it does not appear that he could have accomplished any other kind of revolt.

What then is the essential issue of authenticity? The question is ambiguous, because it is clear that, for Sartre, it is both a social and an individual issue. In the abstract, each individual is a sovereign. Authority thus flows from the bottom up. In practice, this sovereignty of the individual has been usurped by those in power and institutionalized as a function of the few. That certain people have to be in charge of tasks does not mean that authority *naturally* flows from certain functions. In the student uprising of 1968, Sartre was one of the very few intellectuals who took the part of the students. This was the sin against the Holy

Ghost, which the French academic community could never forgive. Raymond Aron accused Sartre of deserting the responsibilities of his status: a university is a collection of professors; students don't know what they really need. For Sartre, a university is primarily a collection of students. If authority flows from the bottom up, it is the students who have given professors the right to have authority over them, and they can take this authority back.

Finally, the task of being authentic is different, depending upon where one is on the social strata. Sartre implies that the authentic person always aligns oneself as much as possible with the most disadvantaged members of a community. For the disadvantaged, the task of being authentic is precisely their challenge to the image of themselves as being naturally disadvantaged; and they challenge this image not so much by trying to succeed, but by denying the justification of the image. For the advantaged members of the community their task is to see that their position is not merited, for no matter how hard they work, their wealth and power come to them through the collective efforts of others, who work just as hard as they do. In the concrete, this historical picture must be balanced by the conditions of the immediate environment, particularly the family environment. Also, the type of work that an individual is doing has to be taken into consideration. A woman who teaches large classes of poor children has, practically speaking, no obligation to better the historical situation. She has a right to enjoy her middle class home in a secure neighborhood. Although she would be the first to condemn the social practices that divide neighborhoods by race and color, it is to much to expect her to have the energy to fight this situation. Nevertheless, she would not be justified in actively attempting to further the segregation of neighborhoods. If it was unrealistic to expect Flaubert to leave the bourgeoisie class, it would have been unjustifiable for him to advance his bourgeois condition by further oppressing others.

It is now clear why authenticity cannot be described as self-realization. In the concrete, the self to be realized exists differently in each family environment and on each social level. The situation is thus complex. The views and actions of others toward us affect the core of our being, altering the most intimate awareness of ourselves. Frequently others see us from the perspective of their own bad faith. This bad faith can be either individual, social or historical. A person with an inferiority complex disparages the efforts of others. An anti-Semite forces the Jew to choose Jewishness as a confrontation. But most important, our deep-rooted Manicheism has created a condition of scarcity. Our world is characterized not by its natural scarcity of goods, but by the cultured scarcity that we sustain in existence by our choices. We choose to spend money on weapons, *in order that* we cannot have money to raise the standard of living for all. And if the money were not spent on weapons, it would be spent on something else; for example, being able to fly to Tokyo in three hours. For a long time, we have had the technology to feed and clothe the world. We have chosen, rather, to create a world of luxury for the elite. And we are responsible for this choice.

An authentic life, no matter how tragic, reveals human action to be at the root of all our accepted values, and it indicates the possibility of altering the very historical structures that we have collectively produced. For Sartre, there is no privileged self to which we can turn for direction, no poetic insight into Being to guide us. We cannot wait for some God to help us. We cannot rely on humanism or on historical laws. By our victories and defeats against oppression, we create the limits of our humanity and inhumanity. If certain people did not fight against the role of woman as the helpmate of man, that role would now still be the truth of being a woman. "Tomorrow, after my death," Sartre writes, "some men may decide to establish Fascism, and the others may be so cowardly or so slack as to let them do so. If so Fascism will then be the truth of man, and so much the worse for us."[28]

Notes

1. An early, shorter version of this paper was given at the annual meeting of the American Psychiatric Association, 10 May 1988, Montreal, Canada.

2. In his *Critique of Dialectical Reason* Sartre reveals privacy and other directed behavior to follow from the more basic condition of seriality. In a series, members are mutually related in their otherness. *This* individual helps build nuclear weapons, because if he didn't do it, someone else would. Even if he is against building these weapons, he helps build them, because he can see himself as the other who would do the work, if he did not. Seriality does not excuse the behavior; it is rather the condition for the possibility of acting in such a way that responsibility can be kept, as it were, at arm's length.

3. I am thus interpreting Sartre's notion of scarcity as a condition produced and sustained by our social practices. It does not, in my view, refer to the natural scarcity of goods.

4. This confusing footnote apparently alludes to a recovery of one's fundamental project, or purpose in life, in the sense of owning up to it. It no doubt also says something about this project; for example, that it should be directed towards a development of freedom and not an attempt to hide from it. My own disinterest in searching out the possible meanings of this note of Sartre's is not

meant to detract from the interesting studies that have developed by taking this footnote seriously. In particular, Thomas C. Anderson has given an excellent study in his *The Foundation and Structure of Sartrean Ethics*, (Lawrence: Regents Press of Kansas, 1979). The difficulty that I have with this general approach to the fundamental project is that, as I will attempt to show, it is difficult to see in what sense this recovery can eliminate the tragedy arising, when one attempts to live in good faith, although others are in bad faith. Further, I do not think that Sartre's notion of the group-in-fusion can viable replace that of the recovery of the fundamental project, since the former can occur only in very restricted social conditions.

5. I wish to thank the readers for their suggestions that led to the following clarification of my project and to the addition of several footnotes.

6. I explained above in chapter 2 of this second part how both weak and strong notions of good and bad faith are implicit in Sartre's early ontology. The weak notion has the broader extension and points to some socially constituted bad faith that Sartre does not explicate. In today's world, we might say that we are all in bad faith, in the weak sense of the term, insofar as we at least passively allow the build up of nuclear weapons, or insofar as we allow ourselves to function in a white male dominated society. Aside from this broad socially constituted bad faith, there is still the more restricted notion of being in bad faith, such as a being a racist. This latter kind of bad faith can be avoided even though one is in bad faith in the weaker sense of the term.

7. I am presently engaged in writing a book that develops this aspect of Sartre's thought.

8. Jean-Paul Sartre, *The Transcendence of the Ego*, trans. Forrest William and Robert Kirkpatrick (New York: Noonday Press, 1957), 104, Sartre's italics. Hereafter referred to as *Transcendence*.

9. Jean-Paul Sartre, *Critique of Dialectical Reason*, Vol. I *Theory of Practical Ensembles*. trans. Alan Sheridan-Smith (London: New Left Books, 1976; Verso, 1982). Hereafter this work will be frequently referred to as *Critique*. See also my *Commentary on Jean-Paul Sartre's 'Critique of Dialectical Reason Vol. I, Theory of Practical Ensembles* (Chicago, University of Chicago Press, 1986), 99–101.

10. See Jean-Paul Sartre, *Being and Nothingness*, trans. Hazel E. Barnes (New York: Philosophical Library, 1956), l–lvi; 150–170. In the text this will be cited as BN. See also my book, *A Commentary on Jean-Paul Sartre's 'Being and Nothingness'*, New York: Harper and Row, 1974; Chicago: University of Chicago Press, 1980, 30–35.;125–131.

11. My entire analysis of pure reflection and its relation to the ego, both in the preceding and the subsequent paragraphs, is an interpretation of Sartre's texts.

12. I think that the notion of pure reflection is viable, even though a problem

arises, because, while all consciousness is a nonthetic awareness, pure reflection seems to be both thetic and nonthetic. I believe that the paradox can be resolved along the following lines: All consciousness is not only a nonthetic awareness of its "object," it is also an *indirect* awareness of the *I*. This quality of consciousness is the reflexivity of consciousness as distinct from the reflective aspect of consciousness. If I am absorbed in my reading, I am not explicitly aware that *I* am reading, but, as Sartre says, using a different example, if someone asks me *who* is reading, I answer *I* am. Of course, in this case, I stop my reading to answer. In my view, pure reflection is a momentary awakening to the ego that "haunts" our every act. It is not like impure reflection, a different state of consciousness, but it is the prereflective cogito as momentarily aware of its own ego on the very edge of consciousness. The point is that, although I may be absorbed in my reading, at times I do become momentarily aware, for example, that this is indeed a good book that I am reading. In a similar way a tennis player can hear the sound of the ball hitting the racket and become momentarily aware that her entire body is moving *just right*, even as she follows through with the motion, and becomes absorbed again in the act of playing tennis.

13. I think that it is thus incorrect to refer to the prereflective cogito as *impersonal*; it is rather *prepersonal*.

14. For the following discussion on bad faith, see *BN*, 47–70; 433–531; 557–575. "If we admit that the person is a totality, we can not hope to reconstruct him by an addition or by an organization of the diverse tendencies which we have empirically discovered in him. On the contrary, in each inclination, in each tendency, the person expresses himself completely, although from a different angle . . ." *BN*, 563.

15. See chapter 4 of this second part.

16. See *BN*, 67–70; "Bad faith does not hold the norms and criteria of truth as they are accepted by the critical thought of good faith." (67). See also, *BN*, 472–475.

17. I do not mean to imply that Sartre held to a fact-value distinction. He did not. The human reality is the origin of all value. From this perspective, there is responsibility in every project, for we have chosen it, and it is us. Further, it is indeed true that, in the concrete, responsibility, even in the reflective sense, is one with consciousness. However, it is still possible and important to make conceptual distinctions, and these distinctions indicate very different possibilities, that is to say, different possible ways of existing, whether in good faith or bad faith. As I will try to indicate below, Genet was responsible for choosing to be a thief and in *loving* evil. But do we want to say that he, Genet, was evil? Further, in my view, bad faith involves a successful self-deception. See my article cited note 15.

18. "In the first place Hegel appears to us to be guilty of an epistemological optimism. It seem to him that the *truth* of self-consciousness can appear; that

is, that an objective agreement can be realized between consciousnesses—by authority of the Others's recognition of me and my recognition of the Other.'' (BN, 240, Sartre's italics) In this section, Sartre is intent on showing that there is no self prior to action, and that, since the action can change, the self is always in question. Further, the other has the same self that is in question, and his objectification of me is tainted by his project. In this sense it is impossible to know the self apodictically as an object reflected in the other's knowledge of me. But, if we take the self as that ideal sustained by my present acts, than there seems no reason why this self can not be known. Indeed, the entire section on existential psychanalysis, (*BN*, 557–575) presupposes that my self can by known by the analyst and also by me. Of course, it is never known as a thing, but as a project that can change even as I sustain it in its present being. A person with an inferiority complex can be made to see his ideal of being superior that he hides from himself. But, it would seem that the very moment of seeing this is to have also rejected the complex, and to have already made it to exist in the past as an object of our reflection.

19. It is now clear that Sartre did write a several hundred pages of an ethics that was to follow BN, but never completed it. It has recently been published as *Cahiers pour une morale*, edited by Elkaim-Sartre (Paris: Gallimard, 1983) and it has been translated by David Pellauer as *Notebooks for on Ethics*, Chicago: University of Chicago Press, 1992. For an early study of this work see, Sonia Kruks, ''Sartre's *Cahiers pour une morale: failed attempt or new trajectory in ethics*,'' *Social Text* 1986; 13/14:184–194. Sartre later worked on an ethics based on his *Critique of Dialectical Reason*. See *Rome* and *Cornell* lectures in index.

20. Jean-Paul Sartre, *Anti-Semite and Jew*, trans. George J. Becker (New York: Schocken Books, 1948), p. 45. This work will frequently be hereafter cited as *Anti-Semite* (Published in England as *Portrait of the Anti-Semite*, Trans. by Eric de Mauny, London: Secker & Warburg, 1948.)

21. *Anti-Semite*, p. 146.

22. Jean-Paul Sartre, *Saint Genet, Actor and Martyr*, trans. by Bernard Frechtman (New York, George Braziller, 1963) 55. Hereafter, this work will be cited as *Genet*.

23. I am tempted to claim that it is not implicit, but, as I have already noted, I am concerned here with the viability of certain notions and not with the issue of the textual accuracy of my interpretation of Sartre's texts.

24. See, Jean-Paul Sartre, *Search for a Method*, trans. by Hazel E. Barnes (New York: Alfred A. Knopf, 1963), 80. In the French, this work was published together with the *Critique*.

25. See *Critique*, 642–654. Also, my *Commentary*, 222–224.

26. See *Critique*, 770–781.

27. Jean-Paul Sartre, *The Family Idiot*, Vol I, trans. by C. Cosman (Chicago: University of Chicago Press, 1981), 40–51. For an excellent study of all three

volumes, see Hazel E Barnes, *Sartre and Flaubert*, (Chicago: University of Chicago Press, 1981.)

28. Jean-Paul Sartre, ''Existentialism is a Humanism,'' contained in Walter Kaufmann's *Existentialism From Dostoevsky to Sartre*, (New York: New American Library, 1975), 358.

Index

AAUP. *See* American Association of University Professors

abstraction, 93

action, 9, 26–27, 34–40, 56, 102, 116–17; false ideal of, 27–30

acts: good faith and, 54; oppressive and repressive, 5, 122

AFCT. *See* American Federation of College Teachers

AFL-CIO, 47–48

alienation, 14, 24, 33, 56, 64

American Association of University Professors, 47

American Federation of College Teachers, 47–48

anarchosyndicalism, 42

Anderson, Thomas, 53, 72n39, 72n49, 73n52, 172n4

anthropocentrism, 3, 21, 25, 52, 62, 65

anti-praxis, 40

anti-Semite, 102–3, 119, 137, 141, 162, 170

Anti-Semite and the Jew, 103, 110n3, 118–19, 141, 163

anti-Semitism, 102–3, 119, 137, 161–63

anti-violence, 16

a priori, 20–21, 26, 45, 57–58, 105

authenticity, 12, 17, 19, 27, 34, 77, 110n3, 169–71; the term, 151–54

bad faith, xii, 4, 25, 41, 130, 145–46; and authenticity, 77 cynical aware-ness of, 82; defined, 81–82, 104; distinct from good faith, 79–81, 86–87, 158–64; ideal of, 29, 91 and ideal of good faith, 79, 81, 138–40; weak and strong notions, 88, 99, 100, 102–10

Barnes, Hazel, 68n5, 111n4

Beauvoir, Simone de, 51

being, 21, 33, 115–16, 171

Being and Nothingness, x, 6, 7, 8, 18–19, 24–25, 36–37, 77–78, 89, 92–94, 99, 109, 116–18; and bad faith, 25–26, 91; methodology of, 127–28; and oppression, 117–18

belief 28, 82, 138, 145; critical, 79, 83; ideal of, 28; simple, 81; uncriti-cal, 80

Bell, Linda, xi, 51, 55

body, 14, 124n2, 131

bourgeois, 166–67, 169–70

Bowman, Elizabeth A., vii, 15–16, 51, 55–57, 72n47

Buber, Martin, 20, 21–22, 154

Cartesian dualism, 124n2

change. *See* conversion

collective, 34–40

The Communist and Peace, 139

177

About the Author

Joseph S. Catalano lives in Manhattan and is a professor emeritus at Kean College of New Jersey. Until his retirement in 1991, he was a professor of philosophy at Kean and had also taught courses in existentialism at the New School of Social Research. He attempts to balance his writing with modest activities in radical causes and is a longtime member of the Radical Philosophers Association and the Sartre Society of North America. Aside from his interest in Sartre, he has completed a manuscript on nonreductive materialism and has recently published articles on the nature of writing. Catalano is the author of two commentaries on Sartre's major philosophical works: the first, *A Commentary on Jean-Paul Sartre's "Being and Nothingness"* (Harper and Row, 1974; University of Chicago, 1980); and the second, *A Commentary on Jean-Paul Sartre's "Critique of Dialectical Reason, Vol. 1"* (University of Chicago, 1986).

The present volume brings together his major articles on Sartre's ethics and also includes a long introductory essay, which outlines a unified Sartrean moral perspective.